Yale Publications in American Studies, 8
David Horne, Editor
Published under the direction of the
American Studies Program

Fenollosa:

The Far East and American Culture

BY LAWRENCE W. CHISOLM

NEW HAVEN AND LONDON, YALE UNIVERSITY PRESS, 1963

To William Garnett Chisolm

πολλῶη δ᾽ ἀνθρώπων ἴδεν ἄστεα, καὶ νόον ἔγνω·

PREFACE

Ezra Pound called Ernest Fenollosa's career "the romance par excellence of modern scholarship." That Fenollosa realized his extraordinary opportunities was due to his rare combination of sensibility, energy, and disciplined intellectual boldness. As a philosopher, historian, and reforming prophet he searched the cultures of East and West for the outlines of an emerging world civilization. He interpreted Japanese art to the Japanese in the 1880s with the authority of his position as a resident professor of Western philosophy; then he returned to the United States to interpret Far Eastern civilization to Westerners and to work vigorously toward "the coming fusion of East and West." This vision of a world civilization whose prelude was visible in the evolution of art set the framework for his widespread activities and speculations; this vision animated his religious experience, his poetry, his oratory, his zeal for education and reform, as well as his philosophical writings and his great history of East Asian design. Although a specialist, in a sense, as the world's leading authority on Japanese art history, Fenollosa never narrowed his view for long and seldom hesitated to push his ideas to the limits of action and speculation.

Yet specialization has fragmented Fenollosa's reputation. He is remembered in literary circles primarily in connection with Ezra Pound and William Butler Yeats as a translator of Chinese poetry and Japanese drama, although a few recall him as a friend of Lafcadio Hearn. Among art historians Fenollosa is noted for his pioneer Far Eastern studies, particularly *Epochs of Chinese and Japanese Art*. Among museum curators and art collectors he is known for the superlative collection of Japanese painting bearing his name in the Boston Museum of Fine Arts and for his work in establishing that museum's Department of Chinese and Japanese art as a training center for a generation of scholars and curators. Less well known is his role in developing the Freer collections, now a part of the Smithsonian Institution in Washington.

In honor of Fenollosa's services to the art of Japan annual ceremonies are held by his grave at Miidera overlooking Lake Biwa and by his monument in Tokyo's Uyeno Park. A recent monograph by

Mitsugu Hisatomi has recorded in detail Fenollosa's important activities in Japan. But in the United States there are few who remember his campaign to awaken America's art consciousness, a campaign waged across the country in schools, clubs, and Chautauqua meetings and carried on after Fenollosa's death by his collaborator, Arthur Dow, the influential Director of Fine Arts at Teachers College, Columbia University. And among philosophers Fenollosa's aesthetics remain in a limbo shared by non-Western theories of art and philosophies of art history, with one notable exception—Donald Davie's analysis of Fenollosa's poetics. In *Articulate Energy: An Enquiry into the Syntax of English Poetry* (1955) Davie analyzes Fenollosa's essay on "The Chinese Written Character as a Medium for Poetry" and ranks this "great seminal work" alongside the poetic manifestos of Sidney, Wordsworth, and Shelley.

The aim of this first biographical study is to see Fenollosa's career as a whole and to explore the continuing life and importance of his ideas.

For their generous contributions to this book I would like to thank the following: Mrs. S. T. Whatley and Alan Chester for perceptive recollections of their mother and their stepfather and for the privilege of examining and quoting from Fenollosa family papers; the late Brenda Fenollosa Biddle for her memoir of days in Japan and for the privilege of quoting from her father's early poetry; the late Moncure Biddle for genealogical data on the Fenollosa family; Mrs. Russell Robb for access to the papers of her father, Edward S. Morse; Mrs. Margaret Dole McCall for being allowed to utilize the papers of her father, Nathan Haskell Dole; Mrs. Ward Thoron and Mrs. Roger S. Warner for recollections of their cousin William Sturgis Bigelow; the late John F. Fulton for Bigelow biographical information; L. Bancel LaFarge for suggestions and encouragement; Ralph Ladd for access to and quotations from the papers of Arthur Wesley Dow and Arthur Warren Johnson; Ezra Pound for permission to quote from Ernest Fenollosa's lecture, "Landscape Poetry and Painting in Medieval China"; Thomas C. Mendenhall II for the privilege of examining the autobiographical notes of his grandfather T. C. Mendenhall.

I want to thank as well: Johannes Rahder for bibliographical suggestions; Miss Tana Takahashi and Mrs. Anne Phipps Sidamon-Eristoff for acquiring several rare Japanese journals; Burns A. Stubbs and Mrs. Bertha Usilton of the Freer Gallery of Art for aid in examining the papers of Charles L. Freer and for patient assistance with Fenollosa's slide collections; Kojiro Tomita of the Boston Museum of Fine Arts for encouragement and for drawing my attention to the sale at auction of Fenollosa's library; David Little, registrar, for information on Boston Museum of Fine Arts trustee actions relating to Fenollosa's departure; Miss Marjorie Childs of the Boston Museum of Fine Arts Library; Miss Evelyn Burr of the Isabella Stewart Gardner Museum; Miss Doris Bry; Donald C. Gallup for Pound bibliographical assistance and the help of the staff of the Yale Collection of American Literature; the staffs of the Essex Institute and the Peabody Museum in Salem, the Houghton Library at Harvard, the Library of Congress, the New York Public Library, the Sterling Memorial Library at Yale, and the Metropolitan Museum of Art.

I am grateful to Mikiso Hane, especially for his care and patience in translating Japanese materials, and I want to thank William Jordy for encouragement and suggestions in the early stages of research, the late George Rowley for an eloquent introduction to Chinese painting, Nelson Wu for stimulating discussions of Far Eastern aesthetics and art, and Norman Holmes Pearson for introducing me to Fenollosa's poetics and for decisive support from the beginning.

I wish also to express my gratitude to the United States government, without whose financial assistance in the form of veteran's educational benefits this project might never have been undertaken, and to Yale University and the Colonial Dames of America for a generous fellowship in the early stages. Mrs. Lucille Siebert typed two complete versions of the manuscript patiently and accurately. Ruth A. Chisolm and Elizabeth R. Chisolm have helped considerably and cheerfully with details of manuscript preparation.

The book has benefited from the criticisms and suggestions of many readers at several stages, and I wish to thank them. Theodore Sizer, George H. Hamilton, George W. Pierson, Lamont Moore, David M. Potter, David Horne, and Albert E. Stone commented on all or portions of an early draft. The final version has profited from the comments of Mary C. Wright, John W. Hall, Nelson Wu, and Norman Holmes Pearson. Any errors of interpretation remain, of course, my own.

Acknowledgment is made to New Directions, New York, for permission to quote "Song of the Bowmen of Shu" from Ezra Pound, *Personae*, and for permission to reproduce a passage from "Canto 77" in *The Cantos of Ezra Pound*; to Harvard University Press for permission to quote a portion of "Elegantiae" from Ezra Pound, *The Confucian Odes*. Georgia O'Keeffe's water color, *Abstraction No. 10—Blue Lines*, is reproduced by courtesy of Miss O'Keeffe and the Alfred Stieglitz Collection, Metropolitan Museum of Art.

Lawrence W. Chisolm

New Haven, Connecticut
July 1963

CONTENTS

xi

Contents

ILLUSTRATIONS

PART 1 · *Possibilities*

We are ahead of the European races in the fact that more than either of them we can deal freely with forms of civilization not our own, can pick and choose and assimilate and in short (aesthetically etc.) claim our property wherever we find it. To have no national stamp has hitherto been a regret and a drawback, but I think it not unlikely that American writers may yet indicate that a vast intellectual fusion and synthesis of various National tendencies of the world is the condition of more important achievements than any we have seen.

Henry James to Thomas Sergeant Perry, September 20, 1867

1 · PRELUDE 1906

In a quiet apartment on New York's West Twenty-third Street in the spring of 1906 Ernest Fenollosa worked steadily and rapidly on a history of East Asian civilization. He wrote seated at a large table which served as a desk, its top piled with notes for lectures on Chinese and Japanese art and outlines of Far Eastern history—events, biographies, doctrines. Alongside a stack of magazines lay notebooks filled with comments on recent art exhibitions and drafts of articles for current issues of the *Golden Age,* a monthly journal he was editing. In a separate corner were outlines and sections of several plays and novels in progress. Most of his other manuscripts and books were in Spring Hill, Alabama, at "Kobinata," a rambling frame house where he hoped to relax with his family after finishing his regular summer lectures in Indiana at Winona Lake's Chautauquan camp meeting. The manuscripts in Alabama included several essays on aesthetics, lectures on Spencer and Hegel given while teaching philosophy at Tokyo University, analyses of Chinese and Japanese poetry, a history of English literature, a systematic exposition of Fenollosa's theory of art education, a report of his world tour of 1886 as Japanese Imperial Commissioner of Fine Arts, a work on Northern Buddhism, and notebooks filled with observations on Japan's Noh theater based on personal study and the lore of his teacher, Minoru Umewaka. At fifty-three Fenollosa's cosmic imagination had been disciplined by thirty years of scholarship; his intellectual ambition remained boundless.

On the walls of his New York apartment hung several kakemonos, favorite landscapes he had managed to hold on to despite frequent sales from his collection. A number of the gorgeous yellow and blue screens he loved remained in Kobinata, although over the past few years he had sold several to Charles Freer. Fenollosa found comfort in knowing that his screens would be enjoyed and permanently tended; the federal government had finally accepted Freer's gift of a superb collection which combined Far Eastern paintings and pottery with the work of the American painter Whistler. The collection as a whole drove home the importance of Far Eastern art for Western development, a theme Fenollosa had himself made central in his work at the Boston Museum of Fine Arts in the early '90s.

More recently, after his final return from Japan in 1901, Fenollosa had devoted his lecture tours and meetings with art teachers to spreading an awareness of how much could be learned from the Far East, particularly from the art of Japan. Since leaving Boston he had developed a missionary zeal for the cause of a democratic art revival in America, an awakening of art consciousness which might widen a man's sense of possibilities and educate his eye toward seeing new wholes, new ways of selecting, as the painter does, from virtually limitless possibilities. He felt sure that if a citizen developed an artist's eye he would never conform timidly to narrow rules of living and the deadening "pressure of the average."

In the spring of 1906 Fenollosa was very much alive to possibilities, still searching for the forms of thought and art which might make beautiful sense out of his own life and the world's experience. Whatever social and intellectual fashions he may have accommodated when younger, his ambitions were now his own in the special sense of an independent scholar and man of letters. The scandal of his divorce and second marriage had never really subsided in Boston. A close friend observed at the time that Fenollosa had "perhaps too audaciously realized his own unusual genius . . . feeling justified in being a law unto himself, thus transcending some of the conventions and suffering the inevitable consequences." [1] In New York, however, the consequences of a Boston scandal were reduced. And Boston itself had become less important as an intellectual and artistic center in the ten years since Fenollosa's abrupt departure. New York was closer to Fenollosa's dreams of cosmopolis, its polyglot energies more suited than Boston's to continental programs and international ideas. For all its bustle, Manhattan's impersonality offered the quiet freedom of privacy.

Fenollosa and his second wife, Mary, lived simply. Their pleasures were books, music, theater, and serious talk. Money came from lecture tours, commissions on art sales and authentications, occasional fees and royalties from writings. To meet special demands some work of art from Fenollosa's own collection could be sold. Mary Fenollosa's writing was going especially well. That year she published her third novel, *The Dragon Painter,* which she dedicated to her husband, using his Japanese name, "Kano Yeitan." Ernest Fenollosa had been adopted into the Kano family some twenty-five years earlier during his studies in Tokyo with the master painters of the traditional Kano school. "Yeitan," or "Long Search," recalled his archaeological explorations and the historical and philosophical probings of his art criticism and connoisseurship. In New York Fenollosa continued his long search as he outlined his pioneer interpretation of the development of Sino-Japanese civilization.

He worked undisturbed from early in the morning until late at night, indifferent to his surroundings, ignoring meals—to his wife's dismay. Usually he paused for a walk at twilight, his favorite time of day. He walked vigorously, head high, shoulders back, "as though breasting an invigorating gale," a sturdy, thick-chested figure, two inches under six feet tall. His full dark beard was now streaked with grey, his long hair almost white and brushed straight back from the temples, forehead broad and lofty, cheekbones high, nose strong and straight, mustache accenting a full lower lip in a firm mouth and jaw—the whole focused by unusually deep-set eyes. The eyes were a surprising green, very light, animated and sparkling when he

1. Nathan Haskell Dole in *Ninth Report of the Class Secretary of the Class of 1874 of Harvard College* (Cambridge, Mass., 1909), p. 42.

talked. He spoke with a clipped, cultured New England accent, his voice an even baritone rising typically with enthusiasm, seldom brusque, never ironic. When relaxing in Kobinata, Fenollosa usually wore loose kimonos with tabi and sandals, but in public he dressed elegantly: a Prince Albert for lecturing, full dress at dinner. Meticulous in habit and grooming, his skin "seemed to literally shine." The public figure was that of a gentleman. This gentleman spoke powerfully, eloquently, with an assured clarity. He was strikingly handsome, with the romantic aura of a man who has searched for beauty and knowledge in strange and distant places. A friend described him as "finely organized, sensitive, full of noble ideals," a man who was many things—"musician, poet, painter, dreamer, prophet, philosopher, mystic." [2]

In private Fenollosa shaped his own conclusions out of a lifetime's varied experience and sustained study. He was the first philosopher, perhaps the first modern writer in any field, to think in a genuinely historical world perspective—that is, with respect for the particulars of non-Western cultures and a regard for their own patterns of development. His ability to avoid the intellectual ethnocentrism of a Voltaire, a Hegel, a Kipling owed much to his several careers in two cultures: Japanese and American. And both these cultures were changing internally at a rapid rate. When Fenollosa returned to Japan in 1896, he found it altered substantially from the '80s. The Salem and Harvard of his youth were quite different from his Boston milieu in the early '90s; and life in New York and Alabama presented still further contrasts. In a way Fenollosa experienced four worlds, possibly five, so great were the changes going on around him and so dramatically did these changes affect his personal fortunes. To cope with the sharp reversal of his fortunes in Japan, for example, he was forced to become a historian in more than Hegel's philosophical sense. What sustained Fenollosa and made these changes an intellectual tonic was the habit of serious hard work acquired young, added to limitless curiosity and a speculative bent.

Equally important for the substance of his speculations was his faith that the universe was a cosmos not a chaos, that the world was basically harmonious and orderly. This faith was Emersonian in its universality and frequent pantheism; it was Hegelian in its lust after logical system; by 1906 it had become stubbornly empirical in

2. Ibid.

6

its attention to unique objects and events, although his analogies, drawn from biology and opposed to physics, kept a transcendental tone. "Thought grows like a living tissue," he editorialized in *The Golden Age*. "A keen historian's reasoning is the key to all reasoning, since its test of truth, of reality, is just the organic interplay of all the facts. . . . Thinking is *thinging*, to follow the buds of fact as they open, and see thought folded away within thought like so many petals." [3] The image recalled the lotus blossom and its special significance for Fenollosa: the sensuous lotus of Tendai Buddhism; the lotus of "individuality" unfolding from within outward; the lotus as symbol of a Far Eastern harmony with nature which might complement the West's imposition of technology on nature; the lotus flowering in Indiana not to bring forgetfulness but rather a wider consciousness of "world-embracing cultures."

Fenollosa's belief that all experience occurs in a cosmos helps explain the tone of assurance in his writings. His sense of life as an infinitely complex web of forces seldom baffled him, partly because he accepted no limits to the mind's capacity to create order, to discover significant unities in the sweet various stream of things. The things he dealt with seem almost too various to a later age of specialists, yet the connections which he drew are still alive. For example, one of his essays comparing Chinese and English poetry led Ezra Pound in the excitement of discovery to entitle it, "An Ars Poetica." "We know as we read," a later critic declared, "that this is a great seminal work, speaking with the authority of a devoted and passionate solitary thinker." In Pound's *Cantos* the petals of Fenollosa's lotus continue to unfold within a cosmic design. In the paintings of two Americans, Max Weber and Georgia O'Keeffe, the buds of Fenollosa's educational theories flower freely. And, more generally, the cosmopolitan perspectives Fenollosa championed have flourished in a world acknowledging slowly the historical varieties of cultural experience.

These future possibilities were scarcely glimpsed in 1906. Max Weber was then in Paris roaming the basement of the Louvre and the Musée Guimet and the Trocadero, finding confirmation of the Fenollosa-Dow theories of spacing in the art of Egypt, the Orient, and Africa. Georgia O'Keeffe was studying academic painting with little enthusiasm, not yet freed by the same Fenollosan language of

3. Editorial in *The Golden Age*, 1 (June 1906), 263–64.

space-art. Ezra Pound was just starting on his world-wide search for Beauty, and as Fenollosa reflected on the historical pattern of East Asian design, Pound was in southern Europe investigating the rhythms of Provençal poetry.

What was beginning to be clear as early as 1906 was an emerging Asian nationalism signaled by Japan's startling victories in her war against Russia. In one generation the land of chrysanthemums and two-handed swords had produced a modern war machine, the best card of admission into the community of nations. The guns at Mukden and Tsushima Straits announced a meeting of East and West on new terms; Japan had clearly imported Western scientific and industrial techniques with success. Her victory added urgency to Fenollosa's broad concern with "the coming fusion of East and West" and his continuing efforts to interpret each to the other and to itself. He was convinced that future historians of mankind would consider the twentieth century as, most significantly, a time of re-union for civilizations which had grown apart since their last meeting under the sword of Alexander and the image of Buddha. A new kind of world civilization was developing. Russia's defeat dramatized the appeal to the East of the West's industrial culture; what the East would mean to the West remained uncertain. Japanese art had already quickened Western eyes; Japanese guns made broader historical perspectives a plain necessity. Fenollosa was alarmed by Japanese militarism but excited by the stir of Asian energies.

In the United States in 1906 the energies of "Progressive" reforms were upsetting customary practices. Although many reformers urged a social and economic individualism modeled on simpler times past, attention to present complexities foreshadowed a weakening of conventional attitudes, a reviving sense of possibilities not limited to the merely commercial. To many scientists and philosophers the publication in 1905 of Einstein's *Special Theory of Relativity* revealed the inadequacy of basic conventions underlying man's knowledge of physical reality, namely long-held assumptions of absolute time and absolute space, anchors of certainty in modern conceptions of the universe. At a more general level William James, lecturing on "Pragmatism" in 1906, was attacking the pretensions of a variety of "block universes" which seemed to close the future. James pictured reality as multiple and moving, a various stream of possibilities ordered by the purposive force of thought into solutions which were tentative, not certain. Fenollosa's attacks on cultural parochialism

and on formalisms of every sort—social, educational, artistic, philosophical—anticipated a looser, relational pattern of thinking; his
respect for craft and his own disciplined work complemented a view-
point anarchic in another man. A trained eye alert to novel combinations might find a path to progress in a pragmatic, relative world.

An ability to recognize unfamiliar possibilities and a willingness
to act without being sure of the outcome have become particular
assets in modern life. The freedom to select from among the most
various possibilities and the skill to make fit selections have come
to determine the quality of life in societies where conventional se-
curities—individual, social, international—weaken amid changing
conditions. Art, to return to Fenollosa's conception, requires analogous freedom and trained selectivity, for only by free selection from
among infinite possibilities can an artist discover that unique arrangement which is beautiful. To live artistically, in this sense, is to
live as an individual. Fenollosa pointed out that even in a traditional
culture Kuo Hsi, the great Chinese painter, urged his son "to throw
away what is old and take in what is new," to "let the mind play
in the sphere of Art." [4]

"It is a vain cry that the Golden Age lies all behind us," Fenollosa
announced in the spring of 1906, "that romance is dead, that poetry
is old-fashioned, and that ours is a dry, decrepit humdrum world.
There never were greater dramatic crises for man than lurk in present
history. No greater marvels of human thought and industry ever
stimulated imagination than now. There was never a time when the
heroic in our nature, the responsibility upon our finer powers, stood
at tenser strain. We should read our morning papers as if some sibyl
had written us a new Arabian tale over-night." [5]

Fenollosa's wonder at the world's ordered variety survived personal
disorders and grew with the varieties of his experience. Viewed
retrospectively, across the last fifty years of turmoil, his confidence
stirs wonder that he could have been so hopeful. It is part of his
achievement that in seminal speculations and in the style of his life
he rouses the suspicion that he might have been right.

4. *Epochs of Chinese and Japanese Art* (rev. ed. New York, Stokes, 1921),
2, 13.
5. Editorial in *The Golden Age*, 1 (April 1906), 128.

The world owes all its onward
impulses to men ill at ease. The
happy man inevitably confines
himself within ancient limits.

Nathaniel Hawthorne, *The House
of the Seven Gables*

2 · THE FENOLLOSAS OF SALEM

"My father's full baptismal name," Ernest Fenollosa recalled, "was
Manuel Francisco Ciriaco Fenollosa del Pino del Gil del Alvarez, the
names Francisco and Ciriaco standing for the two patron saints,
according to Spanish custom. Pino was the family name of his
mother and Gil and Alvarez of his two grandmothers. The Alvarez
he supposed to be a modified form of the family name Alvarado, so
famous in Spanish history, not impossibly the direct descendants of
Alvarado, the Lieutenant of Cortez in Mexico, who married the
daughter of the king of the Tlascalans." [1] The story of Ernest Fenollosa's long search and many voyages begins with one particular
voyage westward to the New World from Spain, from the sunny
southern port of Málaga, home of a young musician, Manuel Fenollosa, "not impossibly" heir of Tlascalan kings.

Manuel Fenollosa's emigration westward from Spain to the New
World at the age of fourteen started as an adventure. When the
first Carlist war broke out in 1833 and an army draft seemed sure,
his parents urged him to join a military band scheduled to leave
for the United States aboard an American frigate. The young man
was already an accomplished violinist and pianist but the sole opening was in the brass section. He practiced all night on the French
horn, passed the examination in the morning in time to sail out of
Málaga harbor to the Balearic Islands and thence, after a narrow
escape from officials, across the Atlantic westward never to return.

1. Preface to *Epochs of Chinese and Japanese Art*, 1, vii.

Manuel Fenollosa's father, also a musician and a veteran of the Napoleonic wars, had come from Valencia to settle in Málaga, where he married Isobel del Pino of nearby Canillas de Aceytuno. Their only son, Manuel—there was a daughter, Isobel—was a musical prodigy. At six he stood on tables in crowded halls to sing Italian operatic arias; at ten he was playing in public on both piano and violin; and before long he became leader of the boys choir in the cathedral. The French horn came easily.

Manuel's musicality and good spirits made him a favorite with the military band, and he sat regularly at stage front playing the piano and assorted wind instruments. The band's violin soloist and leader was his sister Isobel's fiancé, Manuel Emilio. The band enlivened the crossing and the members decided to stay together after their arrival in the United States. For several years they toured the Atlantic seaboard from Washington, D.C., to Portland, Maine. They featured Italian opera but introduced some of the new German music as well: Mozart, Beethoven, Meyerbeer. By 1838 the band had separated, and Manuel Fenollosa joined the violinist Emilio in settling down in Salem, Massachusetts, at the special urging of George Peabody, a wealthy patron who was himself a fine cellist and an amateur painter.

Salem was then a major seaport rivaling Boston in her trade. The peak of her prosperity was past but the fine houses on Essex Street overlooking the busy wharves represented a cultivated community where musicians could count on a regular income from lessons and concerts. The two young Spaniards were soon comfortably established, and Isobel Fenollosa, Manuel's sister, was persuaded to come over from Málaga. She married Manuel Emilio in February 1844, and soon afterward her parents made the voyage to Salem for a visit. The elder Fenollosas were not happy. The father returned alone to Spain before the year was out. The mother stayed on for three years, possibly to rescue her children from apostasy; baptized as Roman Catholics, they had both become Protestant Episcopalians. She prayed devotedly in the church at Salem, but in vain; perhaps the alien priests and their Irish congregation made her ill at ease. Once back in Málaga she lived in religious retirement, communicating at rare intervals with her son and daughter in Salem.

Manuel Fenollosa lived pleasantly in Salem, visiting most of the large houses as music teacher, directing a variety of musical societies, and playing in orchestras in Boston. There were few evening trains from Boston to Salem in the early days, and after a concert he would walk back the sixteen miles, often in the snow, violin slung across his back, arriving in time to join the Emilios for breakfast.

When his father died back in Málaga, the last tie with Spain was broken, and in 1851 Manuel Fenollosa married one of his pupils, Mary Silsbee. She was thirty-five, one of seven homely children of a beautiful mother; Manuel was thirty-two. The Silsbee family was prominent in Salem. Through this marriage the young Spanish violinist entered the upper levels of a society noted for the authority of its leading families and now becoming more conscious of rank as the town's maritime vigor declined.

Mary Silsbee's mother, Mary Hodges, came from an original Salem family. Her father, William Silsbee, had not so ancient a claim, but the Silsbees had a most distinguished recent history. William Silsbee's father, Captain Nathaniel Silsbee, had missed the wealth of the earliest Salem mariners, but William's older brother Nathaniel rose rapidly. He went to sea at fourteen; he clerked aboard the *Astrea* on its pioneering voyage eastward to China; at nineteen he captained the Derby ship *Benjamin* around the Cape of Good Hope to Mauritius. In twenty years as master and merchant he pyramided a fortune. Leaving the quarterdeck, Nathaniel Silsbee served as United States congressman and as president of the Massachusetts upper house; from 1826 to 1835 he represented Massachusetts in the United States Senate. His marriage to the daughter of Mary Derby Crowninshield allied him with the most powerful families of Salem.[2] William Silsbee followed the sea, as did his younger brother, Zachariah, and the three sons of old Nathaniel shared management of prospering family ventures. When Manuel Fenollosa married a Silsbee he was clearly rising in the world of Salem.

Mary Silsbee Fenollosa's first child was born on February 18, 1853, baptized in the Episcopalian Church, and christened Ernest Francisco—Francisco after his father's patron saint. A second son, William Silsbee, arrived the following year shortly before Christmas, and Manuel Fenollosa moved his family into a fine new house, Number Three Chestnut Street, in the most fashionable part of Salem.

Ernest Fenollosa's earliest memory was of lying in the sun on a floor near a window hearing Beethoven's *Sonata Appassionata* played

2. Through the marriages of Nathaniel Silsbee's children the Silsbee line was joined to Devereux, Appleton, and Saltonstall, leading families in Essex County and Boston.

12

by his father on the violin accompanied on the piano by his mother. The house on Chestnut Street was filled with music and with the sounds of talk. Along with the clipped twanging speech of his mother and his playmates the young boy listened to the voluble Spanish of his father and the Emilios. From the beginning his ear noted differences in rhythm and gesture which raised questions beyond the experience of his Salem friends, rending, if only slightly, the seamless web of childhood.

The two Fenollosa boys grew up hearing stories of Spain to match their mother's memories of an earlier and more adventurous Salem. To the classic tale of Manuel's escape by French horn were added stories of boyhood pranks in the Málaga cathedral, of the delights of exploring dark lofts and towers, and of how Manuel Fenollosa committed sacrilege by hiding all night in the church. Or the boys' father might tell of being punished for serenading an aristocratic young lady one evening below her balcony; or he might point to the large scar on his forehead and recount his climbs and falls around the steep ruins of the last Spanish fortress to be held by the Moors. The stories seemed all the more real when supported by boxes of raisins and casks of wine sent direct from Málaga by grandmother Fenollosa.

The boys' mother had lived as a girl in a big colonial house on lower Essex Street looking down the hedged and arbored hillside across Derby Street to the seashore. She told them how her mother had in childhood peeked through the blinds at the British redcoats marching down the street, and how she herself had watched for the first white flash of foretopgallant sails over Naugus Head and had listened excitedly for the gunshot announcing the return of a Silsbee ship from the Indies. Out her windows she had watched the brigs and slim schooners, none of them over five hundred tons burthen, fold their white wings wharfside. She had seen the treasures drawn from their holds: silks, porcelain, and lacquer; Polynesian curios; pepper, ginger, and mocha coffee; cottons from the East— Mull Mull, Beerboom Gurrahs, Madras chintzes. The wonders were unloaded in a steady line of bales and barrels and boxes, while rising shrill above the clatter of the wharves could be heard the chatter of Anjer monkeys in the rigging. She listened to tales of the hazardous passage up the Hoogly to Calcutta and tales of brushes with Malay pirates in the Sunda Straits. In 1833, the year of Manuel Fenollosa's arrival in America, a Salem brig lost five men to cannibals in Fiji.

If the risks of voyages to the Indies were great, so were the profits. For fifty years after the *Astrea's* return to Salem from Canton in 1790 the East Indies were a rich preserve for Salem merchants, who enjoyed a virtual monopoly by the tacit consent of Bostonians, whose ships sailed westward around the Horn to load furs on the northwest coast for trade in China. Salem stood for the United States along both coasts of Africa, at Mauritius and Manila, and throughout the Dutch East Indies. In fact, in Quallah Battoo, Malaya, to one wealthy merchant—Po Adam by name—Salem was clearly "a country by itself, and one of the richest and most important sections of the globe." [3] The Salem city seal pictured a Parsee and a palm tree along with a ship; its bold motto: *Divitis Indiae Usque ad Ultimum Sinum* (Of the riches of Ind, to the uttermost gulf).

The riches of the East built the mansions of Salem, but the sensuous arts of the East made little impression at first. Traditionally, New England Protestants regarded appeals to the senses as snares of the devil. The merchant-captains who dominated Salem were generally bluff, rugged men with little taste for lavish and colorful trappings or the nuances of Chinese porcelain. Their houses tended toward the clean spare lines of their ships, and the interiors were often as bare and functional as a captain's cabin.

As the second and third generations enjoyed their wealth, the houses became grander in their decorations, although never ornate or elaborate. As the mansions' treasures mounted, chests and corner cupboards overflowed, and pieces of Chinese porcelain and Japanese lacquer came out for display along with other curios. By the 1850s the interiors of the great houses had more color, more objects that caught the light, more visual texture. The rooms in which Ernest Fenollosa played as a child with his Silsbee cousins had become less stark and subdued than the rooms of his mother's childhood.

Although Salem avoided some of the drabness of other nineteenth-century New England towns, it shared the passion for business that stirred the energies of Massachusetts. Emerson remarked that "from 1790 to 1820, there was not a book, a speech, a conversation, or a thought in the state." Commerce absorbed men's best energies. In the next generation the balance was righted somewhat. Great books were written; scholarship advanced; and to some observers the great merchants seemed already figures of the past. But the main stream

3. Quoted in S. E. Morison, *Maritime History of Massachusetts* (Boston, Houghton Mifflin, 1921), p. 84.

was economic. "In Boston in the middle of the nineteenth century," a perceptive onlooker noted, "no one who was ambitious, energetic, or even rich thought of anything but making a fortune; the glamor was all in that direction. . . . The great affair, the aristocratic path to success and power was business." [4] These remarks apply equally well to the Salem of Ernest Fenollosa's youth and to its esteem for the individualism of business enterprise.

Manuel Fenollosa, Ernest's father, did not fit this pattern of success. He was a businessman, the Salem representative of Chickering and Company, manufacturers of pianos; he gave musical instruction at a price; and he was clearly an individualist, a man of boldness and talent. But he had little eye for the main chance. Santayana, a fellow Spanish-American, put the matter well. "The Spaniard is an individualist; he can be devout mystically, because that is his own devotion to his own duty; but socially, externally, he distrusts everything and everybody, even his priests and his kings." [5] Manuel Fenollosa had not fled from King Carlos to pay homage to "King" Derby. His Alvarez blood was as aristocratic as any in Spain; he reserved his devotion for his music. This was clearly not the kind of individualism which carried weight in Salem in the 1850s and '60s. On the contrary, an individualism that did not dream of wealth implied a criticism of the dominant dream. Criticism is rarely welcome, even to the most secure people, and during Ernest Fenollosa's childhood Salem's eminence was no longer secure. The town's economy was undergoing a forced shift from wharf to mill.

The opening of the Naumkeag Steam Cotton Mills in Salem in 1848 signaled the closing of Salem's maritime frontier in the Indies and indicated the town's need for new sources of wealth. No longer could a young man go to sea in hopes of making his way quickly up in the world; nor could maiden ladies send their savings off with a young captain to trade in Calcutta, reasonably certain of success. It became doubly important for those on the make to be prudent and for those who had arrived to avoid losing what they had, whether money or social position. The leading families continued to ally themselves with new wealth even after Salem's decline as a center became evident. Mary Fenollosa's first cousin, Georgiana Silsbee, for example, was married in 1855 to Henry Saltonstall, a leading mill industrialist. By contrast Mary's own marriage to an unconnected

4. George Santayana, *Persons and Places* (New York, Scribner's, 1944), p. 68.
5. Ibid., p. 24.

Spanish musician of limited prospects placed her near the fringes of her milieu. Very likely the town did not allow her to forget it, completely. To the socially minded it was clear that Mary Silsbee Fenollosa had married down and to a foreigner besides.

Not that there was any direct hostility on the part of native Yankees to the few Spaniards who settled in Salem. The town was more cosmopolitan than most, its experience of the world extended by trading and travel. Her ships' crews were polyglot and her waterfront too. Furthermore, Spaniards were rare, Spanish musicians rarer still. And they did not compete for jobs. The shadows of popery were removed when the Fenollosas and the Emilios became Protestants, Episcopalians at that. Yet the anxious nationalism of the 1850s aggravated that widespread intolerance of differences often noted as American by foreign observers. Echoes of this demand for consensus may well have affected an economically declining Salem. The Know-Nothing or American party, center of nativist bigotry, was strongest in the larger cities—Boston, New York, Philadelphia—but in the election of 1854 it carried Salem easily in its sweep of Massachusetts. Manuel Fenollosa had influential patrons, but his English was never perfect, and his sister and brother-in-law, Isobel and Manuel Emilio, still spoke Spanish, a curiosity to the children on the streets and to storekeepers who knew that their tills would never be kept filled by violinists. The Northern victory in the Civil War restored general confidence, and suspicions of foreigners tended to be dismissed as new waves of immigrants were welcomed to the great enterprise of continental development.

To Ernest Fenollosa, a child in the '50s and early '60s, these general currents of economic decline and nativist excitement meant little; odd tones of voice and challenging glances were taken merely as signs of the way things are. Nor does the war appear to have made very much of a mark on his imagination. When Lee surrendered at Appomattox Court House, Fenollosa was still a student in Hacker Grammar School. His later writings make no mention of the war, the only legacy of the great struggle being a few martial poems in a school notebook, most of them addressed to Greeks and Romans in the high-flown rhetoric of the day.

More important to Fenollosa's development were personal matters which gave rise to precocious speculations about the meaning of life and the direction of his own career, speculations which foreshadowed many of the major concerns of his later years. The philosophical cast of mind evident in the poems written during a period from February 1866 to August 1868 may have been a result of the emotional pressures of two experiences which followed quickly on each other—the death of his mother and an unhappy love affair. In the autumn of 1866 Fenollosa entered Salem High School at the head of his class. In November his mother died. The next summer found him walking often with the girl of the poems, golden-haired Lizzie Millett. The young poet appears alternately meditative and rhapsodic, focused on his own emotional unfolding. The last poems, including an extended dramatic narrative, were written the following winter after Lizzie had broken off apparently for good, submitting, Fenollosa contends, to social pressures—

> My station far inferior to hers
> My habits so disliked by all her friends.

Fenollosa's development during this short period is evident in the ideas expressed in the poems, the forms of verse, even the handwriting. The changes are pronounced. The first set of poems is written in an ornamental, copybook script, and they treat nature, ancient history, and angelic love in the doggerel rhythms and cute rhymes of childhood. The last poems are composed in dramatic blank verse with variations and written in a script very close to Fenollosa's mature handwriting, slightly tighter and more careful. These last are all love poems, but the rhetoric is less inflated, sharpened by disillusion. The love scenes have become particular, the setting social. Although the long central poem involves an ascent from Nature to God, and is written in language that seems abstract and conventional, the occasion for the poem was clearly a matter of deep feeling.

This central poem of the last series tells a story of love and self-discovery. In the course of glances, walks, encounters, an intimacy develops, hampered at first by "her relations or familiar friends by whom I was regarded as a boy of dark reserve and gloomy character." When alone with her, however, he talks with eloquence and passion until her bashfulness vanishes. She asks why he stays so much alone with nature or a book. Thereby, he replies,

> I tear myself away
> From fashion and society and all
> Those pleasures of the sense one ever meets
> Within the rich man's palace, and to shun

> The sickening hypocrisy I see
> In everything, and that great thirst for gain
> That swells in every heart. Of what result
> Are all the objects of all persons' lives
> In these degenerate times. My spirit aches
> Within itself. Attraction for the woods
> And fields and rugged rocks, all nature's scenes
> Draw me from home. . . .

Great opportunities to benefit the race, the poet continues, are sacrificed to society's "idolatry" and to "idle pleasures." For his part, should he mix in gay society and learn the "vices of the rich . . . I should be drawn in the great whirlpool down forever lost. My nature flows that way."

As the poem's narrative continues, the dialogue of Fenollosa's inner struggle pivots on the ambiguities of Love as Life and as Death, Love as sweet tie to earth and Love as Vice, a dreadful path to dissolution. But he does not stop with the revivalist's simple dualism of Sin and Virtue; he sets a Faustian goal, admitting that his soul's thirst for ultimate knowledge of itself nearly tears him apart. Above all, his soul "longs to wander in a freer space where it can view itself." Ambition, variously directed, is the middle term in Life's dialogue with Death.

In this immediate struggle between Ambition and Death each individual confronts a variety of possible lines of action, which Fenollosa proceeds to examine as a final prelude to the two lovers' meeting of hearts. Pursuit of military fame and glory he dismisses summarily. Descent to Hades through sampling sins leads only to doubt and fear. The "petty cares" of business prove no comfort, nor do wealth and honor won abroad put anxiety to rest. Not even Nature's art with all the power of Niagara Falls can give shape and purpose to his loneliness. At last Poetry fires Ambition (which is allied with Life) with a sense of "mine own worth" and "tunes my heart to loveliness." Yet even Poetry turns out to lack the potent charm he seeks. Only God approached in prayer gives meaning and release. At this point the lovers embrace and give themselves in a flood of rhetoric "to pleasure's ravishment," pledging to love forever, oppose who may; but not before the poet himself challenges all pessimisms, divine and human, with the cry, "O man! Thou art the king. To thee are given the keys to all these beauties." [6]

6. "First Love," in "Poems Written in Boyhood," pp. 124–59, MS in possession of Brenda Fenollosa Biddle estate, Haverford, Pa.

This poem was oddly prescient. Ten years later in 1878, death, ambition, and love combined again to shape the pattern of Fenollosa's life. More important, this early love, when grasped imaginatively, confirmed for Fenollosa a sense of unfolding possibilities at a time when his mother's death might have separated him further from the world. Drawn toward solitude by temperament and experience, his ambitions might have turned completely inward, isolating him from the world of his "higher ranking" Silsbee cousins and Salem's pattern of success. But this world was the world also of Lizzie Millett, whom he eventually married, and the world of the Salem men who went on to Harvard. Ambition and precocity drew Fenollosa toward Harvard and "a freer space."

> And, as for me, if, by any possibility, there be any as yet undiscovered prime thing in me; if I shall ever deserve any real repute in that small but high hushed world which I might not be unreasonably ambitious of . . . then here I prospectively ascribe all the honor and the glory to whaling; for a whaleship was my Yale College and my Harvard.

Herman Melville, *Moby-Dick*

3 · HARVARD WAS MY WHALE-SHIP

As a young man Fenollosa shared an American faith in progress, and throughout his life that faith seldom wavered. In his schoolboy writings the "world's advancement" was assumed to be both likely and the most important task for able men. One hopeful prospect which Fenollosa noted early (1866) was a "world community," a brotherhood of men not confined, as some would have it, to "some portion of the race, for God did not intend that we should bind our love to any country, class, or place." [1] This was the cosmopolitan spirit of Emerson, Thoreau, and Whitman and in many ways the spirit also of James Russell Lowell and of Doctor Oliver Wendell Holmes, who proclaimed that "like the Romans we are the great assimilating race."

In the 1870s America's gates opened wide to the thousands of workers needed to build railroads and to man factories and mines; foreign capital and technology were equally welcome. The transatlantic flow of men, money, and technique seemed a tribute from the old world to the special destiny of the new. While the bulk of American energies was directed inward on continental development,

1. "Poems Written in Boyhood," p. 29.

American intellectual life was at the same time becoming more inter-national, quickened by European scientific work. The confident ad-vance of knowledge matched the pace of economic expansion. Theo-ries, like railroads, webbed over wide territories and were considered clear evidence of progress.

In the autumn of 1870 Ernest Francisco Fenollosa embarked on his studies at Harvard College. He was fortunate to find a milieu where success was not defined narrowly and where possibilities were not mainly commercial. At Harvard he encountered a variety of in-tellectual possibilities which both stimulated and satisfied. For a great part of his life Fenollosa lived most intensely in the world of ideas; his furthest voyages were philosophical and contemplative. In a real sense Harvard was his *Pequod* or, perhaps better for a Silsbee, his *Benjamin,* the ship of his wanderings through the philosophical tra-dition of the West. Harvard studies provided the idiom which Fenol-losa would use in a lifelong search for a world-view spacious enough to contain the far reaches of aesthetic and religious experience as well as the historical particularities of his own cosmopolitan career.

Socially Fenollosa stood back from the swirl of college life. As a boy he had been sensitive to imagined slights. At Harvard he was re-served. "Few knew him well," a close friend recalled later.[2] He was one of a small minority of students to enter from public high schools, and he seems to have had little contact with those classmates whose ideas of success left scant room for philosophy, poetry, and music. He had nothing to do with his cousin and classmate, George Saltonstall Silsbee, for example, whose career developed vigorously in an estab-lished pattern: from a Salem private school through Harvard, high-lighted by crew and the Porcellian, and on to eminence in textile manufacturing. Fenollosa's few good friends were men who shared his interests: Arthur Foote of Salem, his freshman roommate, a com-poser and later organist at the First Unitarian Church in Boston; and Nathan Haskell Dole, writer, editor, and translator of the Russian novelists. Pictures show Fenollosa as a lean young man of rather som-ber look: straight black hair curling over the ears, eyes set deep in a long, oval face. He is handsome, serious, sensitive, and seems some-what withdrawn.

After freshman year Fenollosa roomed with his younger brother William (Class of '75) in the west entry of Gray's, sharing a single

2. Dole in *Ninth Report of the Class Secretary of the Class of 1874 of Harvard College,* p. 40.

room. Nathan Dole's good-sized sitting room across the way was their meeting place. The three men boarded together. "We enjoyed walking," Dole recalled, "and after we had boarded awhile in Commons in Memorial Hall, where portraits of ancient worthies looked down pityingly on our meager fare, we got our breakfasts and suppers at the Prospect House in Cambridgeport. In our last year we boarded with two friendly maiden ladies who lived in a tiny house directly opposite the Saunders." [3] Week ends spent in Salem at the Fenollosa house were made particularly congenial by Manuel Fenollosa's pretty young second wife, whom all the students called "Annie." Music was likely at all hours. Both Fenollosa boys sang in the College Glee Club and the Handel and Haydn Society, and Arthur Foote recalled an evening serenade of the Fenollosa house in Salem by sixteen or twenty members of the Glee Club and Pi Eta. No drinks were offered the serenaders.[4]

Fenollosa continued to write poetry in college, again as an imaginative exploration of lines of action and philosophical principles. Emerson, in particular, incited an enthusiasm which grew with the years; Fenollosa read Emerson all his life. His admiration for the Emersonian ideals of contemplation and action is evident in his "Class Poem" and in "Pantheism," an essay written as a commencement part in 1874. In the essay his rhetoric mounts until the world is revealed as a progressive organic unity in which the individual, if he will but reverence all nature, can grasp the Ideal and synthesize Subject and Object, Force and Being to become absorbed, finally, in God. His graduation poem is not so breathlessly abstract—"I only sing the song we all are singing." Its pantheist mysteries are lighted by flashes of scholarly wit, although its message remains Emersonian, calling for a native literature and art, and urging "greater earnestness," "childlike reverence," and "steadfast individuality."

At about the same time, in the spring of 1874, Fenollosa wrote in his Harvard Class Book an autobiographical sketch which placed a

3. Dole, "Autobiography," p. 110, manuscript in possession of Mrs. Margaret Dole McCall, New York, N.Y. The only other boarder was Parker C. Chandler, son of the Honorable Peleg Chandler of Brunswick, Me. Dole also recalled pleasant summer excursions around Mt. Washington, meeting Ernest and William Fenollosa at Tasker's in Upper Bartlett near the Conway meadows.

4. Arthur Foote, *An Autobiography* (Norwood, Mass., Plimpton Press, 1946), p. 21. Ernest Fenollosa belonged to Pi Eta and was also a member of the Christian Union and Phi Beta Kappa. Arthur Foote composed the music for the class song; Nathan Dole wrote the words. Fenollosa was class poet.

noble savage alongside Emerson's noble seer. In the midst of the proudly understated Anglo-Saxon pedigrees of most of his classmates, Fenollosa set the figure of a dusky Aztec princess. In her name he attacked those prejudices and habits of civilization which destroy man's view of the whole of "rich throbbing natural life."

> My interest in the aborigines of America and especially in the more civilized races of them has always been intense. To my fancy their story contains a history of Human Nature, with its loves, wars, aspirations, and development, more impressive than that furnished by the annals of people better known; and undiscovered America, with its beauty, its rich throbbing natural life, and its dusky children a part of that life, seems to me to afford the truest image of the world and man unclouded and untainted by the prejudices of Eastern [United States] civilization, which though in themselves are natural, blind us by their proximity when we look at the world as a whole, and seem to set themselves up in opposition to Nature. I have therefore often wished that some of my ancestors were to be found in these races; and I have found a clue which affords not merely a possibility, but a strong probability of such ancestry. . . . My very great, great grandfather, I am bound to believe, was Xicotencatl, chief of the Tlascalans in Mexico at the time of Cortes' invasion, which chief gave his daughter baptized Louisa to the Spanish captain Alvarado. History says that from this pair have sprung many of the most aristocratic families of modern Spain. . . . My great grandmother was an Alvarez who married a man below her station, yet a man of some intellectual and musical ability, Don Francisco del Pino of the town of Canillas de Aceytuno near Málaga. Of their several children Ysabel del Pino, who died in 1866, was my grandmother.[5]

This sketch made it clear that Fenollosa took his stand with cosmopolitans rather than nativists. The American past with which he identified himself was inclusive rather than exclusive, eclectic in its welcome of variety.

The spirit of variety was nowhere more evident than in the philosophical milieu of Fenollosa's Harvard years, and this was the milieu in which his deepest interests ranged. He graduated with first class

5. "Harvard Class Book, 1874," pp. 285–87; one of a series of handwritten autobiographies. MS in Archives, Harvard University.

honors in philosophy; he held a Parker Fellowship as graduate resident in philosophy for two subsequent years; and he studied at the Unitarian Divinity School for an additional period, withdrawing finally from formal study in the spring of 1877. During these years Harvard's new president, Charles Eliot, developed an elective system which expanded the curriculum and opened the way for new lines of intellectual activity. The rigid requirements of an education geared to the classics and the ministry were suspended and the orthodoxies they represented were opened to challenge. The intellectual stir was considerable. In philosophy the new spirit confirmed the separation of professional academic theory from theology. German idealism led a successful assault on the orthodoxy of Scotch "Common Sense." Fenollosa's teacher Francis Bowen, for example, introduced a course in the history of philosophy, and soon "French and German Philosophy," as the course was entitled, became a primary vehicle for the new idealism.[6]

Nonetheless Fenollosa's allegiance as an undergraduate went to Herbert Spencer, and he joined in forming a Spencer Club at Harvard. More than any other philosopher, Spencer struck the dominant American chords of faith in progress, perfectibility, and science. Even William James in his early years fell under the spell. Spencer had all the answers, and they were couched in terminology sufficiently obscure to confuse the opposition. Civilization as a part of nature was of necessity progressing, and Spencer assured his readers that "the ultimate development of the ideal man is logically certain." [7] Once man overcomes his "non-adaptation of constitution to conditions," as he inevitably will, society will reach a state of "equilibration," a state "of the greatest perfection and the most complete happiness." In the '70s Spencer seemed a giant, one of the great comprehensive minds of the century.

However scientific Spencer might be, he was primarily concerned with making the inner tally with the outer. To Fenollosa the inner was more significant than the outer. His soul's search for the free space of self-knowledge was a matter of the mind. He moved naturally

6. For details see Benjamin Rand, "Philosophical Instruction in Harvard University from 1636 to 1906," *Harvard Graduates' Magazine*, 37 (Dec. 1928), 146–47, and 38 (March 1929), 188–200, 291–311; also Bowen, *Modern Philosophy* (New York, 1877).

7. *Social Statics* (New York, 1864), p. 79. Classmates in the Spencer Club included Lewis Dyer, the classicist, and Samuel Behler Clarke, later Elihu Root's law partner.

toward Hegel in his graduate years. Hegel made the mind ultimate and adequate; his logical architecture was spacious and firm, inviting metaphysical adventure and offering rational faith. Hegel interpreted all human history and every facet of human experience in terms of the development of Absolute Spirit, a development focused on the growth of individual awareness of freedom, an infinite freedom of a spirit "an-sich-und-bei-sich-und-für-sich-sein," potential (an sich), self-sufficient (bei sich), and self-fulfilled (für sich). The progressive movement of Hegelian ideas from birth to opposition to new birth drew Fenollosa into a dialectical web whose apotheosis of thought offered a persuasive alternative to Spencer's mechanical materialism. Most important, Hegel's combination of metaphysical adventure with rational faith left room for novelty and for individual search.

Fenollosa had been prepared for Hegel's world-spirit by Emerson, by the widespread belief in America's spiritual destiny as the light of the world, and by news of distant lands now accessible through photographs and travel. Hegel's was a world history; like Emerson he told a tale of the universal bond of spirit which links men of all places and all times. "The History of the World travels from East to West," wrote Hegel, "for Europe is absolutely the end of history, Asia the beginning." In the New World he found "only an echo of the Old World," and he urged that America "abandon" the old ground of development, for "America is the land of the future." [8]

Hegel's monarchism presented obstacles in the United States in the seventies, but it was speedily democratized. William T. Harris, superintendent of schools in St. Louis, interpreted Hegel as a spokesman for an ethical state keyed to laissez-faire initiative, a state in which St. Louis would act as mediator of East and West, its spiritual force strengthened by its pivotal geographic position. What was needed in the wake of Civil War political dialectics was a broad formulation of philosophical issues—or so Harris contended. The journal he founded was the first wholly philosophical magazine published in English. Graduate students in philosophy, Fenollosa among them, would be sure to give it respectful attention.

The *Journal of Speculative Philosophy*, launched in 1867 with Harris as editor, aimed to create a new American philosophy by resolving the opposition between anarchic Emersonian intuitionism and systematic Spencerian mechanism. To open the campaign Harris

8. Hegel, *Lectures on the Philosophy of History*, Eng. Trans. J. Sibree (London, 1867), pp. 109, 90.

selected the field of aesthetics, perhaps because Spencer's ponderous system pushed art into an ornamental corner, or because Emerson had merged art into the formless circles of the Oversoul. Hegel's analysis of romantic art, in particular, forced aesthetic experience inward to an ultimate subjectivity akin to Emerson's views, but the structure of Hegelian aesthetics was highly systematic; Beauty joined Goodness in a magnificently "philosophical" movement toward Truth. The publication of Bénard's "Analytical and Critical Essay on Hegel's Aesthetics" in the early volumes of the *Journal* marked the beginning of systematic consideration of aesthetics by American philosophers.[9]

Fenollosa's aesthetics developed within this idealistic tradition. As a graduate student he may well have discussed Hegel's proposals with a Harvard professor, Charles Carroll Everett. Everett had studied in Germany, and in *The Science of Thought: A System of Logic* (1869) he acknowledged Hegel as a master. Everett intended his work to mediate the antagonism between science and religion by weaning logic from "formalism." The plan was predominantly Hegelian, although his discussion of aesthetics avoided Hegel's tight categories by concentrating on the romantic stage of artistic development. "The aesthetic judgment," wrote Everett, "recognizes the free play, the uncontrolled spontaneity of the result which it contemplates."[10] Yet art for Everett as for Hegel was historical, a developing unity with a com-

---

9. Emerson's reflections on Beauty were intentionally unsystematic. Occasional earlier essays by Americans on aesthetics are mentioned by William Knight in the chapter "The Philosophy of America," in his *The Philosophy of the Beautiful* (2 vols. New York, 1891–93). The democratization of Hegel found further expression in the exuberant "aesthetics" of Walt Whitman. In the early seventies Whitman was outlining a series of lectures on Hegel and German idealism. "Only Hegel is fit for America, is large enough and free enough. Absorbing his speculations and imbued by his letter and spirit, we bring to the study of life here and the thought of hereafter, in all its mystery and vastness, an expansion and clearness of sense before unknown. As a face in a mirror we see the world of materials, nature with all its objects, processes, shows, reflecting the human spirit and by such reflection formulating, identifying, developing, and proving it. Body and mind are one; an inexplicable paradox; yet no truth truer. The human soul stands in the centre, and all the universes minister to it, and serve it and revolve around it. They are one side of the whole and it is the other side. It escapes utterly from all limits, dogmatic standards and measurements and adjusts itself to the ideas of God, of space, and to eternity, and sails them at will as oceans, and fills them as beds of oceans." *The Complete Writings of Walt Whitman*, edited by his literary executors (10 vols. New York, Putnam's, 1902), 9, 170–71. See also ibid., 9, 167–86 and 4, 318–22, for more on Hegel, "the grand ensemblist."

10. *The Science of Thought*, p. 153.

mon life running through all the works of an individual artist and all the historical moments of composite artistic achievement. For Everett the "science of criticism" rested on a base of sympathetic eclecticism. He wrote:

> The critic must not stand on the outside and apply external and foreign measures. He must penetrate to the very heart of what he is examining, must discover the ideal, or the idea, which is its heart, must see how, and how perfectly, it has developed itself, and thus judge every work by a standard of its own. . . . Every period of the history of art has had its own ideal, and thus also its own methods. Each, thus, must be judged by its own principle.[11]

Everett saw no laws for the creation of art, only a succession of original works of genius codified into rules by lesser men. This critical eclecticism characterized Fenollosa's own later approach to the inner ideals of Far Eastern art; its antiformalism anticipated Fenollosa's response to the broader arts of living.

The connections between the fine arts and the arts of living were drawn carefully by Charles Eliot Norton, another Harvard teacher who broadened Fenollosa's sense of possibilities. Norton's enthusiasm and moralism carried the added excitement of breaking new ground in the teaching of history. As early as 1779 Thomas Jefferson had recommended a professorship of ethics and fine arts in his proposal for revising the curriculum of William and Mary; and in 1832 Samuel F. B. Morse had been appointed to the first professorship in fine arts at New York University. Thirty years later James Jackson Jarves had recommended the establishment of professorships of art in order to teach "the relation of art to civilization." But not until the '70s was a start made, notably by Norton at Harvard.

A letter to President Eliot outlined Norton's aims:

> In a complete scheme of University Studies the history of the Fine Arts in relation to social progress, to general culture, and to literature, should find a place, not only because architecture, sculpture, and painting have been, next to literature, the most important modes of expression of the sentiments, beliefs, and opinions of men, but also because they afford evidence, often in a more striking and direct manner than literature itself, of the

11. Ibid., p. 227.

moral temper and intellectual culture of the various races by
whom they have been practised, and thus become the most effective aids to the proper understanding of history. . . . We need
to quicken the sense of connection between the present generation and the past to develop the conviction that culture is but the
name for that inheritance, alike material and moral, that we have
received from our predecessors, and which we are to transmit,
with such additions as we can make to it, to our successors.[12]

To his Harvard students Norton conveyed his own love of beautiful
things and the obligation to consider them historically, the whole
enterprise charged with his ideals for the conduct of life. Norton's
teaching was a second career; and he spoke from a background of
broad experience in the world. He had worked in the East India trade;
he had been a founding editor of the *Nation;* he had written widely
and was a close friend of Ruskin, Carlyle, and the Brownings. The
range of his activities reflected a missionary zeal for public service.

It may well have been Norton who drew Fenollosa toward art and
away from Hegel's "bloodless dance of categories" and the mild theology of the Unitarians. In the spring of 1877 Fenollosa withdrew from
his philosophical studies to work in Boston at the new Massachusetts
Normal Art School and to study painting under Emil Otto Grundmann at the Boston Museum of Fine Arts.

Fenollosa's shift toward art reflected his own uncertain prospects
and a continuing pattern of self-exploration and development. Harvard had opened the way into a world of ideas where he felt very much
at home. He had been powerfully attracted to universal philosophies:
Emersonian pantheism, Spencerian mechanism, Hegelian metaphysics. Teachers like Everett and Norton had confirmed and widened his
own freethinking and cosmopolitan ideals of individualism. But with
sights set so high, it was difficult to be sure of the right beginning. The
sensuous delights of painting could serve to complement the abstractions of the pure philosopher. As a practical matter, academic appointments in philosophy were scarce, especially for a young man with few
connections and heterodox religious inclinations.

At home in Salem prospects were nil. Manuel Fenollosa had remarried and had all he could do to provide for the three young sons
born to him by his second wife, Annie Kinsman. The Salem wharves
were quiet, and the mills had little to offer a young philosopher.

12. C. E. Norton to Charles W. Eliot, January 15, 1874, in Archives, Harvard
University Library.

Fenollosa lived frugally. He often lost track of time and missed meals without caring; aside from art and books he had few expensive tastes. But if he were ever to marry, he would have to have some means of support, especially if the girl were of "higher station," as was his boyhood love, Lizzie Millett. In fact, this same girl drew most of his attentions. In 1877 a career as art teacher and painter seemed a possibility. He had always liked to draw and welcomed the chance to assess his talent properly. Furthermore, the experience would be valuable for a philosopher or a historian of art and might lead in unforeseen directions.

The Boston Museum of Fine Arts and the Massachusetts Normal Art School represented new developments in an American art world riding the crest of a general post-Civil War expansion. Private wealth and public concern rallied to support art under banners of culture and economics. The openings of New York's Metropolitan Museum of Art (1871) and Washington's Corcoran Gallery (1872) were followed by Baltimore's Peabody Institute Art Gallery and art museums in Philadelphia and Boston. Art schools kept pace, stimulated by America's poor showing in art industries at the Philadelphia International Exposition of 1876. As was the case in so many areas of public enlightenment Massachusetts led the way. In 1870 the Massachusetts legislature passed an act whereby all children in tax-supported schools were to be taught to draw. To implement this act the first normal school for training art teachers was established in Boston and opened in 1875.

Fenollosa studied in the makeshift classrooms of the Normal Art School during its third year of operation, working on mechanical drawing, perspective, and historical ornament. Over at the Museum of Fine Arts he rounded out a program of academic art training. There he made careful drawings from the antique and a few studies from life; he learned the techniques of oil painting from a new teacher, Emil Otto Grundmann. Grundmann was himself trained in the atelier of the Düsseldorf painter Julius Hübner, and the characteristically dark Düsseldorf palette is evident in the Fenollosa paintings which have survived. Fenollosa's *Head of a Boy*, however, recalls by its slashing brushwork and dramatic contrasts the Munich style patterned after Franz Hals, which created a stir in Boston when introduced in 1875.[13] In landscape—Fenollosa's abiding enthusiasm—his taste ran

13. Frank Duveneck (1848–1919), from Cincinnati, the first American painter to return from study in Munich, exhibited at the Boston Art Club in 1875. Fenollosa's *Head of a Boy* is in Cismont, Virginia.

not to the meticulous realism of what a later generation has called the Hudson River School but to the delicately muted harmonies of greens and browns achieved by the Barbizon painters. Millet's mastery of dark-and-light relationships set a mark for Fenollosa's later judgments.[14]

For nearly a year Fenollosa studied drawing and painting almost as though waiting for something to happen. His chance when it came was extraordinary and altered the entire course of his life. Early in the winter of 1877–78 he was recommended to fill the first chair of philosophy in Tokyo University, Japan's new institution for the modernization of her knowledge. After generations of isolation Japan had determined to join the modern world, on the best terms she could fashion and with whatever help was most suitable. That Ernest Fenollosa, barely turned twenty-five, should be selected to instruct the future leaders of a nation in the mysteries of Western philosophy was the result of a series of events not even Herbert Spencer could have foreseen, although evolutionary theory offered both an occasion and an explanation.

The man most responsible for Fenollosa's extraordinary chance was a Salem neighbor, Edward S. Morse, a Harvard-trained zoologist. Morse visited Japan in June 1877 in search of brachiopods to test Darwinian theory. His energy and candor so impressed the Japanese authorities that he was invited to organize a department of zoology at the university and to establish a museum of natural history. He accepted and worked in a whirlwind until November, then returned to the United States to fulfill lecture obligations, to bring his family back to Tokyo, and to secure the services of a physicist and a philosopher for the new university. The physics chair offered little difficulty. Morse had a wide acquaintance among scientists, and while lecturing in Columbus, Ohio, his proposal was accepted by Thomas C. Mendenhall, who was then teaching at Ohio Agricultural and Mechanical College. With philosophers Morse was less familiar. His friends at Harvard pointed to the brilliant record in philosophy made by a young Salem man, Ernest Fenollosa. Fenollosa had left the Divinity School to study art, a rather unusual course possibly, but Morse had no sympathy for religious orthodoxy. A philosopher was wanted, not a missionary. He

14. William Morris Hunt (1824–79) introduced and supported Barbizon work in Boston; an opening show at the Boston Museum of Fine Arts in the winter of 1875–76 included seven paintings by Jean François Millet.

talked with his man and sent off a strong recommendation, backed by President Eliot and Professor Charles Eliot Norton.

To Fenollosa the offer was providential. The last several years had been filled with uncertainties, climaxed that January by his father's sudden death. Manuel Fenollosa drowned, an apparent suicide, by walking into the sea at Salem on a Sunday evening. His hat was found on the beach; his body was discovered in April after the spring thaw and was identified by his sister, Isobel Emilio. The Salem newspapers, the *Gazette*, the *Post*, and the *Register*, all reported the "mysterious disappearance" of the music teacher who was the Salem agent for Chickering and Company. No explanation was offered. His health had been good. He had no debts. There had been no gossip. The newspapers reported "no blemish" on his name.

If Manuel Fenollosa left no debts, he left no estate either. To his son Ernest the Japanese government's liberal salary sounded like a fortune. Morse advised him that he could easily save half and still live in princely style. The contract was for two years, but it might be renewed; and there would surely be an audience for lectures once back in the United States. Morse himself was earning over five thousand dollars annually in his public lectures, and Fenollosa's handsome profile and fine voice—he had won the Boylston elocution prize at Harvard—might well lead to a platform career.

For the moment the most important result of the Tokyo post was that Fenollosa could now marry and support a wife in nearly any style to which she might be accustomed. At Harvard he had again courted Lizzie Millett, the girl of his boyhood poems. At last he could offer more than promises. Confirmation of his contract arrived in April. On June 12, 1878, in Salem, Massachusetts, Ernest Francisco Fenollosa was married to Lizzie Goodhue Millett, the only child of Mary Elizabeth Goodhue and Needham Chapman Millett. In July he and his bride sailed westward for Japan.

If the voyage was a honeymoon, it was also an escape from the shadows of Manuel Fenollosa's sudden death. Once again love and death gave a deep urgency to Fenollosa's personal and professional ambitions. The Tokyo opportunity meant more than an exotic interlude; its possibilities were crucial. Fenollosa committed himself totally. The discoveries which might follow were apt to be personal as well as public. Fenollosa was, in a sense, following Melville's Ahab in search of the white whale in Japanese waters, but Fenollosa sought

31

freedom not in death but in life, a freedom not single in its compelling order but multiple in its imagined possibilities. Most important for this heir of Silsbee sea captains, the *Pequod* was not his Harvard. Fenollosa's passage lay among the same "milky-ways of coral isles, and low-lying, endless, unknown Archipelagoes and impenetrable Japans"; but Harvard had shown him the landmarks to guide his philosophical voyages.

Fenollosa's westward voyage marked a new stage in American explorations of the Orient. In Salem the East India Marine Society's collections had become part of the Peabody Academy of Science; the Salem East Indies had been consigned to history as a chapter in the march of scientific progress. The passage to India which excited the best minds of Fenollosa's generation was now an imaginative passage, a probing of time and space which sought to chart the depths of human origins and the breadth of human cultures. The passage was part of the great Western dream of progress. Fenollosa believed in the dream, and like Emerson and Whitman he was prepared to find the cosmos in a blade of grass and to seek cosmopolis in every village and town.

PART 2 · *In Search of Cosmopolis*

To the merit of our Sensei, high
like the mountains and eternal
like the water.

Inscription on the Fenollosa
Monument in Uyeno Park, Tokyo

4 · DAIJIN SENSEI (TEACHER OF GREAT MEN)

As Fenollosa steamed across the Pacific with his bride in August 1878
he may have sensed something of the wider significance of his voyage.
His cosmopolitanism was already clear, rooted in family experience
and articulated in the spirit of Emerson and Whitman, and his enthusiasm for Spencer and Hegel had vitalized his sense of historical
development. More certainly Fenollosa realized that his own future
depended on the outcome of the voyage, that his career would have
to be of his own making. As it turned out, the extraordinary opportunities of a brief historical moment challenged his talents in unexpected and decisive ways.

Part of Fenollosa's opportunity lay in Western ignorance of Japanese culture, an ignorance to which Americans could claim no exception. To the boys of Salem "impenetrable Japan" had been one of
a line of dangers for American sailors in Far Eastern seas. Shipwreck
on the Japanese isles meant imprisonment or death. The treaties of
the 1850s reduced these hazards and opened several Japanese ports
for trading, but foreign "barbarians" were restricted to treaty ports,
and the first accounts of Japan were little more than fragments suggesting an exotic land of toylike savages. Walt Whitman had characteristically raised high his "perpendicular hand" in "Salut Au Monde"
(1856) to hail "You Japanese man or woman! You liver in Madagas-
car, Ceylon, Sumatra, Borneo." But Japan remained blurred amid
hazy notions of the far-away Orient, merged with Ceylon and Borneo
and other "low-lying Archipelagoes."

In the United States the first particular stir singling out Japan fol-

35

lowed the Japanese treaty mission of 1860, which visited several American cities. When the envoys joined a parade up New York's Broadway, Whitman took occasion to muse over the full circle of the human passage westward, now reversed. As he phrased it in a poem in the *New York Times*, "To us, then at last the Orient comes," from "Niphon"

> Courteous, the swart-cheek'd two-sworded envoys,
> Leaning back in their open barouches, bare-headed, impassive
> Ride to-day through Manhattan.

More significant in terms of popular attention was P. T. Barnum's quick promotion of Japanese curiosities—coins, lanterns, autographs. What interest there was about Japan among Americans in the '60s and early '70s focused on tales of exotic customs brought back by a very few travelers and more usually contained in missionary reports. The missionaries alternately boasted of sweet, mild-mannered converts to Christianity and inveighed against the pagan immoralities of the natives, notably their quick violence and easy sexual customs. A stereotype of the Japanese was already forming in the double image of the gentle savage in a barbarous toyland, an image developed for a later generation of Americans into the seeming paradox of the chrysanthemum and the sword.

These scraps of exotic information were little help to prospective visitors, and Fenollosa was fortunate in having Morse at hand with advice as to what a young American professor might expect. Morse was a brilliant observer, with an anthropologist's eye for significant detail and a quick pen for sketching pictures to document his encyclopedic curiosity. He was a cataloguer, however, a natural scientist intent on classification; he had little to say about the beauties of Japanese art. In this regard Fenollosa was completely unprepared for the magnificent paintings and sculpture he encountered. It could not have been otherwise, given the widespread ignorance of these areas throughout the West; even Japanese prints were little known outside avant-garde circles. Most Americans in the middle '70s were unaware of Japanese art in any form. The Japanese exhibit at the Philadelphia Centennial Exposition in 1876 was "a revelation to most people," as Fenollosa's colleague T. C. Mendenhall remarked.[1] The following year in New York Tiffany and Company offered for sale 1900 lots of

1. Thomas C. Mendenhall, "Autobiographical Notes" (1904), 4, 102, MS in possession of Thomas C. Mendenhall II, Northampton, Mass.

curios selected in Japan, and a Japanese vogue gained momentum. That same year the Kiritsu Kosho Kaisha, chartered by the Japanese government for encouragement of native art industries, opened a branch office in New York. The craftsmanship of these curios was often excellent, but there was no Japanese painting or sculpture, nor even any woodblock prints.

The absence of painting and sculpture from Japanese exhibits abroad was not accidental. It was part of a conscious effort to break away from whatever traditions might impede Japanese progress toward equality with the modern industrial nations of the West. The inferiority of the material culture of former times seemed clear in the face of Western guns; weakness was humiliating and the old ways were bound up with weakness. After the fall of the Shogunate and the restoration of the Emperor in 1868, Japan reversed the Tokugawa policy of hostile isolation and set out to master the secrets of Western power in order to preserve national dignity and sustain national aims. If the pursuit of power required a wholesale adoption of Western ways, so be it. The ensuing vogue of things Western on the surface of daily life among "advanced" Japanese reflected the prestige of Western power. The practical focus is clear in a song for children composed in 1878, the year of Fenollosa's arrival. Called the "Civilization Ball Song," it tallied the bounces of the ball by the names of ten exemplary Western objects: gas lamps, steam engines, horse-carriages, cameras, telegrams, lightning-conductors, newspapers, schools, mail routes, and steamboats.[2]

Ernest Fenollosa and his young bride—he was twenty-five, she twenty-four—arrived in Yokohama in August 1878. They took the train up to Tokyo and were soon established on the grounds of the University in a comfortable house, Number One Kaga Yashiki. Edward Morse was already there in Number Five, and T. C. Mendenhall arrived shortly to occupy Number Two. The Fenollosas' one-story house was solidly built and compact, not large by Western standards but well suited to the young couple. As befitted honored guests of the Japanese Government, special care was taken to provide every amenity. Servants tended to household needs, and Professor Fenollosa's monthly salary of 300 yen (raised to 370 two years later) permitted them to live well. Beautiful things and a prospective summer house in the mountains added a note of luxury. Lizzie Fenollosa must have

2. Cited in G. B. Sansom, *The Western World and Japan* (New York, Knopf, 1950), p. 383.

been charmed; her ample scale of living may even have quieted her parents' misgivings about their only daughter's adventurous marriage.

Even before Fenollosa and Mendenhall were properly settled, their talents were pressed into service by their eager hosts. Along with Morse the two American professors were engaged immediately, before term opening, to speak every Sunday before the Lecture Association, a group of leading Japanese, primarily civil servants and mature students. For a time they were the only foreigners giving these public lectures, and their audience sat in close attention throughout the day as long as the lecturers would stay. Morse continued his teaching of Darwinian evolution; Mendenhall lectured on "Physical Science"; and Fenollosa expounded Herbert Spencer's scientific philosophy.[3] Then back to the three houses in Kaga Yashiki.

"Kaga Yashiki" signified the official residence of the Lord of Kaga province. Quarters for his retinue clustered around the main house, and the grounds were entered through a red lacquer gateway built in 1828 for the marriage of the Shogun's daughter to a Kaga heir. The presence of the three Americans, two scientists and a philosopher, living and teaching on the grounds of this feudal estate indicated the seriousness of Japanese efforts to enter the modern world of science and industry.

The Satsuma Rebellion of the summer before proved to be the last stand of warrior diehards. The central government's conscript army had defeated a strong samurai force, serving notice of a crucial shift of aristocratic energies from swords to pens. An imperial edict of 1876 had banned samurai wearing of swords, the traditional badge of rank, and samurai class privileges had been steadily reduced. In 1871 the government had revoked the samurai prerogative of cutting down any commoner thought insulting. In 1873 the vendetta was made illegal (duels were not banned until 1889). Most important, the economic base of samurai social position had been eroding for some time with the decline of the feudal land-revenue system which had supplied rice allowances. These allowances had declined in value even before the Restoration, but now they vanished, and what pensions were granted in compensation left the samurai generally impoverished, their status further threatened by newly mobile, property-owning commoners.

3. For an account of these pioneer lectures see Mendenhall, "Autobiographical Notes" (1904), 4, 121 ff., and E. S. Morse, *Japan Day by Day* (Boston, Houghton Mifflin, 1917), 2, 428–29.

Nevertheless the samurai, some four hundred thousand strong, remained the major resource in building the new Japan. Able young samurai, partly because they had little to lose, committed themselves to the new order and were soon established as a self-perpetuating oligarchy, monopolizing posts in the government bureaucracy and the armed forces. Very few of the old feudal lords played major roles in the Meiji years; the new leaders were nearly all former samurai of modest origin, men who believed in disciplined firmness and in duties over rights. Traditional samurai contempt for commercial careers persisted for some time, leaving the struggle for political power at the center of the national stage.

The political center was Tokyo, and the energies of national growth radiated outward in systematically centralized procedures and institutions. Although social ferment was widespread, the forces of modernization were guided by a relatively small group of ambitious men who held power in the name of the Emperor. Since the acquisition of modern knowledge was considered essential to national aims, Tokyo University (named Imperial University in 1886) was an instrument of national policy. As such its classes offered access to national careers as well as to Western knowledge. For a short while knowledge actually meant power. Knowledge of Western ways and Western learning carried not only the prestige of fashion but the authority of superior culture and superior personal prospects. It is not surprising that Fenollosa's students were eager to learn or that there were so many future leaders of Japan among them that Fenollosa became known as *Daijin Sensei*—Teacher of Great Men.[4]

For his part, Fenollosa was impressed by the quality of his students from the very first, as is evident from a letter to one of his classmates in April of 1880: "I found the University in remarkably fine condition, considering that the country had so lately emerged from what must be termed, at least relatively speaking, a state of profound ignorance. Some two hundred students were at work in the special elective courses, reading English books, and speaking and writing that lan-

4. Fenollosa's students included the following distinguished scholars and intellectuals: the philosophers Yujiro Miyake and Tetsujiro Inouye; the Buddhist scholar Enryo Inouye; the novelist and teacher Yuzo Tsubouchi; the historian of Japanese literature Kenzo Wadagaki; the president of Waseda University, Sanae Takada; the painter Jigoro Kano; the social economist Noboru Kanai; the constitutional scholar Yatsuka Hozumi. For a more extensive list see Mitsugu Hisatomi, *Fenollosa* (Tokyo, 1957), pp. 81–82.

guage fluently. A finer set of young men, or more earnest workers and keener thinkers, cannot, I venture to say, be found in any university in the world." [5]

The 1870s in Japan were extraordinary years for a philosopher. The times gave such vital relevance to ideas that their reality seemed self-evident. Theories of society and development, moral, political, economic, were not merely academic to Fenollosa's students, some of them already holding responsible posts. Japanese leaders sought guidance for framing long-term plans; a theory persuasively expounded might thus find application on a grand scale. Or, more certainly, theories propounded one day might be cited on the next as authoritative arguments to support a maneuver for political power. On a more personal level, a general theory might persuade a student, for a moment, that he had made sense out of the world, that all experience hangs together somehow, and that this particular rational, consistent account of things offered a special key to the secrets of the West—and possibly the world. Ideas meant policy, argument, explanation, even conversion. The intellectual milieu of Tokyo was unusually receptive to the kinds of sweeping speculative systems that Fenollosa was drawn to both temperamentally and by training.

Fenollosa began his lecturing by expounding Herbert Spencer's systematic theories of social development. The young philosopher had been enthusiastic about Spencer at Harvard, and since Morse's lectures on evolutionary biology were so successful, Fenollosa concentrated on evolutionary sociology in the Sunday talks he gave with Morse before university classes convened. Spencer complemented Darwin and was well-suited to the members of the Lecture Association, many of them ranking civil servants who would have listened attentively all day if the Americans could have been persuaded. Fenollosa may have been asked specifically to expound Spencer, since the English philosopher seemed to explain Western progress—and everything else for that matter—in scientific and authoritative fashion. Spencer's reputation in Japan in 1878 was already considerable. A Japanese translation of his *Social Statics* had been published the year before, and many of those who could read English had sought in his other voluminous writings a key to Western learning. Spencer revealed the universe as a simple system, and his synthesis of all knowledge prom-

5. Letter of April 16, 1880, from EFF probably to George Sanger, secretary of Harvard's Class of 1874, quoted in *Class of 1874 of Harvard College, Third Report*, 1880, p. 20.

ised to be supremely useful—a staple of argument and a frame for understanding complicated kinds of new information. The laws of progress revealed by social Darwinism provided grounds for optimism, and the slogan *Yusho Reppai* (Superior Wins, Inferior Loses) readily justified consolidation of power and the centralizing trends inherited from the Tokugawa period and elaborated in the course of modernization.

Spencer's economic individualism offered difficulties, especially to men oriented toward family and clan, but instruction was eagerly sought. Smiles' *Self-Help*, the manual of success so popular in England and the United States, was received enthusiastically in many editions after its first translation into Japanese in 1870. Even *Robinson Crusoe*, recurrently popular, served to instruct; as one translator put it in his preface, "If men will read it carefully they will see that it shows how by stubborn determination an island can be developed." [6]

The English example of an island kingdom which had risen to imperial eminence was widely admired in the '60s and '70s and lent authority to British writers. The Japanese mission to Europe in 1861 had been much impressed by British power, wealth, and institutions. The study of English had been pressed energetically, and the adoption of English as the major language for education was under consideration for some time; in fact English language and literature held a strong position well into the nineties, particularly at Tokyo University. All of which evidenced an intellectual atmosphere hospitable to Spencer's theories.[7]

One of Fenollosa's distinguished colleagues, a professor of literature, Shoichi Toyama, had returned from the University of Michigan in 1876 thoroughly imbued with Spencer's system, which he presented to good effect. The combined advocacies of Fenollosa and Toyama have been credited with making a lasting impression on Japanese thinking; certainly the moment was suited to Spencer.

Fenollosa's original two-year appointment as professor of political economy and philosophy was renewed in 1880 and 1882, and in 1884 he became professor of philosophy and logic. During the first three

6. Quoted in Sansom, *The Western World and Japan*, p. 398.

7. As late as 1892 Spencer's advice on racial intermarriage was sought officially to resolve the question of improving Japanese stock by marriage with occidentals. Spencer replied that intermarriage should be forbidden on biological grounds. See Chitoshi Yanaga, *Japan Since Perry* (New York, McGraw-Hill, 1949), p. 97. The proposal involved Japanese males only.

years his teaching centered on Spencer, gradually extending to include contrasting currents traditional and contemporary (he introduced his Harvard teacher Bowen's book, *Modern Philosophy*), but as his own artistic activities increased he was pulled more strongly toward German idealism. When another professor became available to instruct in political philosophy and a Japanese returned from Europe to expound political economy, Fenollosa was free to follow his special interests in aesthetics, logic, and religion. And he found a Hegelian framework not only congenial but peculiarly suited for holding together his broad speculations and his personal responses. The courses which Fenollosa presented in 1884 to each of his undergraduate classes indicate the direction his thinking was taking: Freshman— Synthetic Logic; Sophomore—History of Modern Philosophy to Hegel; Junior—Hegel with Side Glances at Spencer; Senior—Ethics, Aesthetics, and the Philosophy of Religion.

Hegelian idealism did not have Spencer's practical appeal to Japanese intellectuals; Hegel was not scientific in Spencer's materialist sense. Although Hegel was satisfyingly systematic and sweeping, his language was difficult or, more likely, opaque. Hegel's particular appeal lay in his support of the State as an Absolute, an idea quickly applied to buttress Japanese efforts to build a stable nation on a base of absolute loyalty to the Emperor. The Imperial Rescript of 1886, for example, reorganized national education to stress obligations to the Emperor and the respect due to ancestors and to the process of national growth. A Japanese Hegelian could view the Emperor and his counselors as the culmination of social development. In this context Fenollosa's Hegelian enthusiasm lent support to the assertive nationalism of the late '80s and '90s. As part of a general pattern of Japanese intellectual development Fenollosa's lectures have been called "the turning point of Japanese thinkers toward German philosophy." [8]

Although the impact of Fenollosa's interpretations of Spencer and Hegel was due largely to the prestige of Western thought, his personal enthusiasm made his lectures striking. Lectures of any sort were still very much a novelty in Japan. Public speaking was a Western innovation, and a British historian has noted that among most cultured Japanese it was considered "slightly improper for a man to presume

8. Yujiro Miyake, "The Introduction of Western Philosophy," in *Fifty Years of New Japan*, Eng. trans. by Marcus B. Huish (2 vols. London, Smith, Elder, 1909), 2, 231.

to disclose his views aloud and without decent restraint." [9] In England and America, by contrast, the orator was in his heyday. The lecture platform offered a prestige and influence which drew the most distinguished men of the day, and Fenollosa's ambition ran early in this direction. He had a fine voice and a confident bearing. Although not a large man by American standards, he was considerably taller than most Japanese, and a bristling black beard helped conceal his youthfulness in a land where age carried authority. If his enthusiasm seemed barbarous to some of his listeners, it was none the less persuasive, even contagious. The critical comments of a nationalistic Japanese philosopher are revealing: "Professor Fenollosa's discourses, lacking in subtlety and exactness, gave an impression akin to that produced by scratching one's feet outside one's shoes [not in direct contact], yet his eloquence had no small influence upon students." [10]

Fenollosa was an enthusiast in a moral sense that reflected the strong ties of New England and Harvard with the great Victorians. His enthusiasm was rooted in sensibility; virtue was felt to derive its vitality from those noble emotions which can lead men into the delighted service of a high ideal. This kind of enthusiasm did not preclude moral discipline and a dutiful seriousness; it was a matter of emphasis.[11] Fenollosa was impatient of limitations, more admiring than critical, and his eloquence drew his students to expand their speculations in all directions, to explore the cosmopolis of the intellect.

Fenollosa's lack of arrogance is equally important to an understanding of his relations with his Japanese students and friends. Representatives of the West spoke of their civilization with a confidence which reached a peak in the 1870s and '80s. Progress seemed assured; nothing was impossible. The superiority of Western civilization was assumed in ways not always pleasant for non-Westerners. The arrogant Western imperialists of the '90s were not yet in full cry, nor were the more strident racists yet in evidence, but many of the Europeans and English in Japan tended to lump all Japanese together in a native class. Accustomed to class deference at home, these foreigners

9. Sansom, *The Western World and Japan*, p. 351.
10. Miyake, p. 231.
11. In *The Victorian Frame of Mind* (New Haven, Yale University Press, 1957), Walter E. Houghton ascribes this kind of enthusiasm to a minority group —Mill, Morley, Browning, George Eliot—and contrasts it to a dominant moral earnestness which stressed conscience, mastery of passion, and willed duty. Earnestness and enthusiasm often complemented each other, however.

lived apart in Western style with an air of condescending superiority not endearing to members of a culture unusually sensitive to status and face. Japanese manners, obsequious by Western standards, puffed up Western egos and often confirmed Westerners in their indifference to Japanese culture, a basic complacency which permitted a taste for the exotic, since exoticism also preserved social distance. The American scholars, on the other hand, tended to approach the Japanese more as equals,[12] which may help account for the extensive use of American advisers, especially in the educational field. Certainly Fenollosa refused the refuge of an easily assumed superiority of culture or race. Here again he was fortunate in having Morse as guide.

Morse had come to Japan with few preconceptions and had been delighted at the enthusiastic response to his scientific programs. His direct observations had given him broad respect for Japanese energies and hospitality. Morse's open, hearty manner and his vigorous candid approach embodied the best elements of America's egalitarian ideals. Attitudes of racial superiority and inferiority were simply not part of his make-up, and he had little patience with self-righteous missionaries' strictures on Japanese life or with the condescension of foreigners.[13] From the beginning Fenollosa was impressed with Japanese abilities and by the richness and complexity of their cultural tradition. His students were disciplined and attentive; they were willing to make real sacrifices for their education; and he reported that he had soon found out they were worthy "antagonists at dialectics."

12. T. C. Mendenhall commented on this in his "Autobiographical Notes."

13. Morse was convinced, as he confided to an old friend, "that the expenses of the missionaries are entirely out of proportion to the good they accomplish and that the teaching of peculiar religious views are [sic] an obstacle in attempts to change a people. When the people change their habits, it is from imitation or because experience shows it to be more successful, and the logical absurdity of doctrine for these people arises when the city which contains the greatest number of representatives of Christian nations is notoriously the most licentious, profane, indecent and corrupt city in Japan. The banks are gouges, the merchants are horse jockeys and the whole foreign settlement given up to debauchery. Now, please don't publish this, but I assure you it is a fact without the slightest exaggeration. Yokohama is a bad place and for that reason I scrupulously avoid going there more than I can help. The Japs know this and they don't want the religion of the [Yokohama] people. . . . Understand there are some delightful people there among the missionaries but as a town it is reckless and asbolutely indecent." E. S. Morse to John Gould, Tokyo, July 14, 1878, quoted in Dorothy Wayman, *Edward Sylvester Morse* (Cambridge, Mass., Harvard University Press, 1942), p. 250.

Fenollosa's respect for his students gave a special quality to their loyalty to him, a loyalty strengthened by traditional Japanese feelings of obligation toward one's teacher. A man's teacher was due lifelong deference from his students and suitable offerings of thanks over the years. The great respect for teachers stemmed traditionally from the moral character of instruction. Education was designed to lead a young man toward virtue, to shape his character so that he might take a fit part in society. The teacher was respected for his learning; he was reverenced for the quality of his ideals and the wisdom of his conduct. These traditional attitudes were marked among the former samurai and their sons seated at Fenollosa's feet in the early years of the University. Nor has the more impersonal utilitarian mode of modern education displaced this tradition completely even today, especially since Imperial University has retained its command over access to many careers.

What was particularly significant about this esteem for Fenollosa as a teacher was that it gave him crucial help in his exploration of the arts of Japanese life and the traditions of Japanese art. His major work in art criticism and art history owes a great deal to the help provided by his students. He came as a philosopher; he remained as a teacher. The moment made him a teacher of great men.

In fact we are a live Art Club
right out here in the East.

Ernest Fenollosa to Edward
Morse, April 26, 1884

5 · AN AMERICAN REVIVAL OF JAPANESE ART

Fenollosa's position as teacher of philosophy to a new generation of
political and intellectual leaders was instrumental in enabling him to
influence the direction of Japanese artistic development. Again, the
unique conditions which prevailed in Japan in the early '80s created
the extraordinary opportunities which led a young American philosopher to play a leading role in restoring the prestige of traditional Japanese art and, in effect, reviving Japanese nationalism in the arts. Ironically, it was easier for Fenollosa as a Westerner to lead the national
revival. For a brief moment his authority was real; Western approval
was important, particularly for anti-Western opinions. Fenollosa
would have become a connoisseur in any case, but his swift rise to a
position of national leadership stemmed from the conditions of the
moment, notably from twin Japanese attitudes of adulation of Western art as Western and contempt for native art as "uncivilized."
When Fenollosa's researches led him to reverse this judgment he became a national figure, his eminence a measure of the intensity of the
Westernizing purpose in the '70s and '80s and a sign of nationalist
reactions to come.

When Fenollosa arrived in Japan in 1878, Japanese painting and
painters were in dire straits. The break-up of the feudal power of the
clans and the reorganization of the court had deprived the hereditary
artists of their positions, and the new Japan tended to discard traditional art along with its feudal past. The artists of the Kano family no
longer had the patronage of the daimyos, and the official court school
of Tosa painters lost all support. Many of the art collections of the

clans could be bought for a pittance, and the great temple collections had fallen into disorder and decay, the more so with Restoration disestablishment of Buddhism.

Although Western techniques of painting had been introduced during the Shogunate by the Dutch, not until the 1860s and '70s did Western art begin to dominate the scene. The Institute for the Investigation of Foreign Books, founded in 1857, offered instruction in Western drawing, a practice followed in the early '70s by the art schools of Takahashi and Kunisawa. In 1876, the newly organized Imperial Engineering College placed the Italian artist Fontanesi in charge of the art department, and a succession of Italians taught young Japanese painters elements of perspective and anatomy and the "correct" use of shadow and light. A generation of painters was growing up who had never heard of the Kano or Tosa styles or of Sesshu, or of the great Chinese painters of the past.

Among Japanese of traditional education the vogue of Chinese *bunjingwa* (*wen jen hua*), or "literary men's paintings," had swept all other styles aside. Anyone who wanted to be thought cultivated stroked his brush elegantly and proclaimed his work art. When Fenollosa began his investigations, many cultured Japanese dismissed as vulgar all art but *bunjingwa*, saying "nothing but ink rocks and black bamboos are refined enough for a gentleman to paint." [1]

Art industries also suffered in the early years of the Restoration. Sword-guards and gilt lacquer were no longer in demand, and many craftsmen, deprived of feudal patronage, were forced into other work. In an attempt to expand foreign markets, Western styles were widely imitated, and articles of inferior craftsmanship poured from Japan in response to supposed Western taste.[2] The Japanese commissioners to the Vienna International Exhibition of 1873 returned with a recommendation that the development of national characteristics would provide the best entry into foreign markets. Four years later the first National Industrial Exhibition was held, with a special department for applied arts, this time resolutely "Japanese" and understandable to Westerners as such. But this was a commercial matter, and many of the samurai leaders of the new Japan retained a traditional disregard for the cultural value of commerce.

1. Fenollosa, *Epochs of Chinese and Japanese Art*, 2, 165.
2. Morse noted in 1879 the marked inferiority of Japanese articles made for the barbarian export market; see E. S. Morse, *Japan Day by Day* (Boston, Houghton Mifflin, 1917), 2, 185–86.

The Japanese commissioners to Vienna also brought back the contemporary Western distinction between the applied arts and the fine arts, and the term *bijutsu* was introduced to refer to the higher arts of painting, drawing, sculpture, and architecture.[3] There was a discreet silence on the question of whether *bijutsu* should apply to the art created under the Tokugawa shoguns and earlier. But the junk heaps of the old temples and the discard of family collections indicated acceptance of the Western standards of Fontanesi and the drawing instructors at the engineering schools, standards of a narrowly representational art. By these standards the work of the Japanese masters was amateurish because inaccurate, regardless of the traditional Japanese assumption that to copy nature was to do the work of a mere artisan, since a true artist sought not realistic detail but the informing spirit.

To make matters more confusing for Japanese judgments, it seemed that there were some Westerners, few in number but possibly influential, who regarded wood-block prints as Japan's best and characteristic form of pictorial art. To a Japanese gentleman these were common and ordinary, not *bijutsu* in any sense; the Western vogue for prints seemed patronizing, even insulting. In private this strange taste was doubtless dismissed as a sign of Western barbarism.

This was the situation, then, when Fenollosa began his studies of Japanese art: Western standards controlled the fine arts; the Western market determined the quality of the applied arts; cultured Japanese still esteemed calligraphic *bunjingwa* as a major gentlemanly accomplishment.

Fenollosa's activities led him into archaeology and art criticism and on into art education and administration, but he started as a collector. Trained as a painter himself along the lines of meticulous realism made fashionable by the Düsseldorf ateliers, he was intrigued at first by paintings he bought from the Tokyo dealers who supplied Westerners with curios. The subjects of the paintings were exotic, their compositions curiously spacious although not unified in perspective, their brushwork thin almost like water color but surprisingly solid. Fenollosa showed them to his friends rather proudly; a collection of paintings would complement his mentor Morse's Japanese pottery collection. However, when he showed his prizes to Kentaro Kaneko, a

3. Traditionally in Japan only painting had been regarded as a noble art, with an exception made for Buddhist sculpture. All other artistic activities were esteemed by the Japanese as crafts.

former noble recently returned from study at Harvard, Kaneko advised him that the paintings were poor imitations of famous works, and it was arranged for Fenollosa to see the art collection of Kaneko's former lord, Marquis Kuroda. The Kuroda collection was dazzling, rich in the authentic works of such masters as Sesshu and Motonobu. Fenollosa was overwhelmed.

The Kuroda collection set Fenollosa off on the explorations and speculations of a lifetime. With the special help of two students, Nagao Ariga and Kakuzo Okakura, he undertook systematic investigation of these beautiful paintings and of the circumstances of their creation. He began compiling charts of Chinese and Japanese history, especially intellectual history or, as he called it, a history of doctrines. He read biographies of painters and what commentaries on painting he could find, relying heavily on Ariga and Okakura for translation and interpretation. Most fortunately he gained access to the surviving members of the Kano and Tosa schools of painting, the last in a long line of painters to the courts of shogun and mikado. Morse's interpreter, young Miyaoka, introduced Fenollosa to Tomonobu Kano, who in turn managed to borrow from the family of Katsukawa Kano the *Koga Biko*, a rare, forty-eight volume biographical dictionary of artists compiled and illustrated with copies by Asaoka Kano. Shortly thereafter, toward the end of 1879, Fenollosa began receiving instruction from the patriarch Eitoku Kano, who interpreted the ancient canons with the aid of model books handed down for generations. At the same time Fenollosa studied with Sumiyoshi Hirokata, the Tosa elder, who advised him of the secrets of the Yamato school painters.

The few collections of traditional painting which Fenollosa could find in Tokyo made him all the more anxious to investigate farther afield. An elderly connoisseur told of notable collections in old temples and castles spread across Japan, especially in the area around Kyoto. The contents of these collections were known largely by hearsay, and Fenollosa determined to see for himself. Travel by foreigners outside seaport areas was still substantially restricted, but since Fenollosa was a government servant and a Tokyo professor with well-connected friends, he had little difficulty. In the summers of 1880 and 1881 he traveled extensively, beginning in Nara and Kyoto, visiting all the temples and castles he could find, persuading priests and daimyos to let him examine some of the old relics—paintings and statuary—many of them regarded by their owners as worthless. It was on that first summer trip that he bought the six-panel Korin screen now in the Boston Museum of Fine Arts, its wild swirling waves suggestive of Fenollosa's own mounting enthusiasm.

As Fenollosa rummaged through piles of statuary and patiently unrolled scores of paintings, he found a world of great beauty, a world whose sensuous delights were heightened by the excitements of discovery and by a growing sense of the world-historical implications of his finds. Here was evidence of a civilization virtually unknown to the West, a civilization which had risen, flourished, and declined, its artistic height a match for anything produced in Western history. If an outline of this flowering of Sino-Japanese civilization could be reconstructed, it would stand alongside accounts of Greece and Rome as a record of major human achievement. Revelation of Asian greatness might well spur the scholars of a new Renaissance toward a cosmopolitan culture whose history was not parochially Western but a genuine world history. The prospects were intoxicating. Even Hegel had not imagined the energies of Asian development. Hegel's view of the East in terms of static despotisms, a widespread Western attitude, simply did not tally with the evidence of evolutionary change discernible in Sino-Japanese civilization. Much more work was needed, but it was increasingly clear to Fenollosa that the Japanese were denying an artistic heritage which they should honor and which the West could no longer overlook.

By the spring of 1882 Fenollosa had become convinced that the Japanese artistic tradition included works by master painters who could match any artists in the world. On May 14, in a speech before the Ryuchikai, a club of aristocrats, he opened a broadside attack on the Japanese craze for Western art, which had led to derision of classical Japanese painting as inferior to the representational art popular in the West. This craze meant losing sight of the primary purpose of art, expression of the idea at the heart of the painting. Fenollosa's philosophical frame of reference was idealism. His aesthetic judgments were highly personal. The effect of his speech was to stir currents of nationalism. "Japanese art," proclaimed Fenollosa,

> is really far superior to modern cheap western art that describes any object at hand mechanically, forgetting the most important point, expression of Idea. Despite such superiority the Japanese despise their classical paintings, and with adoration for western civilization admire its artistically worthless modern paintings and imitate them for nothing. What a sad sight it is! The Japanese

should return to their nature and its old racial traditions, and then take, if there are any, the good points of western painting.[4]

It was an Emersonian invitation to the Japanese to paint their own paintings, to close their ears to the muse of Europe, to graft onto the native tree only those foreign elements they found fit.

The young Westerner's strong opinions acted to crystallize many of the doubts in the minds of his aristocratic audience, and as Fenollosa embarked on specific programs to promote the national art revival which he urged, official support swung behind him. Among those who heard his Ryuchikai talk were men of wide influence, including Count Sano, the club's founder, and Fukuoka, the Minister of Education. That summer instructions went out from Tokyo to the district governors of all provinces, requiring them to compile lists of the art works of the temples. In the autumn the government prohibited the display of Western-style oil paintings at the art exhibitions sponsored by the Department of Agriculture and Commerce in Tokyo's Uyeno Park; Fenollosa was on the jury. Most significantly, the art school of the Imperial Engineering College was closed; the stronghold of Western artistic instruction was overthrown by simple fiat. As further evidence of this new attitude an official exhibition of Japanese art in Paris in June 1883 was careful to exclude all Western-style paintings and *bunjingwa*, the calligraphic work which Fenollosa opposed steadfastly after his study with professional artists of the Kano and Tosa schools.

In all these policy reversals Fenollosa's ideas were evident, and the young professor found himself a prominent national figure. One result was that his researches received more encouragement than ever. On his summer trips in 1884 he was accompanied by a special commissioner assigned by the Ministry of Education to observe his methods and to smooth the way. Fenollosa's investigations of Buddhist temple art were never easy. Buddhist priests could still remember the anxious times of the *haibutsu kishaku* (exterminate Buddhism) movement of 1869–71, when hundreds of temples had been closed down. In some

4. "Truth of Fine Arts," address of May 14, 1882; under the title "Bijutsu Shinsetsu," Fenollosa's address was reprinted in *Meiji Bunka Zenshu* [Collection of Works on Meiji Culture], (Tokyo, Nihon Kyoronsha, 1928–30), 12, 159–74. For translation of this and other Japanese material I am indebted to Mr. Mikiso Hane, Assistant Professor of History, Knox College. The excerpt here quoted is taken from Taro Kotakane, "Ernest Francisco Fenollosa," *Bulletin of Eastern Art*, no. 16 (April 1941), 22.

areas Buddhist shrines had been ransacked by Shinto priests with the support of daimyos long jealous of the Buddhist establishment. The priests were wary of intruders and had no notion that old statues might be important for archaeological reasons, or that works of art might bring international acclaim to the new Japan. Okakura's account of the discovery of the long-hidden Buddha of the Yumedono suggests the excitement of Fenollosa's archaeological tours:

> In 1884 Fenollosa, Kano Tetsusai and myself appeared before the temple priests and asked them to open its gates. The priests said that opening the gates would certainly produce a clap of thunder. In the first year of Meiji, when there were disputes over the confusion of Shintoism and Buddhism, the gates were temporarily opened; suddenly the whole sky was overcast, there was a burst of thunder, and everyone was much afraid. The whole matter was suspended at this point. The previous example was still so conspicuous that they did not easily comply with our request. And when we began to open the gates they were so afraid that they fled. When we opened the shrine gates, the stench of almost one thousand years assailed our nostrils. Brushing aside the cobwebs, we saw a low table of the Higashiyama period. When we cleared this aside, there, directly before us was the sacred statue which measured some eight or nine feet in height. The statue was wrapped in many layers of cloth. Surprised by the presence of human beings, snakes and mice suddenly scampered, frightening us. We approached the statue, and when we removed the cloth wrappings there was underneath a covering of white paper. This was the point which had been reached in the first year of Meiji, when the clap of thunder had been heard and the uncovering of the statue was suspended. We saw behind the white paper the serene face of the statue. This was truly one of the greatest pleasures of a lifetime. Fortunately, there was no clap of thunder and the priests were greatly reassured.[5]

Fenollosa's discoveries on these summer expeditions confirmed his feeling that he was opening an important new field. In a letter to his old mentor Morse, who was back in Salem, he recounted proudly the progress being made; the work was extraordinary for a thirty-year-old philosopher from Salem, Massachusetts.

5. Quoted in Masaaki Kosaka, *Japanese Thought in the Meiji Era*, Eng. trans. David Abosch (Tokyo, Pan-Pacific Press, 1958), pp. 226–27.

We have been through all the principal temples in Yamashiro and Yamato armed with government letters and orders, have ransacked godowns, and brought to light pieces of statue from the lowest stratum of debris in the top stories of pagodas 1300 years old. We may say in brief that we have made the first accurate list of the great art treasures kept in the central temples of Japan, we have overturned the traditional criticism attached to these individual specimens for ages, the Dr. [William Sturgis Bigelow] has taken 200 photographs and I innumerable sketches of art objects (paintings and statues); and, more than all, I have recovered the history of Japanese art from the 6th to the 9th centuries A.D. which has been completely lost. I have done it by a chain of close reasonings based on a comparative study of all the specimens, many of which have never been shown to any one before. The priests were everywhere greedy for my certificates, and I have issued more than 100 for things which were absolutely unidentified before. I have found Chinese things called Japanese, and vice versa, many Japanese called Corean, new things called old, and even some old ones called new; and as to names of individual artists hopelessly mixed up. Yet this is the result of native criticism for centuries.[6]

So long as art works were considered simply as temple furniture or private luxuries, lists were unheard of; the very idea that art works might be national assets was Western, as was the study of archaeology. Two years later Fenollosa was asked by the government to prepare a list of national art treasures. The subsequent passage of laws for the preservation of old temples stemmed directly from his expeditions and pronouncements.

Fenollosa's star climbed rapidly in the years following his Ryuchikai speech, and his work seemed more and more important in its world-historical implications. His archaeological expeditions and general historical researches combined with his training in the techniques and traditions of the Kano and Tosa schools to give a special authority to his natural connoisseurship. What had begun as a campaign to restore the prestige of traditional Japanese art rapidly became a widespread movement to revive that art in contemporary terms and make it an instrument of national development. But more than this, Fenollosa

6. EFF to E. S. Morse, Sept. 27, 1884, in Peabody Institute, Salem, Mass. (printed in part in Wayman, *Edward Sylvester Morse*, pp. 289–90).

regarded Japanese artistic resurgence as part of a cultural pluralism suited to an emerging world civilization. As an enthusiastic Hegelian he was convinced that the contact of the West with the Far East would lead to a new and broader synthesis, possibly world-wide, in which the thesis of Western values would elicit a responding antithesis restating Eastern values, the cultural dialogue proceeding in dialectical fashion toward the fusion of new synthesis. Since art, in Fenollosa's view, was the most sensitive sign and carrier of cultural values, the lines of artistic development were crucial both in the West and the Far East; the art arising from the meeting of the two cultures would then be both sign and instrument of this higher synthesis. For the moment, that is in Japan of the early '80s, the most important task was to restate Eastern artistic insights. But this was to be part of larger patterns through which Fenollosa's personal ambitions would merge with what he felt to be world-historical forces.

By 1884, two years after the Ryuchikai speech, Fenollosa's art revival was fast becoming an organized movement, organized in characteristically Western forms. An art club was formed to foster art appreciation; a club of artists was founded, exhibitions of their work held, prizes awarded, markets sought and developed (Fenollosa asked Morse to serve as agent for American sales); an art journal was established to report on connoisseurship and exhibitions; book publications were planned; the artistic training of school children was pressed; and a special art school in Tokyo was proposed along with a number of projects for government encouragement of the arts by means of commissions, medals, honor rolls, and exhibitions. To a Westerner, especially an American accustomed to voluntary associations of all sorts, these forms of artistic organization seemed natural, but in Japan they were innovations which transformed earlier patterns of hereditary guilds of painters, on the one hand, and the private cultivation of art by gentlemen on the other. This latter attitude was prevalent among government officials, and Fenollosa had to persuade them to take art seriously, that is, not simply as a pleasure but with a Western earnestness, and further, to support art institutionally. Again it was Fenollosa's authority as a Westerner that gave crucial prestige to the new organizations.

The Kangwakai, the club for art appreciation founded in February 1884, began as an exercise in historical connoisseurship. At its regular meetings ancient paintings were displayed and discussed. Individual works were analyzed by a four-man board of critics, who certified authenticity, if appropriate. At a June meeting, for example, 480 works were examined and 79 certified. Attendance was often as high as several hundred. Fenollosa was a member of the board of critics and became president of the club in April, with Ariga as secretary. He gave regular lectures on art, many of them published in *Dai Nippon Bijutsu Shinpo* (founded November 1883), the new art journal edited by Fenollosa's student and friend Okakura, himself a leading figure in the art revival.

Fenollosa's close identification with the art revival in his position as critic was strengthened early in 1884 when he was adopted "artistically" into the Kano family. His excitement was evident in a letter to Morse:

> I don't know that I told you that I have received letters patent from Kano Yeitoku, the present head of the Kano house, adopting me (artistically, of course, not legally, though under Tokugawa it would have been legal) into the Kano family, and authorizing me to use the name Kano Yei (Yei being the first character of the artistic names of all past men of the line) and I have taken the name Kano Yeitan, the character Tan being that in the name Tanyu. My *nobu* name is Masanobu so that my full name is Kano Yeitan Masanobu. This I write in Chinese characters and have special seals. I give certificates by myself for old paintings in a novel form (I send you a sample) and I sign my name together with the other three critics [Tomonobu Kano, Yeishin Kano, Kangi Yamana] on the certificate of the Club [see Illustrations]. It is quite a thing to have the three greatest critics of Japan admitting me to equality in certifying; and again that Japanese are demanding these certificates.[7]

To complement the Kangwakai, Fenollosa organized a group of Tokyo artists around the central figures of Gaho Hashimoto and Hogai Kano. Both were talented painters who had been deprived of support by the reorganization of Japanese life following the Restoration. Gaho had subsisted as a draftsman in the Navy Department; Hogai had been reduced to painting pots and drawing pictures of dogs. None the less Hogai had maintained a stubborn aloofness from all things Western, and Fenollosa had great difficulty in winning his support for the new club called Shingaku Shokai (New Painters Group Club). But Hogai was at last persuaded; Fenollosa was a Kano, after all. Hogai's paintings drew attentive crowds at the club's

7. EFF to E. S. Morse, April 26, 1884, in Peabody Institute, Salem, Mass. (quoted in Wayman, p. 289).

exhibits and at the exhibitions sponsored by other groups, with the increasing approval of official government circles.

Fenollosa acted as critic for the artists' group and urged the development of original expression built on past insights. In the Japanese context Fenollosa's major innovation was his insistence on the artist's freedom to paint as he pleased, to paint in an individual style rather than to aim at faithful rendering of the styles of past masterpieces. Traditional styles were to be studied for their universal principles rather than as models for sedulous imitation.

In addition to testing Fenollosa's historical and critical theories, the Shingaku Shokai had a practical goal, namely, selling paintings. A market had to be developed to replace court patronage. Accordingly, the Painters Club held its own exhibits, and in December 1884 the group of connoisseurs reorganized their club, the Kangwakai, to focus directly on promoting contemporary national art. At regular monthly meetings the Kangwakai now discussed current work, with Fenollosa discoursing in a less archaeological vein on such topics as the future of Japanese painting, the suitability of Buddhist subjects, and the quality of decorative art. The following September the Kangwakai held its first exhibition of new paintings, most of them the work of Shingaku Shokai artists. Guests were invited to cast secret ballots for their favorites, with votes determining cash prizes. The influential Baron Kuki was honorary chairman, and Fenollosa made the speeches of the occasion. So successful was the exhibit that official support was assured, and at the next Kangwakai exhibition the following April Prime Minister Hirobumi Ito himself was converted to the cause of national art, his conversion due, according to tradition, to Hogai's paintings, notably the prize-winning *Niwo Holding a Soul.*

Although Fenollosa's work with connoisseurs, painters, and the public was directed toward an immediate revival of national painting, he regarded the importance of this revival as a matter of long-term devolopments. In order for Japan to play her role in the approaching fusion of world art in a world civilization, she needed conditions conducive to the development of artistic talent, wherever that talent might lie. On this score Fenollosa feared that the new educational system would destroy a superb tradition of artistic training, which had started at the elementary level with instruction in brush and ink. (During the Westernizing craze of the '70s the brush had been dropped from primary school art instruction in favor of pen and pencil drawings.) He urged restoration of the brush as more suitable to Japan, artistically superior, and an advantageous base for later art training and appreciation. He won over to his views Baron Arata Hamao, an influential official of the Education Department, and in December 1884 Fenollosa was appointed to an official committee to study art education, a committee whose other members were Hogai, Tomonobu Kano, and Fenollosa's former student Okakura. The committee's report the next spring recommended restoration of the brush in elementary schools, along with a Fenollosan innovation—a stress on abstract linear composition rather than the detailed copying of model paintings. On the basis of this report crayons and pencils were replaced shortly by *sumi* (ink) and brushes.

In all these activities, in art training, artists' clubs, public art appreciation, historical criticism, archaeology, Fenollosa moved energetically and enthusiastically, helped at every turn by the students, colleagues, and friends who experienced his missionary persuasions. This missionary enthusiasm was central; it invigorated his work from the smallest details of attribution to the cosmic schemes of world history that framed his speculations. As he put it in a letter to Morse, "We are a live Art Club right out here in the East, and we have a mission to discharge both to Japanese and foreigners." [8]

Fenollosa's "mission" was really several missions. As a Western philosopher, he was engaged in spreading the scientific and historical ways of thinking identified by Westerners with the progress of civilization. As a connoisseur, his mission was to nourish the national cultural roots of Japanese art and at the same time establish international perspectives. As a discoverer of the heights of Far Eastern cultural achievement, his mission meant reporting the news to the unknowingly provincial West from which he had set forth. In this last and perhaps most important mission Fenollosa was advancing an American dream in the cosmopolitan spirit of Emerson and Whitman. Although the American forms of art organization which Fenollosa had helped transplant into Japan were easily made national, the challenge to Western ethnocentricity presented by his estimates of superlative Sino-Japanese attainments pointed toward a cultural pluralism. This pluralism was itself American to the extent that America welcomed variety, to the extent that America believed in a free world's ability to contain multitudes.

8. EFF to E. S. Morse, April 26, 1884, quoted in Wayman, p. 289.

I have no expectation that any man will read history aright who thinks that what was done in a remote age, by men whose names have resounded far, has any deeper sense than what he is doing to-day.

Ralph Waldo Emerson, "History," *Essays: First Series*

6 · LOTS OF THINGS IN THE AIR FOR THE FUTURE

Fenollosa's mission of enlightening the West was subordinated to immediate tasks during his early years in Japan; there was more than enough work close at hand. But the dream was there, a young man's proud dream of revising world history and heralding the dawn of a more cosmopolitan epoch. The rhetoric of the dream was Victorian, as was its confidence in the power of individual reason to cope with a world still conceived and felt as orderly, that is as a cosmos. Fenollosa confided the shape of this dream to Morse in a letter written after returning from a summer spent examining temple art collections.

> For myself, I must confess to you, who will hear me in private without thinking me conceited, that I cannot see why my work this summer was not just as important at bottom as much of that which the world's archaeologists are doing in Greece and Turkey. Of course people don't see the practical importance of Eastern Civilization for the world with the same vividness as they do that of Greek culture. Perhaps it is not so important. But from the point of view of human history as a whole, it is absolutely indispensable. I expect the time will come when it will be considered as necessary for a liberally educated man to know the names and deeds of man's great benefactors in the

East, and the steps of advance in their culture, as it is now to know Greek and Latin dates and the flavor of their production.

Now, as to my book. I am at work on it all the time, but have not given any part its final shape. I am sure I can get a publisher for the text; but as you know my ambition is to have it illustrated with the actual masterpieces of all Eastern art, in a way which will force my conclusions home to people's hearts. I want to fix it so that there will be no question in the mind of an intelligent reader when he has finished. It will not be dry; it will present entirely new views of the origin and nature of culture in China and Japan; it will try to make the great artists real living human beings, but radiant with genius, to the imagination. For this, the illustrations must be absolutely the best that modern methods can supply. Now you say in your last letter that "Mr. Osgood has authorized me to write you and to say that he will do whatever you wish. I have repeatedly talked to him of the immense work you are contemplating, and he didn't scare worth a cent"—all this is very interesting, but I am not sure I understand quite how much it means. . . . Can he produce color plates or fine wood engravings like those of the American magazines? I ask all this, because I am just as much interested as you, that the work should be brought out in Boston for the honor of Massachusetts and the Hub; if it can be well done there . . . Lots of things in the air for the future. Will write more next mail. Love to all, E.F.F.[1]

Fenollosa's pride and ambitions received a fine fillip that same summer with the publication of the first of his interpretations of Far Eastern art directed to a Western audience. It took the form of an extended review of the chapter on painting in the French connoisseur Louis Gonse's *L'Art japonais*; it was published first in the *Japan Weekly Mail* (July 12, 1884) and then in pamphlet form. Fenollosa sent a number of copies to Morse in Salem, and the Boston firm of James R. Osgood and Company reprinted the article for further distribution. Laurence Binyon, a British orientalist of the following generation, called Fenollosa's review "the first adequate survey of the development of Japanese art in its true perspective and

1. EFF to E. S. Morse, Sept. 27, 1884, in Peabody Institute, Salem, Mass. (quoted in part in Wayman, p. 291).

proportions, ever published in a European tongue." [2] Fenollosa was thirty-one years old.

Previous accounts of Japanese art had been distorted not so much by Western critical canons, although condescension on these grounds was frequent, as by simple ignorance. Japanese painting and sculpture were ignored because they were virtually unknown. Handicraft arts and woodblock prints, on the other hand, had acquired enthusiastic followings in the West. In France an avant-garde vogue for Japanese prints, particularly those of Hokusai and Utamaro, was well developed by this time, as was evident in the writings of Theodore Duret, Ary Renan, and the brothers Goncourt, as well as Louis Gonse. The Englishmen Rutherford Alcock, George Audsley, and Christopher Dresser had written on Japanese art industries, and William Anderson had undertaken a historical sketch. In Germany only H. Gierke had broken ground. The number of informed critics was very small. Nevertheless, by the middle '80s interest in Japanese work was rising in European art circles, and Americans were not to be left behind. In fact, two Americans, John LaFarge and James Jackson Jarves, were among the first serious critics of Japanese art. Fenollosa was familiar with their views as were most of the connoisseurs and critics to whom he addressed his review of Gonse's *L'Art japonais*. The opinions of LaFarge and Jarves, so different from Fenollosa's, suggest the surprise which must have greeted Fenollosa's review. The print-loving avant-garde must have been shocked at Fenollosa's attack on Gonse's "Hokusai-crowned pagoda of generalizations."

The American painter John LaFarge's analysis of Japanese art, based on prints and lacquers, was included in his friend Raphael Pumpelly's *Across America and Asia* (1869). Pumpelly, who had been employed as a geologist by the Japanese government in 1861, kept his traveler's eye alive to Japanese sights and customs, but he demurred at art and turned to a professional. LaFarge had bought his first Hokusai book in 1858 and had been collecting Japanese prints since then, acquiring them as rare occasions offered, despite the censure of Victorian moralists, who associated the prints with erotica. LaFarge recalled that his French family laughed at "les amours exotiques . . . but here people thought moral ill of a lover of Jap art—as for the lover of Blake or Goya." [3] LaFarge ignored these

2. Laurence Binyon, "National Character in Art," *Littell's Living Age*, 259 (Dec. 5, 1908), 627–29.

3. Quoted from a 1908 letter to James Gibbons Huneker cited in R. Cortissoz, *John LaFarge* (Boston, Houghton Mifflin, 1911), p. 243.

attitudes; his outlook was securely cosmopolitan. His estimate of the Japanese art he knew stressed design, the decorative qualities achieved by a "distinct civilization where art is happily married to industry." He described Hokusai as a master print-maker and praised Japanese deftness of line, originality of pattern, and sensitivity to moods of nature; but he found Japanese art lacking "that deeper individual personality—the glory of our greatest art."[4] Yet he did not attack Japanese art for its lack of realism; he did not ask, like Ruskin, that art mirror nature. LaFarge's essay stands at the beginning of an understanding of Japanese art as the product of a distinctive way of seeing.

The most extensive account of Japanese art available to the West in the 1870s was written by James Jackson Jarves, a widely traveled, independent critic. The same sensibility which had valued Italian primitive paintings derided by critics as "pre-Giottesque ligneous daubs" led Jarves to explore the new world of Japanese art with sympathy. He saw the Japanese exhibit at the Paris Exposition of 1867 and commented on its quality in his *Art Thoughts* of 1870. In 1872 he wrote several articles on Japanese art for the *Independent*, a New York newspaper, and three years later published *A Glimpse at the Art of Japan* in response to what he termed the "unexpected interest" in his *Independent* articles. Fenollosa had a copy of Jarves' *Glimpse*.

Jarves had studied Japanese culture in Florence with the Paris-trained scholar, Antelmo Severini,[5] and he carried his explorations of Japanese art into mythology, religion, and literature as well as investigating the social conditions confronting the artist. He had written earlier of the eclectic mission of America to enrich its art by "assimilated examples . . . drawn from all sources" and free from any "invidious nationalism"; now in 1875 as an enthusiast rather than a scholar Jarves hoped to "enlarge our own Anglo-Saxon art-horizon." Jarves' approach was Emersonian rather than Hegelian but remarkably similar to the more systematic proposals of the Harvard

4. LaFarge, as quoted in Pumpelly, *Across America and Asia* (2d ed. rev. New York, 1870), p. 201. LaFarge pointed out the neglect of Japanese elements in so recent and compendious a work as Owen Jones's *Grammar of Ornament* of 1851.

5. Antelmo Severini (1828–1909) taught Chinese and Japanese at the Instituto di Studi Superiori in Florence, the first such instruction in Italy. His works on the Far East include a Chinese-Japanese dictionary that was left unfinished when Severini became unbalanced in 1894. See Marcello Muccioli, "Japanese Studies in Italy," *East and West*, 2 (April 1951), 9–13.

philosopher Charles Everett. "In entering the new world," wrote Jarves, "familiar ideals and ordinary rules must be cast aside. Instead we must accept new ideals and rules, and try to enjoy everything good in its principle and sound in its manifestation after its kind, however much it varies from the forms and laws which we have been trained to esteem as the only correct ones." For "the root axiom of Japanese art" Jarves turned, like LaFarge, to Hokusai, who "taught it was easier to invent new forms than to copy exactly what one sees in nature." Yet Jarves was limited in his material to an album of Hokusai, a few books with poor reproductions of temple paintings, and some stray objects of his own. He concluded that the "fine arts" —painting, sculpture, and architecture—"in their supreme significance . . . are not found in the aesthetic constitution of the Japanese." [6] Fenollosa shared Jarves' cosmopolitan sympathies but saw the limits which Jarves' ignorance imposed.

Louis Gonse was far more knowledgeable than Jarves, and Fenollosa welcomed Gonse's work as the first broadly appreciative account of Japanese art to merit "the world's serious consideration." Then he proceeded to demolish Gonse's "Hokusai-crowned pagoda." Gonse had recognized the importance of painting for an understanding of Japanese art, but he had been forced to rely solely on European collections for first-hand judgments and upon misleading Japanese opinions for historical information. Fenollosa offered detailed corrections and attacked Gonse's historical and critical assumptions, based as they were on severely limited contact with Japanese and Chinese work.

Fenollosa confined his review largely to archaeological and critical specifics, but there were indications of the broader, more philosophical approach which had characterized his work in aesthetics and which would enlarge the scope of his final, full-scale account of the history of East Asian design. He wrote of "the several languages" of the arts, attacking the literary approach to musical and visual arts. An accent on storytelling ignored the "utter differences" and "peculiar innate possibilities" of each form of art. The language of an art, then, must be studied on its own terms, and so must the arts of different races

6. *A Glimpse at the Art of Japan* (New York, 1876), pp. 1, 12; *The Art-Idea* (New York, 1864), p. 198; *A Glimpse at the Art of Japan*, pp. 14, 80, 22. Francis Steegmuller, *The Two Lives of James Jackson Jarves* (New Haven, Yale University Press, 1951), recalls Jarves' Yankee background, his experiences in Hawaii, his independent art collections, and his services to American art.

and times. "Painting," Fenollosa concluded, "is not everywhere an identically defined process, extending over all its particular cases the domination of a single set of laws."[7] This opposition to aesthetic monism was extended in his later work on the history of civilization into an opposition to all analogous formalisms—social, political, economic, religious. His experience persuaded him that particulars were too easily subordinated to universals and thereby lost, that artistic and cultural pluralism was essential to avoid parochial blindness and to keep open the many paths of evolutionary progress.

The breadth of Fenollosa's perspective and the validity of his criticisms made his review seem more disinterested than it was. "Of course, in it, I didn't give away any unnecessary points of my own," he confessed to Morse. "I confined myself to those where Gonse was in serious error, and on which it was most important to set people right at once."[8] Within the pattern of Fenollosa's developing cosmopolitanism ran a strand of self-promotion which indicated a possible conflict between his ambition for personal success and his missionary absorption in historically important work. There were ambiguities in pursuing at the same time the two kinds of success, the Salem and Boston kind of success—wealth, social position, reputation —and the other, the success of world-historical acts appreciated by very few. The ambiguities were most apparent in the matter of Fenollosa's loyalties, specifically in the question of his personal art collection.

Fenollosa had been in Japan for six years when his review of Gonse's book appeared, and by that time he had identified himself with Japanese art to an unusual degree. An enthusiast by temperament, he was frequently overwhelmed by the beauty of the paintings he found; repeatedly he lost himself in the sensuous ideal world created by a master's brush, neglecting meals, appointments, even his health. The beauty of Buddhist art and the philosophical scope of Buddhist writings drew him into studies with the Abbot Keitoku, and in September 1885 he was "confirmed" in Tendai Buddhism, the sect of *The Lotus*.[9] Fenollosa's Buddhism at this time involved

7. *Review of the Chapter on Painting in L'Art Japonais by L. Gonse* (Boston, 1885), pp. 1, 13, 14, 28, 35. Gonse leaned heavily on young Tadamasa Hayashi, who was working in the Paris branch of Nippon Kiritsu Kosho Kaisha.

8. EFF to E. S. Morse, Sept. 27, 1884, quoted in Wayman, p. 291.

9. See below, pp. 103–11, for a fuller discussion of Fenollosa's Buddhist interests and activities.

aesthetic and philosophical exploration rather than personal conversion—the lotus offered a sensuous metaphysics—but like his adoption into the Kano family it marked a strong identification with Japanese traditions and ideals.

Yet Fenollosa did not consider remaining permanently in Japan. The Japanese looked forward to replacing all foreign teachers with Japanese, once they were trained and available, and Fenollosa had definite plans to return to the United States and a career in lecturing and writing. Morse started lining up American lectures for Fenollosa as early as 1883, holding off when Fenollosa wrote in the spring of 1884 that he had decided "not to come home 'til 1886," since his teaching duties had been reduced and his art activities looked so promising.

A further pull toward practical considerations and American viewpoints came from the Fenollosa household. Lizzie Millett Fenollosa enjoyed the novelty of Japanese life and the prestige of her husband, and she managed her households well. Servants were plentiful, the Tokyo house was well situated, and a summer house in the lovely hills of Nikko provided relief from Tokyo's heat. But as a foreigner and a woman she did not have her husband's unique access to Japanese life, nor was she sustained by the intense enthusiasms that left Professor Fenollosa often preoccupied. His summer archaeological tours left her alone in Nikko more and more, and frequently there were spring and autumn trips as well. Furthermore, the children were to be considered. A son, Ernest Kano Fenollosa, was born in June 1880; the birth of a daughter, Brenda, followed three years later. The Millett grandparents had never laid eyes on their only daughter's children; they hoped to before long. Under these circumstances Lizzie Fenollosa's outlook tended to remain American. She enjoyed her exotic life, but exoticism inevitably preserved her sense of social distance. Household servants were not samurai students.

The Fenollosa households in Tokyo and Nikko received a stream of distinguished Western visitors, especially those at all interested in Japanese art. There were no hotels in Tokyo, the nearest accommodations being in Yokohama, and summer visitors were prey to dysentery and cholera. The Fenollosas offered an oasis of American style living, and Lizzie's guests included such prominent Bostonians as William Sturgis Bigelow, Percival Lowell, Henry Adams, even Bishop Phillips Brooks and Mrs. Jack Gardner, the unconventional mistress of "Green Hill" in Brookline and later the creator of

Fenway Court. It would have been surprising if Mrs. Fenollosa had not thought of the social possibilities that might develop on returning to Boston.

Fenollosa, too, was flattered by the respectful attentions of prominent American visitors; and the deference of his students and of leading Japanese officials could not fail to whet his personal ambitions. In his letters to Morse a note of self-satisfaction continually creeps in: "You will see in the [*Japan Weekly*] *Mail* that [Captain Frank] Brinkley declares me to be the greatest living critic of Japanese pictorial art. That's a good deal for an Englishman to admit." And again, referring to his critical certifications of art works, "It ought certainly to give me some prestige"; and noticeably when commenting on his "little review" of Gonse's essay: "I intend to follow this up with small publications as opportunity may offer. One has to prepare people a little bit, I suppose, to appreciate the worth of his work." [10]

The matter of the disposition of Fenollosa's personal art collection raised questions of ambition more significant than proud confidences in a young man's letters to an old friend. By 1884 Fenollosa had acquired a number of superb paintings, many of them very old, a collection developed by combining a rare sensibility with equally rare opportunities for purchase. Fenollosa already possessed the kinds of treasures that his art program aimed to preserve as a national heritage. There were no laws as yet which defined national treasures or prohibited exporting them, but Fenollosa was himself a leading promoter of such policies. He was clearly aware of the conflicts of interest involved. As he wrote to Morse from Tokyo in the fall of 1884: "Already people here are saying that my collection must be kept here in Japan for the Japanese. I have bought a number of the very greatest treasures secretly. The Japanese as yet don't know that I have them. I wish I could see them all safely housed forever in the Boston Art Museum. And yet if the Emperor or the Mombusho [Department of Education] should want to buy my collection, wouldn't it be my duty to humanity, all things considered, to let them have it? What do you think?" [11]

It was a difficult question. Morse's superlative, encyclopedic collection of Japanese pottery was already in Salem, but then Morse's connection with the Japanese government had had little relation to

10. EFF to E. S. Morse, April 26 and Sept. 27, 1884, quoted in Wayman, pp. 289–91.
11. EFF to E. S. Morse, Sept. 27, 1884.

pottery. However, the Japanese government made no offer to purchase Fenollosa's collection, which may have made his decision easier. In the latter part of 1886 Fenollosa completed negotiations for the sale of his paintings to Charles Goddard Weld,[12] a wealthy Bostonian, with the understanding that the collection would be located in Boston and that the paintings would be described officially as the Fenollosa-Weld Collection. By this arrangement Fenollosa could count on access to the collection for research when he returned to the United States; and the collection would stir in Boston an interest in the Far East which could only help his prospective career on the lecture platform. More generally, such a group of Japanese paintings, the finest in the Western world, would offer artistic and cultural stimulus to Americans and to the West.

In Tokyo in 1886 Fenollosa's star was approaching its zenith. The artistic revival which he had launched was well established. Art organizations were strong and multiplying, benefiting from a slowly growing reaction against the craze for things Western. There remained as the capstone of Fenollosa's program the establishment of a School of Fine Arts which would assure the continuity of national artistic development. In December 1885 the Education Department had appointed a committee to consider the formation of a national art school. The committee included Fenollosa, Okakura, and Hogai Kano. On the basis of their recommendations the government concluded that the art programs of common schools, museums, and art academies should be carefully integrated and that Japan would profit from examining the art programs of other nations before making final decisions on methods and administration. Consequently Fenollosa, Okakura, and Baron Hamao, the Mombusho's Director of the Bureau of Colleges, were appointed Imperial Commissioners and charged "to investigate thoroughly all fine art institutions, educational, industrial, and preservative," the journey to include England, France, Germany, Austria, the Low Countries, Spain, and the United States. Such a touring mission followed a conscious pattern of cultural assimilation. The Japanese wanted to be sure that the very best

12. Charles Goddard Weld (1857–1911) was interested by Edward S. Morse in things Japanese. Weld spent a year at Harvard College (1875–76) and three years at Harvard Medical School (1876–79), receiving an M.D. in 1881. He soon retired from surgery, while continuing generous and intelligent gifts to hospitals. In addition to his purchase of Fenollosa's collection of paintings and their donation to the Boston Museum of Fine Arts, Weld donated the wing of the Peabody Museum in Salem to house Morse's Japanese ethnological collection and memorials of Salem's clipper trade.

available forms of art organization had been examined before final decisions were made on the basis of suitability to Japanese conditions and aims. The pattern was unashamedly eclectic on the surface, but the results in institutions and customs formed a consistent pattern that was clearly national—and before long militantly nationalistic.

In accepting appointment as Imperial Commissioner, Fenollosa transferred (effective August 1886) from the faculty of the University to the Education Department, with a four year contract to serve the Japanese government, including service in the Ministry of the Imperial Household. Before departing on this world-wide mission, Fenollosa and his fellow commissioner Okakura were decorated by the Emperor in token of their service to the national interest.

Back in Nikko preparations for an extended visit home went forward rapidly. The children and their Chinese nurse, Ah-Ching, would, of course, stay with Grandmother Millett in Salem. Presents for everyone would have to be carefully selected and packed. Fortunately the Japanese government made travel arrangements as easy as possible. And to make matters even more pleasant the Fenollosas would be able to sail east by steamer with their companions of the summer, John LaFarge and Henry Adams. Adams had written ahead to a friend in Washington to assure smooth entry into San Francisco for everyone, especially the Chinese nurse.

In the eight years since Fenollosa's departure for the Far East, anti-Chinese agitation on the West Coast had intensified to the point of winning passage in 1882 of a federal law excluding Chinese immigrants. The predicament of young Ernest Kano's Chinese nurse lent an ironic touch to Fenollosa's return to his native land as an ambassador from the East. Not even an apostle of cosmopolitanism would evidently be able to ignore parochial nationalisms. Although there might be a way; Adams' letter, which might ease the predicament, suggested the convenience of having friends in high places, all the more for a young philosopher who had become an art critic and whose career might need help.

At the moment, however, Fenollosa was an Imperial Commissioner. It was curiously appropriate that Henry Adams should serve Fenollosa's world-historical mission, even in this slight way, for despite the provincialism of Boston culture, which Adams was quick to admit, American ties with the Far East were already a tradition in Massachusetts. And the influence of a New England Adams, even at this late season, might still have some effect in the San Francisco Customs House.

Those childish days of revery,
when he played at priests, played
in many another day dream,
working his way from the actual
present, as far as he might, with
a delightful sense of escape in replacing the outer world of other
people by an inward world as
himself really cared to have it,
had made him a kind of "idealist."

Walter Pater, *Marius the Epicurean*

7 · A SEASON FOR NIRVANA:
HENRY ADAMS AND JOHN LAFARGE AT NIKKO

As Henry Adams and John LaFarge prepared to return to the United
States, it was apparent that the summer in Japan had served each as
a mirror of his own particular outlook. Adams and LaFarge were
unusually cosmopolitan visitors; they had seen much of the world
and were accustomed to meeting new experiences confidently and
with a certain detachment which enabled them to compare and
classify and savor. Their summer, spent mostly in the cool, wooded
hills of Nikko as neighbors and guests of the Fenollosas, offered novel
occasions and time for reflection. The responses of these two cosmopolitans to Japanese life and art, responses very different in attention and implication, differed also from the attitudes of their
host Fenollosa—"a kind of St. Dominic," Adams called him. Fenollosa's particular kind of cosmopolitanism comes into sharper focus
in the picture of the three Americans in Nikko: LaFarge sketching
by a waterfall in the garden; Adams on his back reading Dante;
Fenollosa, at dinner, discoursing enthusiastically on an unknown

classical past. "One sees what one brings," Adams wrote later.[1] What these three men saw in Japan helps define what they brought.

Dr. William Sturgis Bigelow had helped persuade Adams to come to Japan, and he acted as master of ceremonies for the summer visit.[2] He met Adams and LaFarge at the pier, introduced them immediately to Fenollosa, and initiated them into the arts and customs of the land. LaFarge responded with enthusiasm. He set out to learn Japanese and looked closely at everything around him. Adams preferred to keep his distance. From his aloof position Japanese life seemed quaint and unreal, like a fairy tale or a dream. "Positively everything in Japan laughs," he wrote to John Hay:

> The jinrickshaw men . . . the women . . . the shopkeepers . . . I believe the Mikado laughs when his ministers have a cabinet council. The gilt dragon heads on the temple are in a broad grin. Everything laughs, until I expect to see even the severe bronze doors of the tombs, the finest serious work I know, open themselves with the same eternal and meaningless laughter, as though death were the pleasantest jest of all . . . This is a child's country. Men, women and children are taken out of the fairy books. The whole show is of the nursery. Nothing is serious; nothing is taken seriously. All is toy; sometimes, as with the women, badly made and repulsive; sometimes laughable, as with the houses, gardens and children . . . I have wandered, so to express it, in all the soup plates of forty-eight years' experience, during the last week, and have found them as natural as Alice found the Mock Turtle. Life is a dream, and in Japan one dreams of the nursery.[3]

A week in Tokyo and a taste of traveling conditions made Adams welcome the sanctuary of a small house in the cooler hills. Bigelow was staying with the Fenollosas at their summer villa in Nikko, and he secured a neighboring house for Adams and LaFarge. It belonged to a Buddhist priest and stood in a wide-walled garden enclosure in one of the first open spaces on the mountain, set against a rocky waterfall and rimmed by pines and willows. LaFarge sketched the

1. *The Education of Henry Adams* (Boston, Houghton Mifflin, 1918), p. 387.
2. Bigelow was a wealthy Bostonian led to Japan by Edward Morse's ethnological enthusiasms. On Bigelow's Buddhist studies see below, pp. 106–09.
3. July 9, 1886, in Worthington C. Ford, ed., *Letters of Henry Adams* (1858–1891) (Boston, Houghton Mifflin, 1930), pp. 366–69.

countryside, delighted with the subtly terraced houses and gardens and intrigued by the flamboyant red lacquer gates and temples which had made Nikko a vast Tokugawa shrine. Adams sat, examining curios which dealers brought to their door from all over Japan. As regular guests at the larger house the two visitors were regaled with Fenollosa's archaeological researches and critical judgments.

Fenollosa decried Tokugawa mediocrity and Meiji commonplaces and championed the more classical past. His enthusiasm for Buddhist art and the masters of traditional Japanese painting had the quality of a crusade. It was Fenollosa's moral fervor, in particular, which Adams resisted and questioned. To his friend Hay, Adams described Fenollosa as "a kind of St. Dominic" who "holds himself responsible for the dissemination of useless knowledge by others. My historical indifference to everything but facts, and my delight at studying what is hopefully debased and degraded, shock his moral sense. I wish you were here to help us trample on him." [4]

Adams was ostensibly observing facts, and the facts indicated that inevitable mixture of good and evil which vitiated all ideals, including beauty. Adams, as historian, jibed at Fenollosa's passion for beauty, but it was this passion which enabled Fenollosa to approach Japanese culture with sympathy and to join hands with the forces of national development. His ability to project himself into Japanese culture was related to his capacity for wholehearted commitment; he was swept along by youthful vigor, intellectual adventure, and a sense of excited discovery. Adams, on the other hand, by remaining aloof, gave no indication that he was aware of the dramatic changes in Japanese life that were taking place at his doorstep. Japan remained a toyland in which to exercise his ironic imagination, a world of children diverting in its way but irrelevant to Western man. Adams' self-concern, which made all enthusiasm suspect, alerted his ironic eye to patterns in history, but it limited his historical perspective to Western civilization.

To commit himself wholly to a course of action jarred with an attitude of detached observation which Adams could never escape. As observer he hesitated to act, balancing alternatives which were never clear cut.[5] For Adams experience was split; and the world's flux reflected a basic cleavage in himself. He stated the dilemma in his

4. July 27, 1886, in Ford, *Letters of Henry Adams*, p. 372.
5. "The more I see, the more I am convinced that to a man whose mind is balanced like mine, in such a way that what is evil never seems unmixed with good, and what is good always streaked with evil, an object seems never im-

own words when he asked, "Do you understand how, without a double personality, *I* can feel that *I* am a failure? One could think that the *I* which could feel that, must be a different *ego* from the *I* of which it is felt." [6] After his wife's suicide this sense of division was strengthened, and the pilgrimage which followed was a search for escape from doubt, at first by avoiding thought and then by pursuit of certainty. It was in this spirit that Adams had set out westward for Japan, in the late spring of 1886, with John LaFarge as companion. In Omaha a young reporter inquired the purpose of their visit to Japan. LaFarge answered that they sought Nirvana, to which the reporter replied, "It's out of season!" [7] For a man whose awareness of himself and the world remained split, it would never be the season for Nirvana.

On later pilgrimages through the East Adams repeatedly encountered forces with which he had no sympathy. With the calm of Buddha he was "bored." Buddha bid him "look in silence on the Lotus," [8] but Adams saw only the silence of death at the beginning and the end of thought. Nirvana recalled the dark hooded figure in Rock Creek cemetery, the memorial to his wife. Nirvana might offer a peace past all understanding, but Adams was too acutely aware of himself to look along Eastern paths. "If only we had found Nirvana—" commented LaFarge, "but he was right who warned us that we were late in this season of the world." [9] Adams felt himself to be late, too late for Chartres or even Quincy. Likewise Western man seemed in his autumn, well along toward a motionless equilibrium. Thermodynamics appeared to confirm the inevitability of Adams' own state of balanced inaction. The dynamics of intercultural forces, the heart of Fenollosa's concern, remained outside Adams' speculations.

---

portant enough to call out strong energies till they are all exhausted, nor necessary enough not to allow of its failure being possible to retrieve; in short, a mind which is not strongly positive and absolute, cannot be steadily successful in action, which requires quietness and perseverance." Henry Adams to Charles Francis Adams, Jr., Nov. 21, 1862, in Worthington C. Ford, ed., *A Cycle of Adams Letters, 1861–1865* (Boston, Houghton Mifflin, 1920) 1, 195.

6. Henry Adams to Charles Francis Adams Jr., Feb. 14, 1862, in *Cycle of Adams Letters*, 1, 112 ff.

7. Henry Adams to John Hay, June 11, 1886, in *Letters of Henry Adams*, p. 366.

8. Henry Adams, "Buddha and Brahma, a Poem," *Yale Review*, 5 (Oct. 1915), 82–89.

9. John LaFarge, *An Artist's Letters from Japan* (London, 1897), p. vii.

Although John LaFarge could agree with Adams that it was too late for Nirvana "in this season of the world," LaFarge had a painter's eye for beauty, an eye which could see Japan fresh. He joined Adams in jests at the bizarre situations which developed in their travels, but his playfulness was free of the relentless self-concern which underlay Adams' ironies. LaFarge's trip to Japan was more clearly for pleasure than was his companion's, perhaps because LaFarge had already won a place in the American art world, more likely because he was a cosmopolitan by temperament and career. He had been interested in Japanese art since the '60s and was delighted at the chance for first-hand observation. LaFarge responded more freely and more sensuously than Adams and discovered many of the qualities of Japanese life and art which had charmed Fenollosa.

What struck LaFarge especially was the Japanese way of seeing, a fresh artistic ordering of materials far more compelling than he had guessed earlier, when writing his pioneer essay. His concern was neither philosophical nor historical; it was visual. He sought to look with eyes innocent of Western lenses and free from intellectual analysis. He found simplicity in place of complexity and suggestion in place of representation. For LaFarge Japanese art reaffirmed "the first primeval needs of the artist . . . the love of certain balanced proportions and relations which the mind likes to discover and bring out in what it deals with, be it thought, or the actions of men, or the influence of nature, or the material things in which necessity makes it work." [10] The Japanese architect, for example, remained concerned with the building itself rather than the appearance of its plans; the gardener practiced his art by subtly improving on nature. Craftsmen of all varieties worked with ideals of excellence in which were mirrored their best selves. Not so in the West. "For us today," wrote LaFarge, "things and realities no longer exist. It is in their descriptions that we believe." [11] The Japanese artist demonstrated the reality of materials rendered individually beautiful by creative imagination.

10. Ibid., pp. 126, 143, 145. On arriving in Japan LaFarge was struck by the quality of light and colors, a continuing thread in his letters: "But the human beings are not the novelty, not even the Japanese; what is absorbingly new is the light, its whiteness, its silvery milkiness. We have come into it as through an open door after fourteen gray days of the Pacific which ended only at sunrise this very morning." Ibid., p. 4.

11. Ibid., pp. 103, 123–25, 104. "You and I know that art is not the attempt at reflecting others, at taking possession of others, who belong to themselves; but

LaFarge was charmed by the Japanese sensitivity to the beauties of nature. It seemed "much more delicate and complex and contemplative, and at the same time more natural, than ours has ever been."

> Outside of Arcadia, I know of no other land whose people hang verses on the trees in honor of their beauty; where families travel far before the dawn to see the first light touch the new buds. Where else do the newspapers announce the spring openings of the blossoms? Where else would be possible the charming absurdity of the story that W——— was telling me of having seen in cherry-blossom time some old gentleman, with capacious sake gourd in hand and big roll of paper in his girdle, seat himself below the blossom-showers, and look, and drink, and write verses, all by himself, with no gallery to help him? [12]

This notion of a natural and easy communion with a landscape felt to be intensely spiritual appealed to LaFarge. He had hoped to find in Japan an atmosphere "not inimical" to miracle, a background suitable for an altar mural in New York's Church of the Ascension. The hills of Nikko offered a suggestive setting. "Here, at last," he confessed, "I am not forced to consider external nature as separate and opposed, and I can fall into moods of thought—or, if you prefer of feeling—in which the edges of all things blend, and man and the outside world pass into each other." His attitude toward this harmony of Japanese life with nature was nostalgic rather than critical.

> This place of dreams is not well chosen for effort. I feel rather as if, tired, I wished to take off my modern armor, and lie at rest, and look at these pictures of the simplicity of attitude in which we were once children. For, indeed, the meaning of our struggle is to regain that time, through toil and the fullness of

---

that it is an attempt at keeping possession of one's self. It is often a protest at what is displeasing and mean about us; it is an appeal to what is better. That is its most real value. It is an appeal to peace in time of brutal war, an appeal to courageous war in time of ignoble peace; it is an appeal to the permanent reality in presence of the transient; it is an attempt to rest for a moment in the true way." Ibid., pp. 112–13. See also John LaFarge, *Considerations on Painting: Lectures Given in the Year 1893 at the Metropolitan Museum of New York* (New York, 1895), p. 163.

12. *An Artist's Letters From Japan*, p. 30.

learning, and to live again in the oneness of mind and feeling which is to open to us the doors of the kingdom.[13]

Japan's refined primitivism attracted LaFarge for some of the same reasons it appealed to other Westerners surfeited with "progress." The pull was strong, but LaFarge kept his balance. For example, when confronted for the first time with Japanese religious painting of great power at Fenollosa's house, LaFarge was struck deeply by its quality of "exalted peace" but never carried away. He referred his response to the passionate delicacy of these paintings back to his earlier enthusiasms for Italian "primitives." His emotional commitments were definite but momentary, set in a frame of cosmopolitan connoisseurship. LaFarge was seldom disturbed by the separation of mind and feeling which plagued Adams; he observed with relish, savoring whatever excellences the moment might offer.

In so far as LaFarge analyzed the culture around him his viewpoint was aristocratic. He was charmed that art seemed so much a natural part of popular Japanese life, but he remained convinced that artistic excellence was incompatible with "the worst public taste, which must be that of the greatest number at any given time." [14] For an art to be popular it must be easily understood and its techniques widely imitated. In the modern world this led inevitably, in LaFarge's opinion, to a confusion of commercial values with art. It was this uneasy alliance of the artist with schools and markets that made him skeptical of Fenollosa's impending mission as an Imperial Commissioner of Fine Arts. LaFarge made his reservations clear in a letter written on the eve of his departure from Japan in company with Adams and Fenollosa:

> Art has always come by the grace of God, to be helped when it was here, or choked out; but no gardener has ever seen its seed . . . Okakura . . . is to inquire with Professor Fenollosa into the education of the artist and artisan with us, and to see "how we do it." I am deeply interested in their undertaking, perhaps the most remarkable of similar inquiries—if honestly conducted. But I see vague visions of distorted values, of commercial authorities looked upon as artistic. . . .[15]

13. Ibid., pp. 172–73, 158.
14. Ibid., p. 219.
15. Ibid., p. 221.

74

For his own part LaFarge was content to look and to enjoy what he saw.

In September 1886 LaFarge and Adams boarded the *City of Peking*, joining the Fenollosa household in a smooth Pacific crossing. In San Francisco the immigration and customs officials had been alerted for their arrival by Adams' friends in Washington, and the whole party swept through, bags, boxes, and Chinese nurse included. The American voyagers had come home again. For Adams return was a prelude to years of wandering, until at last, in *The Education of Henry Adams,* he transformed the story of his personal searches into a history of Western man. For LaFarge Japan had proved a pleasant episode, the results of his journey a book of letters, some beautiful objects, and sketches for a Japanese landscape to serve as background for the Ascension of Christ in an altar mural commissioned by a Protestant Episcopal church in New York.

Despite Adams' preoccupation with his own position in historical time, his eyes had been alerted somewhat by LaFarge's concern with arrangements in artistic space. In turn the Japanese background in LaFarge's Ascension scene may have reflected Adams' ironic historical sense; more likely it was simply an example of LaFarge's cosmopolitan eye. It remained for Fenollosa to consider artistic space historically and to see history on a world stage. If historian and painter could combine visions, an opening toward cosmopolis might emerge.

Yet, remote in time and place, he feels after the Hellenic world, divines the veins of ancient art, in which its life still circulates, and . . . is irresistibly attracted by it. This testimony to the authority of the Hellenic tradition, its fitness to satisfy some vital requirement of the intellect, which Winckelmann contributes as a solitary man of genius, is offered also by the general history of culture.

Walter Pater, *The Renaissance*

8 · IMPERIAL COMMISSIONER OF FINE ARTS

The *Salem Gazette* on Tuesday, October 19, 1886, announced that Ernest Fenollosa and his wife and family were expected in Salem within ten days, arriving from Japan by way of California. On Thursday the *Salem Register* confirmed the prospective return of a native, born the year of Perry's "black ships," now a Japanese Imperial Commissioner of Fine Arts. Fenollosa had left Salem eight years earlier with uncertain prospects; he was well educated and well married but penniless, on his way to an unknown and reputedly barbarous land in the farthest Orient. In a relatively short time, however, the son of a Salem "Puritan" and a Spanish violinist had become the Western world's leading critic of Japanese art, and evidently an important figure in Tokyo's governing circles.

In Salem, as in the world at large, Japanese fine art was still virtually unknown in the middle '80s. Fenollosa's title could have meant very little to the readers of the Salem newspapers. What reputation he had in the United States he owed to Morse's good offices and to the few people in art circles who had read the reprint of his review of Gonse's essay on Japanese painting. Salem welcomed him less as a celebrity than as a man returning home from a long visit. The Milletts were especially glad to see their only daughter, and the grandchildren, Brenda and Ernest Kano, were soon settled in with their mother's family.

The *Salem Gazette's* summary of Fenollosa's work pointed out conflicting Japanese attitudes with a Yankee candor which hit the mark. "We understand that Mr. Fenollosa has encountered the hostility of both the conservatives and the partizans of Western art. The old critics, connoisseurs, and artists resent the intrusion of the more vigorous ideas of a foreigner into the stagnating circle; while the radical young Japanese, who blindly regard everything Western as wholesome, look upon him as a sentimentalist and fanatic." The article went on to state that his present mission, although one of pure aesthetics, had "great economical importance" in view of international competition in art industries.[1]

The *Gazette* also carried the first American account of Fenollosa's hopes for a Japanese art which would join the mainstream of world art without losing its native genius. He was reported as favoring a gradual shift of attention to that Western art "most synthesizable with Japanese quality." The new synthesis would lead the way toward an art appropriate to a world of change in which mere imitation had no place. It remained to be seen whether American methods of art education were "synthesizable" with Japanese art.

Fenollosa and his fellow Imperial Commissioners were well received in Boston and continued on to New York and Washington to study methods of teaching art. Facilities and administrative procedures varied somewhat, but the theory of art education was largely the same wherever they went. In the ten years since the vagaries of American art instruction had been revealed by the exhibit at the Philadelphia Centennial, considerable progress had been made toward uniform standards. The Bureau of Education's voluminous report on drawing in the public schools, the first part of an extensive survey of "Art and Industry," had just been published when Fenollosa and his party arrived from Japan.[2] It recorded in great detail the introduction

1. *Salem Gazette*, Oct. 19, 1886.
2. Isaac Edwards Clarke, *Art and Industry. Industrial and High Art Education in the United States. Part I, Drawing in Public Schools*, U.S. Department of the Interior, Bureau of Education (Washington, Govt. Printing Office, 1885). Of particular interest is "The Democracy of Art," a series of preliminary papers

of drawing into public education and the widespread adoption of the techniques pioneered at the Massachusetts Normal Art School by its first director, Walter Smith. Smith's system was based on English and continental European prototypes and stressed the geometric base of drawing as the key to development of the universal "faculty of imitation."[3] Smith's first job had been to convince teachers and schoolboards that children could learn to draw without being exceptionally gifted. His next hurdle, the opposition of conservatives who opposed art as an unnecessary educational innovation, had been overcome by the combined forces of industry and cultural uplift. But economics and aesthetics remained uneasy allies in the field of public art education. Artists opposed Smith's system as inartistic, and business interests thought it too artistic. In 1886 the industrial drawing proponents were gathering in support of industrial training in order to maximize utility and minimize art.[4]

In the '80s battle lines were forming, but disagreement focused on matters of emphasis rather than basic theory, whether to accent instrument or free-hand drawing, mechanics or antique casts. The universal standard was geometric and realistic in varying combinations. When Fenollosa visited the Massachusetts Normal Art School, he noted facilities much improved in the ten years since his student days but little change in theory. In search of a "synthesizable" art theory he found only the technical facility which he had successfully opposed in the Engineering Art School in Tokyo, an accent on imitation rather than creation. Perhaps in Europe methods would be more advanced.

As the Imperial Commissioners toured Great Britain and the Con-

by Clarke, pp. xxxiii–cclvii. In appendices are reprinted all major documents in the historical development of American public school art education.

3. Walter Smith, *Art Education* (Boston, 1872), p. 46. Smith (d. 1886), an Englishman, graduate of the South Kensington Art School, and Art Master at Leeds School of Art and Science and Training School for Art Teachers, was brought to the United States in 1871 to become Massachusetts State Art Director.

4. Isaac E. Clarke, author of the monumental *Art and Industry* series (Parts I–IV, 1885–98), records his partisan support of Walter Smith in the controversies of the '80s in Part II, *Industrial and Manual Training in Public Schools* (Washington, Govt. Printing Office, 1892), esp. p. xlix; this also contains tributes to the three men most responsible for the success of the Massachusetts Normal Art School: Smith, Charles Callahan Perkins (1823–86), and John Dudley Philbrick (1818–86). Perkins, a Bostonian of independent wealth, was a leading art historian, art lecturer, and promoter of museums and schools. Philbrick was superintendent of the Boston city schools and a professional educator.

tinent, Fenollosa observed the models for American drawing instruction and found attitudes surprisingly uniform. The great international expositions and increasing ease of communication had helped standardize whatever methods seemed to increase the quality of art industries. The official Austrian report on the Vienna Exhibition of 1873 indicated a consensus in European art education:

> The world, so far as it is concerned in drawing, is probably unanimous in the conviction that instruction, in its first stages, must begin with geometrical forms, and that ornament must be practiced, to a certain degree, before figure drawing can be taken up. Differences of opinion have reference to method only; i.e., how shall the several parts be taught? What shall be their proportion, and what models shall be employed? [5]

Failure to discover important art educational advances in the West did not mean that the imperial mission was unsuccessful. On the contrary, this worldwide survey convinced Fenollosa and his colleagues, Okakura and Hamao, that the plans made tentatively in Japan were not only suitable but superior. Their findings in this respect were not too different from the reports of similar Japanese commissioners, who were as much concerned with avoiding a possibly embarrassing ignorance of Western ways as with actively imitating specific Western programs.

For Fenollosa the year of travel presented useful comparisons. He was able to examine European art at first hand, its heritage in churches and galleries and its current work in the ateliers of Paris and Munich, and in Antwerp, Vienna, and Madrid. He found contemporary standards remarkably similar, imitative of past masters rather than original. The work of all the schools seemed fixed at a mediocre level, which made Japanese developments all the more significant.

Late in the summer of 1887 Fenollosa headed back toward Tokyo and the new art academy. He was convinced that Japanese art might lead the way toward the next advance in world artistic development. His excitement at returning was mixed with sorrow, however, as the family made the long voyage west. When the big jin-rikisha finally drew up in front of the Fenollosa house in Kaga Yashiki, the servants saw that a familiar face was missing. Six-year-old Ernest Kano Fenollosa had died of appendicitis in Salem that April. Never-

5. Isaac E. Clarke, *Art and Industry*, Pt. I, pp. 638–39.

theless, the calm elegance of an ordered household was welcome. Brenda Fenollosa recalled in later years how there in Tokyo she "felt at home after so long an absence."

> In front of our house on the lawn, all the servants were standing and bowing low, the better to greet us. Each and every one of them were so nice to me after the death of my brother. I shall never forget their kindly sympathy. We had a large establishment: two butlers, a cook with his two assistants, two laundresses, a seamstress, two gardeners, a night watchman, three jin-rikisha men, the bath-boy, Mother's maid, as well as my Chinese nurse and Japanese maid. The entrance to our house was through a porch, enclosed by glass in winter, some eighty feet long, and filled with tropical flowers and shrubs. . . . The house itself was on one floor, with a big tiled Japanese roof. There was an entrance hall, library, two large drawing-rooms with their respective fireplaces, the dining-room, our five bedrooms, two bathrooms, and, not least important, the small passageway with its low roof to which we all rushed at night whenever there was an earthquake—a thing which happened quite often, and which shook the house and made frightful rumbling noises. The servants quarters were rambling and in Japanese style.[6]

Imperial Commissioner Fenollosa moved back into public life quickly and at the first chance spoke out strongly in support of the national art movement, repeating earlier themes with the added authority of up-to-date comparisons with the West. He concluded that a live and colorful Japanese art was far superior to the static, lifeless forms reproduced almost mechanically by Westerners. This was the gist also of the art mission's official report, although the report was more restrained. And the commissioners set to work to prepare the curriculum, faculty, and regulations for the new Fine Arts Academy which had been authorized. Baron Hamao was appointed president with Okakura and Fenollosa as managers. The painters of Fenollosa's Artists' Club formed the core of instructors,

6. Brenda Fenollosa, "Recollections of My Life in Japan," October 12, 1952, pp. 1–2, MS in possession of Brenda Fenollosa Biddle estate, Haverford, Pa. After the family return in 1887 the rikishas gave way to a stylish landau drawn by a pair of stallions, Tokyo being the district set aside for stallions. Fenollosa rode his own. The three jin-rikisha men were replaced by a coachman, a footman, and a stable boy.

and Fenollosa himself taught aesthetics and art history. Hogai Kano died in the autumn of 1888, but when the school opened in February 1889, Gaho Hashimoto and Yushin Kano were in charge of classes which linked the new system of art training with Japan's classical past. The laws of apprenticeship which had formed the core of artistic training in the guild schools of Kano and Tosa were transformed into a common educational system. After two years of basic instruction students were admitted to a three-year advanced course which included instruction in painting, sculpture, applied art, and design.

Fenollosan principles directed the artist's development: first, training in the unique qualities of the medium, then, familiarization with models, both European and Far Eastern, followed by the creation of original work. In the case of painting the accent was linear. First, the hand must be trained to draw abstract lines, straight and curved, with brush and ink; then study of the spirit of the brushwork of old masters through copying; finally creation of new relations of line and *notan* (light-and-dark) and color. Traditional Japanese art education in painter guilds had culminated with the copying of old masters. Fenollosa's innovation was to accent original creation at an early stage in training. For example, although the basic course stressed learning the language of line, *notan*, and color, a weekly schedule in an advanced course in painting was divided into hours as follows:

	First year	*Second year*	*Third year*
Original work	6	10	26
Drawing from life	11	10	0
Ancient models	6	6	0

Art history and aesthetics were included in both ordinary and advanced curricula, but Fenollosa insisted that each age must create its own art; Japan needed a touch of Emersonian irreverence. A new art would develop out of the artist's personal encounter with the basic elements of his medium, while awareness of traditions would preserve the spirit of earlier triumphs in visual relations made new by contemporary insight. It was Fenollosa's firm belief that "A new art is going to grow in this school, and it will dominate all Japan in the near future and will have a good influence over the world." [7]

7. Taro Kotakane, "Ernest Francisco Fenollosa," *Bulletin of Eastern Art*, no. 16 (April 1941), p. 25. The same critic maintained in 1941 that Fenollosa's

With the Fine Arts Academy in operation along Fenollosan lines the young American's program for a national art revival was virtually completed. The proposals which he had outlined in the early '80s were now a reality. The Academy stood at the top of a revised art educational system which began in primary school with training in the brush and in principles of linear design. Art exhibitions had become regular features of Tokyo life, some of them national, that is, government sponsored, others sponsored by clubs of artists and connoisseurs. In April 1887 the aristocratic Ryuchikai, scene of Fenollosa's first public appeal for the revival, changed its name to Nihon Bijutsu Kyokai and as an art club assumed responsibility for sponsoring important exhibitions. By 1890 Gaho Hashimoto and the Kano painters were leaders among contemporary artists who could now devote themselves to painting supported by prizes, sales, and teaching; in fact, Gaho won first prize at the National Exhibition in March 1890. Further evidence of the restored prestige of painters and their accepted role in the new Japan was the establishment late in 1890 of the Imperial Household honor roll of artists.

As a chronicle of the new art movement and a spur to broad aims a new journal was established in October 1889, the *Bijutsu Zasshi Kokka* or *Journal of National Art-Flowering. Kokka* began its distinguished career with seven articles by Fenollosa, including a series on Ukiyoye and several disquisitions on aesthetics.

In the field of art preservation Fenollosa's proposals were embodied in institutions, and in each case his own direct role was important. An archaeological trip to the Kyoto area in the spring of 1888, on which he was joined by Okakura and Baron Kuki, led to the establishment in September of a Bureau of National Treasures under the Imperial Household Ministry; Kuki was appointed chairman and on his committee sat Okakura, Hogai, and Fenollosa. The following spring saw an art department established in the Imperial Museum; on the board, again, were Kuki, Okakura, and Fenollosa.

In July 1889, when Fenollosa was at the peak of his success, he was invited to take charge of establishing a department of Japanese art at the Boston Museum of Fine Arts. The offer forced important de-

principles "still form the fundamental theory of the present art movement of Japan." Ibid., p. 26. For a detailed curriculum see Odakane, "Ernest F. Fenollosa's Activities in the Field of Art—Part III," *Bijutsu Kenkyu* (April 1941), pp. 115–17.

cisions, and Fenollosa deliberated at length, delaying a definite answer until the following April.

To accept the Boston offer would mean breaking ties with the new art movement before it was fully established. It would require reducing the scope of his art historical researches. It would shift the family scale of living downward, relatively, since in Japan the Fenollosas literally lacked nothing, and for most of their twelve-year sojourn they had enjoyed an eminence that was intellectual, social, even political. The contract with the Mombusho ran until July 1890, at which time some new combination of administration and teaching could very likely be worked out. Remaining in Japan had strong attractions.

Yet there were signs that a general reaction against foreign influences was underway. Although Fenollosa directed his energies against foreign models in the arts—he was a Japanese nationalist in a real sense—he was still a foreigner and therefore limited in his prospects. The University had never intended to employ foreigners as a permanent faculty, and by 1890 foreign professors had either been replaced by Japanese or were retained as visitors on a term basis. Fenollosa's employment by the government as a high official was unusual by the late '8os.

The craze for Western things and Western ways reached the end of its swing in the middle '8os. By 1887 the government's failure to equalize Japanese rights in foreign treaty revisions stirred a public anger that turned quickly on foreigners and the most evident supporters of foreign ways. The government was forced to repudiate the negotiators who had agreed to let foreign judges sit alongside Japanese in suits involving foreigners. Japanese humiliation over imposed extraterritorial rights led to rioting which brought martial law to Tokyo. In 1889, on the very day the Constitution was promulgated, Arinori Mori, the Minister of Education and a symbol of Westernization, was assassinated for an alleged insult to the imperial shrine of Isé. And in 1890 Foreign Minister Okuma, who was closely associated with treaty revision and moderate military policies, was injured seriously by a bomb. The militarists were by no means in control of the government, but nationalism was clearly resurgent and the future of foreigners was at the very least less brilliant than formerly.

In intellectual circles also a conservative nationalism was evident. Supporters of traditional Confucian learning never regained their lost eminence, but reappraisals of national culture attempted to correct an earlier indiscriminate esteem for Western thought. For example, the

Nippon Jin, a magazine founded in 1888, put forward general theories of national superiority which expressed the views of a group led by Yujiro Miyake, a philosopher of broad education in Eastern and Western learning. Miyake was a student of Fenollosa's as were many leading intellectuals, and Fenollosa sympathized with cultural nationalism so long as it was not parochial. In literature developments paralleled those of the earlier art revival. By 1890 an Academy of National Letters, Kokugaku-in, had been founded and a department of Japanese literature was operating in the Imperial University.

Fenollosa's close and cordial relations with many of the most cultivated men of the Meiji era led him to look hopefully on the nationalism which he had, in fact, helped to shape. He saw Japan as a future leader in the Westernization of Asia, her just example a reproach to the rapacity of the West. This view, widespread among samurai officials in the late '80s, was stated aptly in a passage in an 1885 novel, *Kajin No Kigu,* or *Strange Encounters of Elegant Females,* a book so popular that it was said "to have raised the price of paper in the metropolis." The novel's Japanese hero, the Wanderer of the Eastern Seas, gloomy after considering how the strong oppress the weak, draws encouragement from the words of a beautiful Spanish girl:

> Now that your country has reformed its government and, by taking from America what is useful and rejecting what is only superficial, is increasing month by month in wealth and strength, the eyes and ears of the world are astonished by your success. As the sun climbs in the eastern skies, so is your country rising in the Orient. Your August Sovereign has granted political liberty to the people, the people have sworn to follow the Imperial leadership. So the time has come when, domestic strife having ceased, all classes will be happy in their occupations. Korea will send envoys and the Luchu Islands will submit to your governance. Then will the occasion arise for doing great things in the Far East. Your country will take the lead and preside over a confederation of Asia. The peoples of the East will no longer be in danger. In the West you will restrain the rampancy of England and France. In the South you will check the corruption of China. In the North you will thwart the designs of Russia. You will resist the policy of European states, which is to treat Far Eastern peoples with contempt and to interfere in their domestic affairs, so leading them into servitude. Thus it is your country and no other that

can bring the taste of self-government and independence into the life of millions for the first time, and so spread the light of civilization.[8]

Fenollosa's personal experience combined with his world-historical speculations to make this image of benign leadership by Japan seem reasonable. The Constitution of 1889 established the framework for independent self-government, and the flowering of the arts suggested a national competition in the arts of peace which would develop along cosmopolitan lines. Cultural self-government seemed therefore as important as political self-government in creating an appropriate balance between tradition and innovation. Such a balance would present a model for other nations in the world's advance toward cosmopolis.

These peaceful cosmopolitan tendencies reassured Fenollosa about the future of his art program. Yet its very nationalism made continued foreign leadership not only unlikely but undesirable. Furthermore, he could feel sure that his work was in good hands, since the leaders of the art movement were men he respected enormously: Okakura, Hamao, Gaho, Yushin Kano.

Fenollosa had never intended to remain in Japan permanently. In 1890 he was thirty-seven years old and had served the Japanese government for twelve years. They had been good years, but a career in the United States could not be postponed indefinitely. Lizzie Fenollosa had been looking forward for some time to returning home with her husband to familiar friends and places; and young Brenda, almost seven, should be settling into school. They would miss their spacious house and a household attuned to a handclap. But more important, the position at the museum was unique and suited Fenollosa perfectly. As curator of the new Japanese department he would be in charge of his own collection of paintings, which he had sold in 1886 to Dr. Charles Weld, and also Sturgis Bigelow's fine collections of prints and sword-guards. He would be working in the midst of the beautiful things he loved; he would have time for research and writing; and lecturing would follow naturally from exhibitions and the interest they would rouse. The museum's Japanese collections were by far the finest in the West, and Fenollosa was eager to reveal their significance to America and to a progressively cosmopolitan world.

In April 1890 Fenollosa committed himself definitely to the Boston Museum, agreeing to sail from Yokohama in July. In later years he re-

8. Quoted in Sansom, *The Western World and Japan*, p. 414.

turned to Tokyo several times, but by 1890 he had reached the peak of his Japanese career; during later visits his influence was negligible. The special conditions of Japanese life in the years from 1878 to 1890 had determined his particular opportunities. Ten years earlier or ten years later his work would have been impossible. No foreigner could have played so important a role in any other period. The unique conditions in Japan in the '80s virtually forced Fenollosa in his later reflections to think historically, to temper his philosophical inclinations with respect for singular moments. Equally as important, his own intellectual growth was spurred by the innovative atmosphere of an extraordinary time when he saw his ideas literally made real in the lives of his students and in vigorous new institutions. In an address nearly a generation later a Japanese connoisseur summarized aptly Fenollosa's unusual services:

> Since the time of the restoration we had been so enthusiastic concerning western civilization, and blind to our own art as to almost have forgotten it as well as our own literature. At this critical stage of transition his unequalled judgment and his timely warnings regarding the revival of our national arts had most fruitful effects, both at home and abroad, and we owe him deep and grateful thanks.[9]

On the eve of his departure for Boston the young American was given high court rank and decorated by the Emperor Meiji with the Order of the Sacred Mirror. Fenollosa later recalled the high prediction of the Emperor's parting words: "We request you now to teach the significance of Japanese art to the West as you have already taught it to the Japanese." [10]

9. "Fenollosa Memorial Incense Burner Presentation Address" at Miidera Temple, Nov. 28, 1909, by Aiba Komaji, President of Kohukwai, the Association for the Encouragement of National Arts, Preserving and Fostering Their Spirit and Styles. Transcription in Freer Gallery Library, Washington, D.C.

10. The Order of the Sacred Mirror was reserved for those who had performed distinguished personal service to the Emperor; it is said to have been the highest decoration bestowed on a foreigner up to that time. At the same time Fenollosa was accorded the high court rank of third class. The Emperor's words are cited in *Sixth Report, Class of 1874 of Harvard College* (1894), p. 25.

PART 3 · *Apostle*

I came too late to gather much of that quiet spirit of colonial culture, that felt itself to be secondary and a bit remote from its sources, and yet was proud of this very remoteness, which gave it the privilege of being universal and just. In my time this spirit lingered only in Professor Norton, but saddened by the sense of being a survival.

George Santayana, *Persons and Places*

9 · CURATOR AND PROPHET IN BOSTON

The time and place of Fenollosa's return were auspicious for the start of his mission of alerting the West to the significance of Far Eastern art. By 1890 Boston's interest in Japan and China was well established, started by clipper ships and sustained by silks and lacquers. The clipper trade was well past—the last Silsbee square rigger became a coal barge in 1893—but wealthy Bostonians continued to collect Orientalia. *Harper's Magazine* described "Japanism" as "a new word coined to designate a new field of study, artistic, historic, and ethnographic." [1] The collections of Morse, Bigelow, and Fenollosa in Boston and Morse's ethnographic materials in Salem provided an unequaled base for Japanism. A less scholarly Japanese vogue was growing at the same time. When the London *Spectator* referred to "the curious japanolatry which is current in some literary and artistic circles," [2] Boston's Brah-

1. 76 (Feb. 1888), 334.
2. 65 (Dec. 6, 1890), 832. Cf. "examples of the Japanolatry characteristic of this Rococo age," *Athenaeum*, 68 (Aug. 24, 1895), 249. French "Japonisme" was successfully launched by the Goncourts in the '70s after its coterie beginnings in the '60s. Japan's first exhibit at an international exposition, in Paris in

mins, often notably anglophile in cultural matters, could feel themselves at the crest of fashion, even somewhat in advance. Japanese things were sufficiently familiar to William Dean Howells' gentle readers, for example, for him to mention the "Japanese effect" created by a dark-haired heroine in an 1884 novel as she stands before a fire with a fan held before her face. And the same heroine's mother can say, "She can't step out of the house without coming back with more things to talk about than most folks would bring back from Japan." [3] Boston's vast store of Japanese things supported a Japanism nourished by fashion, scholarship, and a pride of accumulation.

Although Boston's cultural eminence in national life was waning by the '90s, her example was still influential. The center of American literary life was shifting to Manhattan; Howells, symbolically, had deserted Boston for New York. But the *Atlantic Monthly* remained, its views a model of gentility; and Boston correspondents reporting on cultural activities were a regular feature of newspapers from New Orleans to Chicago and points west. It was particularly significant for Fenollosa's work that the world of women's clubs looked up to Boston, since any art missionary would probably have to convert women first. In America the arts were considered a special province of women, the more refined and sensitive sex. A man's business was generally regarded as practical, its forms and speculations commercial.

Boston stood somewhat apart from this intense concern with business. Money-making did not seem sufficient in itself to a number of leading Bostonians who had inherited wealth and position and felt a need to do something significant. Nor did the alternative of a political career seem promising: national politics offered a gentleman little more than mugwumpery, and public office in Boston meant dealing with fractious Irish and other aliens. A close observer of Boston's Brahmins remarked that "in the early 1890's the rich dreamt of culture rather than of leadership." [4]

1867, was exciting, but by 1889 the Japanese section of the exposition seemed disappointing and "Japonisme" was fading into the realm of commonplace. With the exception of Whistler and the English painter James Tissot, Anglo-American "Japanism" developed twenty years after its French prototype. See William L. Schwartz, *The Imaginative Interpretation of The Far East in Modern French Literature 1800–1925* (Paris, Champion, 1927), pp. 65–119; and especially Ernst Scheyer, "Far Eastern Art and French Impressionism," *Art Quarterly*, 6 (Spring 1943), 116–43.

3. Cited by Earl Miner, *The Japanese Tradition in British and American Literature* (Princeton, Princeton University Press, 1958), p. 45.

4. Santayana, *Persons and Places*, p. 183.

The Boston Museum of Fine Arts was supported by this dream of culture as well as by a traditional civic pride that relished Boston's eminence in comparison to other cities. The Japanese collections had the advantage of being superlative, the best in the Western world. The *Boston Sunday Herald's* report of Fenollosa's arrival and his prospective work as curator sounded a note of triumph: "The pre-eminence of the museum in its facilities for the study of the art of the most refined of living artistic peoples is practically impregnable." [5]

The size and completeness of the Japanese collections, which guaranteed pre-eminence, made Fenollosa's task as curator cumbersome and complex. The initial problems of shipping, uncrating, and storing complicated the more important matters of organization, research, and exhibition. Fortunately, two wings added to the museum's building on Copley Square were opened in 1890, completing a two-story quadrangular structure which afforded space on the second floor for the new Department of Japanese Art. Nevertheless, exhibition space was limited; only a small sample of the museum's rich collections could be displayed. The Boston newspapers reported the progress of Fenollosa's organizing work, interviewing him regularly on the significance of the collections and noting some of his visitors, notably Walter Crane, the English painter and illustrator, and Samuel Bing, the Paris connoisseur. Fenollosa took keen pleasure in showing off his treasures to such knowledgeable visitors, but generally he worked alone, attending to the details of the new department and planning a series of exhibitions, strolling home in the evening to nearby Newbury Street.[6]

For a first exhibition at the museum, "Hokusai and His School," Fenollosa selected 172 works, primarily paintings and drawings; a few of Hokusai's color prints were included to illustrate his early period. The exhibition opened in the summer of 1892 and was extended on through the following April to enthusiastic notices in such journals as the *Boston Transcript*, the *Congregationalist and Boston Recorder*, and the *Brooklyn Independent*. Starting with a Hokusai show offered many advantages. Hokusai's prints and albums were already well known and popular. The museum's extensive holdings made possible a full chronological study of Hokusai's shifting styles. Most important,

5. Sept. 7, 1890.
6. The Boston city directory listed Fenollosa's addresses as follows: 1891— 272 Newbury St. 1892 and 1893—366 Commonwealth Ave. 1894 and 1895— Charlesgate Hotel (535 Beacon St.).

Fenollosa's revisionist emphasis on Hokusai's paintings opened the way logically toward a historical understanding of Japanese art, a goal of future exhibitions. Furthermore, Hokusai's work raised issues Fenollosa wanted raised, general questions of the artist's role in society, and particularly problems of balancing tradition and innovation and responding to aristocratic and popular tastes. To Fenollosa, writing in Boston in 1892, Hokusai's art seemed to have been weakened at times by popular demands and personal idiosyncrasies. What this "highly imaginative Hokusaiish world" lacked, in Fenollosa's judgment, was "the earnest rendering of a grand conception," a shortcoming due to the low public taste and the social cleavages of the Tokugawa era. Hokusai's outlook, argued Fenollosa, "was on a level with that of the people."

> Cut off from all the higher oriental ideals of religion, of philosophy, of poetry, of refined manners, of prophetic insight, of chastened spirit, he could not rise above essentially vulgar aims. Cut off from contact with the great masterpieces of an earlier Chinese and Japanese art, he was without competent guidance. In his day, there were no public museums. The collections belonging to temples and to private owners were, for the most part, closed to the common people. If Hokusai could have taken Keion for model rather than Utamaro, his might have been a transcendent art. If he could have known intimately the really great men of his day outside of the narrow line of the novelists and the dramatists, if the keen scholars, the profound statesmen, the men of trained insight and judgment could have recognized and deliberately guided his genius into normal channels, as a Medici recognized the new-born lights of his generation, we might have had a Japanese art without rival for centuries.[7]

Hokusai's flawed greatness demonstrated the need for making freely available the highest ideals and artistic traditions of a culture.

Applying this lesson to the United States in 1892, it followed that the very best Far Eastern work deserved the widest circulation, if American art were to point the way toward the cosmopolitan styles of a world culture. The first task was to determine what was the best work on aesthetic grounds, keeping in mind the work's relation to the society in which it was created. Accordingly, Fenollosa followed the Hokusai show with a varied series of exhibitions: early nineteenth-

7. Introduction to the catalogue, *Hokusai and His School*, p. xiii.

century kakemonos by Kaibun and Hoyen and their schools (May 1893 to March 1894); sixteenth-century screens with gold backgrounds (April 1894); several hundred color prints selected by Fenollosa from the collection of Samuel Bing (May 1894); a private collection of pre-seventeenth-century Japanese paintings and metal work lent by M. Shirasu of Tokyo (June 1894); one hundred Chinese Buddhist paintings of the eleventh and twelfth centuries lent by the Temple Daitokuji of Kyoto (December 1894 to March 1895). When this last collection of ancient Chinese paintings was sent to be shown in Philadelphia in March, Fenollosa announced that the next exhibition would focus on the Kyoto school. His program for a full historical series was well begun. Although the series was halted by Fenollosa's dramatic break with the museum in 1895, by then Boston's prominence for Western studies of Far Eastern art was assured. During Fenollosa's five-year tenure the Boston Museum of Fine Arts was established firmly as a center for the training of a generation of curators and scholars.[8]

The Chicago World's Fair of 1892 added stimulus to American interest in Japanese art. Fenollosa was appointed a member of the fine arts jury, and for the first time at an international exposition Japan exhibited under the heading of "Fine Arts" as well as "Industries." The contemporary Japanese work in the fine arts section gave evidence of the new respect for traditional Japanese painting which Fenollosa had encouraged so effectively in Japan and which he was now encouraging in the United States. In a review of this work in the *Century Magazine*, Fenollosa outlined the history of Japan's shift from imitation of Western art toward an art open to Western ideas but built on Japan's national experience.[9] The result was an art which Fenollosa hailed as genuinely contemporary, an example in its high quality of how national artistic traditions could develop toward a world art of many styles.

During the same years that Japanese art exhibitions were drawing attentive crowds in Chicago, Boston, New York, and Philadelphia, Fenollosa was engaged in pointing out the implications of these art

8. According to an authoritative list compiled in 1929 nearly half of the active professional curators of Chinese and Japanese art in the United States "have, or have had, intimate association with the Museum of Fine Arts in Boston." Benjamin March, *China and Japan in Our Museums* (New York, American Council Institute of Pacific Relations, 1929), p. 13 and Appendix A.

9. "Contemporary Japanese Art," *Century Magazine*, 46 (1893), 577–81.

works from the lecture platform. Through the force of personal appearances he hoped to channel fashionable curiosities toward genuinely cosmopolitan tastes. In one Boston lecture he drew implications from oriental design which must have surprised most of his Saturday afternoon audience. As the *Sunday Herald* reported, "The Japanese, he said, would just as lief at first see a picture upside down; that is, they admire beauty of line and color in art, rather than . . . merely depicting nature." [10] Considered somewhat subversive today, this was heresy in 1892.

Fenollosa's reputation grew as he spoke to groups of artists, students, teachers, and in open public forums. The impact of his lectures was heightened by his considerable platform talents: a strong baritone voice and beautiful diction; frequent allusions to more familiar Western art and to music, poetry, and current history; above all, a distinguished appearance and a handsome profile. Confident, passionate, at times mystical, Fenollosa seemed romantic without being alien. By the spring of 1895 Fenollosa was undertaking a six lecture series in Boston's Association Hall on Friday evenings with seats at $3 and $5. Rising interest was encouraging, and rising fees supplemented his annual museum salary of $2,500. The series was titled "History of Japanese Art." It was more than a scholarly outline. Audiences soon learned they would not only see slides of paintings but would hear eloquent discourses on the arts of Japanese life, the illuminations of Buddhism, and the coming union of the civilizations of East and West.

Fenollosa's work on Far Eastern art as a scholar, connoisseur, and critic provided a base for broad speculations on the significance of the West's modern encounter with the civilizations of the Orient. Again his Boston milieu proved unusually sympathetic. This was due in part to civic pride in the museum and perhaps to Fenollosa's familiar Harvard and Salem background; more important was a cultural atmosphere hospitable to ideas which had a transcendental ring. Boston's culture in the '90s was largely secondary, remote from its European sources, and provincial, even insular, but its very provinciality, as Santayana pointed out, allowed Bostonians the privilege of being universal. A tightly knit upper class, whose cultural leaders felt themselves at "the Hub of the Universe"—the phrase was meant only half in jest—was not afraid to speculate broadly. The shallowness of this culture, apparent to an Adams or a James, was no barrier to breadth; it may have encouraged it, especially within a tradition intellectually

10. Feb. 21, 1892.

transcendentalist and theologically Unitarian. Fenollosa spoke as a prophet and poet as well as a connoisseur and specialist; he was fortunate in having an audience which took seers seriously.

Fenollosa's prophecy that a new kind of civilized man would emerge from the coming fusion of the world's cultures appeared in an article published in the June 1892 issue of the *Atlantic Monthly* under the title, "Chinese and Japanese Traits." Fenollosa began by attacking a current stereotyped approach to the Far East which contrasted China's "prudent conservatism" with Japan's "hasty radicalism." He pointed to Chinese ideals of art, literature, and law as the center of Far Eastern civilization and argued that adaptation of these ideals to changing historical situations had determined the present characteristics of Chinese and Japanese culture.

Fenollosa went on to stress the historical fortunes of individualism in the Far East, introducing a theme which he elaborated in later years. Both Chinese and Japanese, he asserted in the *Atlantic*, "have exhibited on the scale of centuries, in grand alternation or in strange mixture, the opposite traits of individuality and formalism." Individuality he distinguished sharply from the "morbid self-consciousness" of "personality."

> I mean by individuality, not the self of which we think, but the self by which we do. It is the power to produce freshly from within, to react and adapt under rapid change of environment. It transcends institution, custom, love of approbation, fear of disapproval, all slowly acting forces of sheer mass. It is spontaneous origination, the salt of social life, the last hope of a race.[11]

In Fenollosa's view the great individuals of Sung China, "innovating statesmen, constructive philosophers, inspired poets, and original artists," had created the greatest illumination of the Far East by attempting to fuse Taoism, Confucianism, and Buddhism. The Mongol conquest and ensuing Confucian formalism had stunted and petrified a native individualism. In Japan, however, "a happy rotation of cultures" prevented exhaustion of mental soil, and the "free shoots of individuality" preserved their flexibility, their "facility to construct and reconstruct under the necessarily ever-changing environment."

This capacity for "self-evolutionary reconstruction" formed the core of Fenollosa's conception of Japanese character. Through the idea of evolution he aligned Japanese development with the basic principle of life. "The very scientific idea of life is perpetual power of readapta-

11. "Chinese and Japanese Traits," *Atlantic Monthly*, 69 (1892), 770–71.

tion; and the highest life is reached when this readaptation implies a synthesis of all the organs and faculties through a free presiding intelligence. Failure to change, through the increasing inertia of the constitution, is the beginning of death." [12]

Currently Japan's unique perspective on cultural change was a result of the speed of her assimilation of Western ideas. Fenollosa had himself watched samurai who had been shaped under the feudal isolation of Tokugawa rush to follow Western examples, study Western civilization intensively, then turn back to view native tradition critically, in order to determine how to preserve the best features of both cultures. This unique perspective, as Fenollosa pointed out, had been gained *"within the lifetime of a single individual."* The leaders of Japan, therefore, would determine the direction of national development with heightened awareness of the issues at stake, an awareness rare in the history of cultural change.

Although Japan might well develop into a military "colossus," Fenollosa concluded, more probably she would pursue her natural advantages in art industries, utilizing her superior design capacity in a peaceful invasion by trade. With her "carefully nurtured refinement" and "creative individuality" Japan's obligation was to preserve Asiatic spiritual ideals in the face of the "materialistic shams" of the West, to act as agent and herald of a newly possible "fusion of Eastern and Western types." This grand theme fired Fenollosa's imagination and guided his career; this initial statement had the ring of prophecy.

> [In this fusion] which shall create in both hemispheres a far more rounded civilization than either has ever known, Japan has the inestimable privilege of becoming our most alert pioneer. Through her temperament, her individuality, her deeper insight into the secrets of the East, her ready divining of the powers of the West, and, more than all, through the fact that hers, the spiritual factor of the problem, must hold the master key to its solution, it may be decreed in the secret council chambers of Destiny that on her shores shall be first created that new latter-day type of civilized man which shall prevail throughout the world for the next thousand years.[13]

Fenollosa developed a similar thesis in *East and West*, a poem delivered before the Phi Beta Kappa Society at Harvard in June 1892.

12. Ibid., p. 772.
13. Ibid., p. 774.

His scale was even broader than in the *Atlantic* article, but his thesis was clarified this time by concrete images, a narrative of events, and occasional dashes of vinegar. *East and West* revealed the world's dialectical progress toward a new global civilization as an unfolding of Spirit. The unfolding was Buddhist, Hegelian, and Emersonian, cosmopolitan in a transcendental mode. "One design unites and animates," Emerson had declared in a Phi Beta Kappa oration fifty-five years earlier, and he had urged the American scholar to trust his own judgment and write books for his own age. Fenollosa's individual eye saw a unified historical design, and in the spirit of Emerson he offered *East and West* as a vision for his own age and for "the conversion of the world."

East and West had a grand theme, and its rhetoric was impressive, at times moving. But the poem was long—fifty-three pages in its published form—and difficult—it attempted to combine a narrative of world history with personal memories and philosophical argument. Fenollosa placed considerable demands on his listeners.

The poem's structure—there are five main sections—established the central thesis. Part I, "The First Meeting of East and West" under the sword of Alexander the Great, sets the stage for analyses of "The Separated East" (II) and "The Separated West" (III), an account of "The Present Meeting of East and West" (IV), and a vision of "The Future Union of East and West" (V). Each civilization needs the other as complement; the West needs the harmonizing feminine insight of the East, spiritual and aesthetic, and the East needs the expansive masculine force of the West, scientific and industrial. The coming union results from this primary marriage, and a secondary marriage supports the final prospect. Christianity serves the West as a feminine eye into the spiritual East, and the martial and self-reliant knighthood of Buddhist and samurai establishes a masculine affinity with the West. "This stupendous double antithesis seems to me," wrote Fenollosa in a preface, "the most significant fact in all history. . . . Within the coming century the blended strength of Scientific Analysis and Spiritual Wisdom should wed for eternity the blended grace of Aesthetic Synthesis and Spiritual Love." [14]

As the poem develops within this dialectic frame it becomes clear that Fenollosa is drawn strongly toward Asian values, especially the kind of aesthetic Buddhism he had studied and practiced. The

14. *East and West, The Discovery of America, and Other Poems* (New York, 1893), p. vi.

97

"golden peace" of Buddhist infinite light contrasts markedly with the "sting of the gold" in the commercial strife of the West. Hogai Kano, pillar of Fenollosa's national art movement, is invoked as a reincarnation of the spirit of Oriental art and as precursor of "the final Asian man" that is to rise in Japan. The history of this rise is primarily the history of Buddhism according to Fenollosa's poetic account. Even Sung China is described in terms of its twelfth-century "Buddhist illumination." And again, it is Fenollosa's Tendai Buddhist mentor, Sakurai Keitoku of Miidera Temple, who prophesies that the West is nearly ripe to receive fresh insight. In preparation all men must follow the way indicated by the Tendai priest and strive to conquer themselves:

> On no external God relying,
> Self-armed, heaven and hell alike defying,
> Lonely,
> With bare will only,
> Biting his bitter blood-stained sod;—
> This for the *world*, as for Japan,
> This is to be a man!
> This is to be a god! [15]

The idea of a higher "individuality" attained by the new type of civilized man acts conceptually in opposition to "personality" and as a synthesis: it is both first and third term in a Hegelian trichotomy. Fenollosa makes this explicit in a note in the published version of the poem: "I oppose personality, the self-centred and self-originated will of an incarnate man, to individuality, the unconscious strength and freedom of an intelligence immersed in the divinity of its work. One is peculiar through the abstract isolation of subjectivity; the other is peculiar through the infinite fulness of the well of Spirit whence it flows." [16]

Fenollosa accepts his own heritage of Western blood as a penitent kneeling in a Gothic cathedral, praying for consecration of Western power to aims more worthy than war. But even the Gothic cathedral

15. Ibid., p. 28.

16. Ibid., p. 212. Fenollosa used the word "peculiar" in the sense of an Hegelian "particular," a subcategory of "Logic" stemming from "Notion." Being, Essence, and Notion are three major subdivisions of Hegel's Logic. Notion, "the principle of freedom, the power of substance self-realised," is characterized by development rather than dialectical transition (which characterizes Being) or reflection (which characterizes Essence). Development is understood in organic terms, i.e. development of a plant from its germ. Notion is further divided

is transformed by Buddhist images. Passions "palpitate in flowers" and pinnacled "crystal darts" merge into "fire-whorls to lap the altars of the moon." [17]

The source of Western power, science, he views with ambivalence. Its passion for conquering facts has widened human horizons, and its insistence on free inquiry, "evolved in self-expansion," has built "structures of world-wide toleration." But science suffers from the "ancestral curse—analysis." Analytical thinking has split ideas into "fine-spun silver threads" and torn the essential fabric of "cosmic synthesis."

To warfare and science Fenollosa adds the "selfish expansiveness of commerce" as a third Western impulse. The forcible exploitation of China in the name of trade focuses the central irony of recent history, the spectacle of Western man assaulting the very princess he is destined to wed. In terms of a future harmonious union of East and West the burning of the Peking summer palace in 1860 is the last ironic service of "the explosive life of competition." [18]

Turning to modern Japan Fenollosa sketches in acid. He pictures the chimney smoke which has already blighted the West threatening to choke Japanese city life. The "steel-bound leap of trade" has arched over the oceans of the world but the new bridges bring to Japan a materialistic culture largely unconcerned with ends. "Sectarian watchdogs religious" snarl round a secular optimism which sees perfection in "nature's selection," hears "bliss roar through the craters of grain-elevators."

> O this spirituality of pure externality!
> Which can patch up disasters with arnica-plasters,
> Pipe the fountain of men's ills with cunning utensils,

---

into three parts: Subject, Object, and Idea. Subjective Notion is again divided into three parts, and these three in a developmental context are most important for Fenollosa's own theories. Subjective Notion "contains the three following 'moments' or functional parts: (1) The first is UNIVERSALITY—meaning that it is in free equality with itself in its specific character. (2) The second is PARTICULARITY—that is, the specific character, in which the universal continues serenely equal to itself. (3) The third is INDIVIDUALITY—meaning the reflection-into-self of the specific characters of universality and particularity—which negative self-unity has complete and original determinateness, without any loss to its self-identity or universality." *The Logic of Hegel,* Eng. trans. William Wallace (2d ed. 1892), p. 291. Reference to Fenollosa's study of Wallace's *Hegel* occurs repeatedly in Mary M. Fenollosa's diary MSS, and Wallace's first edition, published in 1874, was used by Fenollosa in his courses in Japan.

17. *East and West,* p. 32.
18. Ibid., pp. 212, 33, 213.

> Catch a shower of schisms in a cistern of isms!
> Were the world one vast greenery of hot-house machinery,
> Could you speed all creation with the spur of taxation,
> Do you think that would muzzle the asp in the puzzle?
> Would it snuff out the fire of the primal desire? [19]

Fenollosa pictures the current impact of East on West as thoroughly superficial, and he attacks the vogue of spiritualism as an empty masquerade.

Yet Fenollosa sees "The Future Union of East and West" developing from these contacts. Such prophecy seems both utopian and unfounded. How can it be treated seriously? Fenollosa answers that union will begin with art, with a recognition of the essentially musical quality of the art of life and the harmony of all things. Faith apart from creeds, labor filled with joy, creation free from rules and schools point toward Fenollosa's lyric finale. The seeds of love finally burst in a mystical merger of Christ and Buddha in "a dim uncertain form divine," "like God upon a lotus leaf"; the form "fades in formless light. . . ."

> Into the silence of Nirvana's glory,
> Where there is no more West and no more East. [20]

Fenollosa's audience at the Harvard reading of *East and West* could applaud this reassuring finale, but much of the poem was puzzling, even to scholars. Allusions to Far Eastern figures and terms, Roshi and Manwantaras for example, needed the explanatory notes appended to the version of *East and West* published the following year. Rhythmic shifts usually underlined a change of tone, as from spirited to satiric or from satiric to elevated; but the narrative argument, which the shifts in tone supported, demanded close attention from listeners, probably too close for a warm day in late June.

Among Fenollosa's other poems of this period, "The Discovery of America" drew the warmest response, perhaps because unlike *East and West* it avoided erudite argument and moved with striking rhythms, extended alliteration, and flowery images. Its novel form, a "symphonic poem" in four movements, heightened a musical play with themes which were stated clearly, developed broadly, and concluded dramatically. One critic, a close friend, predicted that the poem "will be sometime regarded as one of the greatest things of the

19. Ibid., p. 42.
20. Ibid., p. 55.

nineteenth century." "After I had heard this poem read by the author," he went on, "I felt as though I had been lifted into a new region of poesy. Such absolute mastery of exquisite forms, such overwhelming affluence of diction, such grace of rhythm, such surprising effects, such originality of thought, were a complete surprise to me." He concluded that others present found the poem "incomparable" and that several lady enthusiasts declared it "the greatest poem of the century." [21] A writer in the Chicago *Inter-Ocean*, who had discussed *East and West* favorably, was overwhelmed by "The Discovery of America": "It is the culmination of the great spontaneous and exuberant genius that has expressed itself in this poem. No comparable work has been produced in American literature, and only in Shelley and Swinburne do we find any kindred power and passion." [22]

This kind of adulation, with its reliance on enthusiasm rather than analysis, suggests a particular kind of problem faced by Fenollosa because of his powerful personal presence. There was a danger that simplified emotional response to his vision of Asian civilization would obscure the complex historical particulars necessary for any fruitful understanding. The acclaim of lady enthusiasts—there were many in Boston—was gratifying, but this Boston audience was refined in special ways that set it apart from the mainstream of national life, or even from the women's clubs of a less "cultured" place, such as Terre Haute, Indiana.

If the American people were to be alerted to the significance of developments in the Far East, as Fenollosa intended, then his message would have to reach well outside cultivated Boston. The aristocratic tone of some of Boston's artistic activities limited their relevance in a democratic continental nation. So far as Fenollosa himself considered the matter in the early '90s, he was skeptical of democratic standards. In his appraisal of Hokusai's career, for example, Fenollosa concluded that "an enthusiastic popular environment is not sufficient to create a great national art. The greatest genius can successfully lead the people only through his higher, though intelligible, idealism." [23]

Problems of intelligibility and relevance to national life were crucial for Fenollosa's art mission; they were raised most clearly by a mysticism and aestheticism which attracted an articulate if not happy few of Boston's Brahmins.

21. N. H. Dole, "Notes from Boston," May 19, 1893, in *Book News*, 11 (1893), 423–24.
22. Sept. 15, 1895.
23. *Hokusai and His School*, p. xiv.

Who knows but that the myriad powers of mysticism, today almost abolished in the modern world, will not wake up again, if momentarily paralyzed faculties of the mind will not commence to work again, if our humanity will not see again a period analogous to that of the Alexandrians and the Gnostics, or more correctly of the Brahmans? It would be one of the greatest of those so-called ironies of nature if the future wakening of those so-called occult sciences should have one of its starting points in America.

Paul Bourget, *Outre Mer*

10 · THE LOTUS AND THE BRAHMINS

The mystic overtones and cosmic scale of Fenollosa's major poems matched the dreams apparent in the "White City," assembled as if by civic magic on the shores of Lake Michigan. *East and West* was published in the fall of 1893 to take advantage of the interest in Asia aroused by Chicago's World Columbian Exposition. The exposition buildings, seemingly made of white marble and set in a glistening tracery of canals, looked like a vision of ideal beauty, perhaps the first monument of a world civilization. Among the world congresses which met in conjunction with the fair, the World's Parliament of Religions was an outstanding success. A monthly magazine called *The Open Court* had been featuring popular and scholarly articles on oriental religion since its establishment in Chicago in 1887; now it hailed the gathering of spokesmen for the world's religions as a promising first in the history of mankind.[1] Never before had the prospects for exchange of wisdom seemed so bright. Swami Vivekananda, an unheralded Hindu mystic, became one of the sensations of the fair and a national figure, remaining in the United States for what amounted to a triumphal tour.

Nowhere was Vivekananda more enthusiastically received than in Boston. "Certainly nothing so enchants Boston as mysticism," wrote a lady columnist in December 1894. She went on to describe a Sunday symposium at Mrs. Ole Bull's.[2] Vivekananda spoke in the morning on the spiritual birthright of man, and in the afternoon Fenollosa discussed "Art and Religion," with what the *New Orleans Times-Democrat's* special correspondent described as "a power, a fervor, a splendor of spirited truth seldom equaled." "The name of Buddha is one to conjure with," she continued, and "the term 'American Buddhist' is not an uncommon one at date." She cited the popular French writer, Paul Bourget, in support of mysticism's hold on American life and interpreted the current enthusiasm as evidence that "it is in America that the next round of the highest development will take place."[3] During the same Boston winter the Round Table Club discussed "Some Points in the Ethics of Buddhism," and Professor Rhys Davids, secretary of the Royal Asiatic Society, gave a series of lectures on Buddhism before the Lowell Institute. Fenollosa dissented from Davids on interpretation, asserting that preoccupation with ancient doctrines overlooked the "progressive" character of Buddhism, its capacity to adapt itself to changing needs, and he pointed to Japanese Buddhism as an example of evolutionary growth.[4]

More significant than such scholarly differences was a tendency evident in Boston to treat personal mysticism as a sign of advanced

1. "Parliament of All Religions," *The Open Court*, 6 (1892), 3420.

2. Mrs. Ole Bull, a wealthy Bostonian, was a leading financial backer of the Vedanta movement, inspired by Vivekananda's powerful presence and the universal religion of Vivekananda's master, Ramakrishna. For a vivid account of Vivekananda's American visits see Romain Rolland, *Prophets of the New India*, Eng. trans. E. F. Malcolm-Smith (New York, Boni, 1930), pp. 316–67, 431–40.

3. Lilian Whiting, "Boston Days," *New Orleans Times-Democrat*, Dec. 19, 1894, April 28, 1895. Lilian Whiting (1859–1942) was literary editor of the *Boston Traveller* 1880–90, editor of the *Boston Budget* 1890–93; her books included *Boston Days* (1902) and *Louise Chandler Moulton, Poet and Friend* (1909).

4. "Boston Days," Nov. 13, 1894.

evolution, with the implication that those without occult knowledge or experience would not be saved. To Fenollosa, the Buddhist lotus, especially the lotus of his own Tendai sect, suggested a pattern of human development unfolding from within outward and connected in all its forms, its parts never cut off from one another, not even by saintly excellence. A salvation limited to saints did not tally with Fenollosa's belief in a universal, latent "individuality." Concern about private experience and significance to the exclusion of the experiences of others smacked of egotism, of personality rather than individuality. Such self-concern seemed to Fenollosa to violate the spirit of Buddhism, a spirit often misconstrued in Boston.

In a letter to Mrs. Jack Gardner, whose interest in spiritualism added to the fashion, Fenollosa spoke acidly of the occult "boom." He attacked Buddhist interpretations which were simply "theosophy mixed with a little diluted Hegel" and expressed in categories "neither Buddhist nor Eastern, but a mixture of German Transcendentalism and English Psychical Research. No Buddhist," he declared "talks about Universals, Absolutes, Macrocosms, Essence, Pure Being; at least for the foundation of his practice." As for individual salvation, "conscious mystical practices regarded as ends in themselves are condemned," except for specially consecrated souls who, if they know, do not speak, since their exceptional attainments ought not to draw people away from the world and a proper service of others. Fenollosa contended that although mysticism "anticipates normal human evolution," humanity advances along varied lines.

> A true man or woman whose life radiates sunshine and sweetness, who is sound at the core through love, and devout through reverence for all ideals, may never have had an occult ecstasy, a metaphysical illumination, or a mystic sign, and yet may be nearer Christ, Buddha, Life Eternal, than many an advanced mystic. My Buddhist teacher expressly declared this. So, mysticism is not *the only* "way"; not necessarily even the *best* "way"; certainly not the *normal* "way." [5]

5. EFF to Isabella Stewart Gardner, n.d. (c. 1894), in Fenway Court Museum. Fenollosa's letter was directed at Marion Crawford's views stated on several occasions and evident in his novel then current, *Casa Braccio*. Crawford, a nephew of Julia Ward Howe, was a prolific novelist and journalist and a social lion. Fenollosa had harsh words also for Madame Blavatsky's theosophy and the pseudo-Buddhist writings of A. P. Sinnett. Among Mrs. Gardner's guests at Green Hill in Brookline during the autumn of 1893 were William James, the Paul Bourgets,

Part of Buddhism's appeal to Fenollosa lay in its all-embracing variety. "Where Christianity consigns myriads to Hell, Buddhism allows an indefinite number of trials. Pride in a little occult knowledge," he added tartly, "is about the only cause that delays salvation well-nigh eternally."

Pride in occult knowledge was curiously widespread in New England during the '80s and '90s. Many New Englanders had been intrigued with mesmerism, phrenology, and astral forms in the years before the Civil War, but the spiritualism of the '90s suggested deeper religious doubts and a grasping at psychical mysteries as a means of personal salvation. New England's orthodox religions seem to have declined as the region's relative importance and prosperity diminished. Christian Science, for example, was born and thrived on pursuit of a lost health.

Faith healing had affinities at a philosophical level with transcendentalist denial of material reality and stress on mind. Japanese Buddhism in Boston, even in Fenollosa's "progressive" version, was one more exotic element in a wide spiritualist stream. In the autumn of 1894 the Boston Metaphysical Club began the second year of its exploration of "man's deeper nature, its development and possibilities" in "an age of divine unrest and inquiry." It was probably more than coincidence that at the same time Mr. Kehiro Nakemura opened classes in Japanese, with references from Percival Lowell, Josiah Royce, and William James.[6]

To this spiritualist groundswell William James added a note of empirical analysis and his own intellectual prestige. He was convinced that unusual mental phenomena constitute significant strata of human experience and felt strongly "the contrast between the richness of life and the poverty of all possible formulas." James had grown up in an atmosphere in which heresy was preferred to orthodoxy and in which personal experience was accorded privileged intellectual status. In the middle '90s he was increasingly persuaded of a heretical hypothesis, namely, the "dramatic probability" that "there is a continuum of cosmic consciousness, against which our individuality builds but accidental fences, and into which our several

---

and Ernest and Lizzie Fenollosa, also Sarah Orne Jewett and Edith Wharton. Fenollosa's Green Hill guest book entry for June 10, 1894, read: "No oblivion in the orange poppy."

6. "Boston Days," n.d. (autumn 1894). William James' interest in Japan was probably kindled by Edward S. Morse's Lowell Institute lectures of 1880–81.

minds plunge as into a mother sea or reservoir." [7] While Fenollosa was discoursing on "Religion and Art" and on Buddhism, James was busy collecting data for his classic study, *The Varieties of Religious Experience.*

Material lay close at hand among Boston's Brahmins. Sturgis Bigelow and young George Cabot Lodge were both attracted to Buddhism. Their attitudes underline the ambiguities of a mysticism insulated from the world by the kind of self-concern that Fenollosa called personality, to distinguish it from the individuality he hoped was evolving.

Dr. William Sturgis Bigelow returned to Boston from seven years in Japan and continued Buddhist studies begun in the temples in Kyoto where his friend Fenollosa had also studied. Bigelow's library of occult works kept growing, and on Tuckernuck, a small island off the coast of Nantucket, he gave instruction in Buddhist discipline to a small circle of friends and relatives.[8] Bigelow's interpretation of Buddhism contrasted sharply with Fenollosa's, the issue focused on the social implications of new experience, in this case religious experience.

"Each man," wrote Bigelow, "carries in himself the conditions and

---

See Morse, *Japan Day by Day* (Boston, Houghton Mifflin, 1917), 2, 404. The rise of organized "spirit" religions was marked by Mary Baker Eddy's *Science and Health* (1875); Madame Blavatsky's Theosophical Societies multiplied after 1875; in 1876 Felix Adler founded the Society for Ethical Culture in New York City. Edwin Arnold's *Light of Asia* (1879) circulated widely, also Henry S. Olcott's *Buddhist Catechism* (1885) and Alfred P. Sinnett's *Esoteric Buddhism* (1884).

7. William James, *Memories and Studies* (London, Longmans, Green, 1911), p. 204. In 1894 James became President of the Society for Psychical Research (founded London 1882) and continued to support the American branch (founded 1884). In 1896 he gave a Lowell Institute lecture series on "Abnormal Mental States," in 1898 an Ingersoll Lecture on "Human Immortality," and in 1901–02 the Gifford Lectures, published as *The Varieties of Religious Experience: A Study in Human Nature* (London, Longmans, Green, 1902). Among the "varieties" James recorded the spiritual transformation of Horace Fletcher (1849–1919), originator of Fletcherism and author of *Menticulture* (Chicago, 1895) and numerous optimistic books on nutrition and mastication. Fletcher gave credit to Fenollosa for focusing his religious crisis. See James, *Varieties* (Modern Library edition), pp. 178–80.

8. In Kandy, Ceylon, in 1891, Henry Adams visited "the last remaining watchfire of our church [Buddhism], except for Boston where Bill Bigelow and Fenollosa fan faint embers." Henry Adams to Elizabeth Cameron, Sept. 8, 1891, in *Letters of Henry Adams,* p. 524. On Percival Lowell's Religiosity see my "The Lotus and the Arch," Ph.D. thesis, Yale, 1957.

limitations of his own universe, and it is for him to say how large that universe shall be." [9] Bigelow sought infinite consciousness within a social world which was select and limited but filled with the voice of duty. Like Henry Adams, Bigelow felt the weight of ancestral accomplishment. Only child of a famous surgeon and grandson of another, he felt the pressure of family expectations.[10] His close friends were men of considerable distinction: Theodore Roosevelt, Henry Cabot Lodge, Bishop Lawrence, and Henry Adams. He moved in what Edith Wharton described as a "slightly rarefied atmosphere of mutual admiration and disdain of the rest of the world." [11] His milieu was comfortably insulated, but mutual admiration failed to meet the obligation to be eminent which hung in the back of his mind. On occasion he would point with bantering seriousness to pictures of three generations of Doctors Bigelow as illustration of "the decline in vigor of his race." [12]

Henry Adams interpreted Bigelow's Buddhist preoccupation not in terms of declining vigor but rather as a sign of the common desire for Paradise. In a letter of 1889 Adams focused on his friend's illusion:

> Sturgis is, like everyone else, bound to find Paradise in this world, and seems to be in dead earnest. Thousands and millions of men have taken his road before, with more or less satisfaction, but the mass of mankind have settled to the conviction that the only Paradise possible in this world is concentrated in the three little words which the ewig man says to the ewige woman.

9. W. S. Bigelow, *Buddhism and Immortality*, the Ingersoll Lecture, 1908 (Boston, Houghton Mifflin, 1908), pp. 44–45.

10. Bigelow's mother died suddenly during her second pregnancy when her only son was still an infant. His father, Dr. Henry Jacob Bigelow, was an exacting martinet, who saw medicine as his son's natural career. Sturgis went through Harvard College (1871) and Harvard Medical School (1874) and on to study bacteriology in Europe. He returned to Boston in the late '70s but did not stay with the surgery forced upon him and commenced to wander, spending 1882–89 in Japan. In his Ingersoll Lecture Bigelow stated: "Maternal love is the source and origin of all human virtues." Ibid., p. 35.

11. *A Backward Glance* (New York, Appleton-Century, 1934), p. 150. Mrs. Wharton went on to refer to Bigelow as an "eccentric" whose "erudition so far exceeded his mental capacity."

12. Mabel Hooper LaFarge to John F. Fulton, n.d. (c. 1930), in Yale Medical Library. Mabel Hooper was a cousin of Sturgis Bigelow through the Sturgis family and also a niece of Henry Adams through Marian Hooper Adams (Mrs. Henry). In 1898 Mabel Hooper married John Louis Bancel LaFarge, oldest son of the painter, John LaFarge.

Sturgis calls this the Fireside, and thinks he knows better. He looks for Paradise in absorption in the Infinite. Probably the result will be the same. Sooner or later, fate commonly gets bored by the restless man who requires Paradise, and sets its foot on him with so much energy that he curls up and never wriggles again. When Sturgis can't squirm any longer, and suddenly realizes that Paradise is a dream, and the dream over, I fear that he is too sensitive a nature to stand the shock, and perhaps it wouldn't be worth his while to try.[13]

Illusion or not, Buddhism provided Bigelow with justification for his insignificance in a world which was passing him by. If the "highest virtues" tend to the "extinction of terrestrial types," as he maintained, his own situation was explained. Natural and social struggle reward animal proficiency and ignore the superior merits of the soul's progress toward that "limitless consciousness" which is Nirvana. The fault lay with the world; let the world pass. Bigelow's instructors in Tendai Buddhism had stressed the potential Buddhahood of all "terrestrial types" and a middle way of ethical service, but Bigelow's path led away from the world into the insulation of Beacon Hill and Tuckernuck.

In support of his interpretation of "limitless consciousness" Bigelow cited Dr. Holmes' definition of man as "a series of states of consciousness," [14] but Bigelow avoided the implications evident to many Bostonians, namely, that consciousness carries with it the ideal of service. To Dr. Holmes' son, the justice, as to William James and Fenollosa, the prospect of infinity brought no lessening of individual commitment. "Life seems to me like a Japanese picture," wrote Justice Holmes, "which our imagination does not allow to end with the margin. We aim at the infinite and when our arrow falls to earth it is in flames." [15] Holmes and James and Fenollosa all aimed high and committed themselves. Bigelow did not; and his private pilgrimage stands well to one side. The last of a line of Puritans, Bigelow introspected until he was isolated. His self-concern was critical and demanding, but his sensitivity effected a retreat without issue. His

13. Henry Adams to Anna Cabot Mills Lodge, June 18, 1889, in *Letters of Henry Adams*, pp. 399–400.

14. *Buddhism and Immortality*, pp. 14–15.

15. O. W. Holmes, Jr., to Federal Bar Association, Feb. 29, 1932, in Max Lerner, ed., *The Mind and Faith of Justice Holmes* (Boston, Little, Brown, 1946), p. 451.

legacy is a fine collection of Japanese sword-guards in the Boston
Museum of Fine Arts. The sword-guards relinquished by the samurai
signaled the end of an era of feudal aristocracy in Japan; in Boston
their presence marked the last stage in a Puritanism inherited without a capacity for service.

The same strain of Puritanism may be responsible for Bigelow's
muted response to the aesthetic aspects of Buddhism. He had studied
Buddhism in its Tendai and Shingon forms in Japan, as had Fenollosa, and both sects stress the sensuous aspects of religious experience. Yet Bigelow's writings convey no hint of the vivid visions of
Buddhist scripture and ritual. To Fenollosa, on the other hand, the
beauties of Buddhist worship lent added and perhaps decisive persuasion.

The sacred book of Tendai, *The Lotus of the Good Law*, presents
a richly sensuous divinity:

> Hardly had Bhagavat exposed the subject of his parables dem-
> onstrating the Law, than a heavy shower of Mandarava and of
> Mahâmandarâva blossoms fell from the sky. The hundred thou-
> sand myriads of Buddhas in the hundred thousand myriads of
> Universes, seated on thrones under trees of diamond, were all
> covered with flowers.
>
> Sandal powder fell next, perfuming the atmosphere. In the air,
> timbrels struck by no hands, gave forth delicious sounds. Thou-
> sands of streamers of marvellous stuffs fell to the ground. Gar-
> lands, collars, pearl chaplets, precious gems, immense and re-
> splendent diamonds were suspended in mid-air at all points of
> the horizon. Hundreds of thousands of diamond vases contain-
> ing suave essences advanced from all sides of their own volition.
> And above the Tathâgata, Bodhisattvas supported interminable
> lines of parasols made of gems, which rose to the firmament.[16]

To a New Englander this immersion in sense experience had an added
quality of dream and unreality. Fenollosa had grown up in an atmosphere where human beings seemed little concerned with form and
color. Clothing was generally drab and subdued; schoolrooms were
grey, brown, and dimly lit, as were offices and public buildings. Prot-

16. *Le Lotus de la Bonne Loi*, Fr. trans. M. E. Burnouf (Paris, 1852), p.
200. In this passage I have followed the translation in E. Steinilber-Oberlin, *The
Buddhist Sects of Japan: Their History, Philosophical Doctrine, and Sanctuaries*,
Eng. trans. Marc Loge (London, Allen and Unwin, 1938), p. 92.

estant churches in New England were particularly severe in decoration; the separation of the arts from religious experience, which had begun in the spirit of the Reformation, had left only the rhetoric of sermons and the rhythms of hymns and liturgy to focus the senses of the worshipper. Such concentration may have encouraged aesthetic response, but at the price of visual and tactile beauties.

Fenollosa's own religious feelings were strongly aesthetic. The idea, in which the philosophical perfection of beauty was realized, became an overwhelming persuasion of the presence of divinity in the act of individual worship. In the rites of Tendai Buddhism he found confirmation of the Protestant emphasis on the individual's relation to God, along with a sensuous summons of transforming power. "The ecstasies of this inner vision" could be attained, he felt certain, only by individual effort and concentration, not by "force of sacrament" or by "sentimental Evangel of brotherhood."

"The young soul," wrote Fenollosa,

> had to win the spurs of its knighthood alone, in struggle, in effort to feel and see, in invocation to the gods to tear his heart open—alone before the altar in his cell, or his own chamber shrine. To pray to the spirit beside your bed was as much a part of life as to sleep. But you entered the holy presence naked, with bared motive, with discounted pretensions. Some one of the great Bodhisattva was selected by your preceptor as your most fitting guardian presence, and to him, or her, you made your first trembling prayers, sniffing the rich smoke of incense, learning to tinkle in time your gilded bell, and twisting your fingers into the magnetic language of the *in*. You gaze into the white, round mirror on which is painted in Sanskrit the golden breathing "ah-h!" and you watch while its surface deliquesces, expands to an infinite crystal sphere, in which floats the living soul of the deity you have invoked—Kwannon, perhaps, who now is so white that she burns out the dross in you; or Jizo, who melts you into the torrent of his own pity; or Amida, who lets you sit as calm in his sun as if you were an atom of helium; or Aizen, who kindles your passion till it bursts and reveals itself as no-passion; or Fudo, who ties you to the stake, and lights the pyre, and cuts out your heart, and you sip in the glorious pain as if it were a holy draught.[17]

17. *Epochs of Chinese and Japanese Art*, 1, 156.

In his historic Ryuchikai lecture of 1882 Fenollosa had spoken of art as a religion and of artists as priests. To the appreciator who would make a sustained effort to see the unique idea of a painting as expressed in the right relations of visual elements, the artist would reveal a vision which would transport the viewer away from the world of everyday cares into a world of ease and peace and infinite delight. In Boston Fenollosa's aesthetic Buddhism encountered a persistent self-concern which barred the way to delight.

"The society of Boston," Henry Adams observed, "has always believed itself to have had, from the start, a certain complexity,—certain rather refined *nuances*,—which gave it an avowed right to stand apart; a right which its members never hesitated to assert, if it pleased them to do so, and which no one thought of questioning." [18] But the right to stand apart carried dangers for men equipped with New England consciences. Fenollosa might have added that Tendai Buddhism, for all its sensuous appeal, remained ethical, committed to serving the salvation of all men, others equally with oneself.

As Henry Adams described it, the career of George Cabot Lodge illustrates dramatically the risks of standing apart artistically and socially. Adams was very much concerned with finding his own proper place in the world, a place where social distance and aesthetic distance might be matched most happily. His biography of young "Bay" Lodge developed an image of a sensitive, aesthetic individual who is deprived of life-sustaining sympathy by a society indifferent to imagination. According to Adams, Lodge grew up in an atmosphere where "poetry was a suppressed instinct," where "commonly the poet dies young," in an America where the "instinct of unity with nature dies early." [19] As Lodge's close friends Bigelow and Adams maintained, the fault lay with the world. If it did, then Fenollosa's art mission faced firm obstacles.

George Cabot Lodge was named after his great-great grandfather, Senator George Cabot; his father was Senator Henry Cabot Lodge. The family was a source of both pride and expectation. The pressure of expectation was less, perhaps, than Henry Adams felt, probably more than weighed on Sturgis Bigelow. Family position carried a moral obligation to live and achieve in step with the times. Graduating from Harvard in 1895 Lodge went off to Paris to study literature and philosophy, but his letters indicate a background sense of duty,

18. *The Life of George Cabot Lodge* (Boston, Houghton Mifflin, 1911), p. 1.
19. Ibid., pp. 9, 13.

vague but ineluctable. "Loafing is not fun except in a recognized vacation," he wrote from Paris. "I want something real to do." He struggled with a "crying inability to adapt myself to my time and to become a moneymaker . . . to adjust myself to my age, and try to take its ideals and live strongly and wholly in its spirit . . . work with the tide and not against it." [20]

The previous summer was spent largely at Tuckernuck Island near Nantucket as the guest of Sturgis Bigelow. Bigelow initiated young Lodge into Buddhist lore and continued his instruction during succeeding visits. Lodge embarked on a career of poetry, and Buddhism and Schopenhauer moved steadily to the center of his interpretation of human life. A natural tendency toward introspection developed into a focus on the Ego as the sole tragic actor, "the Me, always maddened by the necessity of self-sacrifice," [21] the necessity of destroying the very attachments most vital to life. In a letter to Bigelow he described Nirvana as "the constant unchanging monotone" or "universal night-blackness." "Nirvana is in-create because never created, and of course complete. Yesterday spurs desire to a state of starvation-grayness because desire and hope look back on every yesterday as a renewed disappointment." [22]

Lodge published a volume of poetry, served in the Spanish-American War, married, and spent pleasant summers on Tuckernuck. He worked on verse dramas for a time and was the toast of his circle of family and friends. However, when his close friend and Harvard classmate, Trumbull Stickney, died suddenly at the age of thirty, Lodge was severely shaken. Stickney, himself a poet and inclined toward Eastern religion, had been a source of encouragement and appreciation; his death turned Lodge more than ever inward. He cultivated an indifference to the world's opinion of his poetry but speculated on the inevitable "consciousness of personal, solitary failure." [23] Only Tuckernuck provided the bliss of "endless air and sea and sun and beauty," and it was on Tuckernuck in the late summer of 1909 that Lodge died, aged thirty-five.

20. Dec. 26, 1895, and Jan. 6, 1896, in *George Cabot Lodge*, pp. 32–34.
21. Ibid., p. 109.
22. Dec. 10, 1897, in *George Cabot Lodge*, p. 70.
23. G. C. Lodge to Marjorie Nott, Sept. 30, 1907, in *George Cabot Lodge*, p. 184. Trumbull Stickney died on the eve of a visit to Tuckernuck; he had studied the Upanishads and the Bhagavad-Gita as a fellow student of Lodge's in Europe, and Stickney's last years followed a parallel development toward a philosophy of life denial.

Theodore Roosevelt called Lodge a "genius." Another close friend, Edith Wharton, referred to his prolonged state of "brilliant immaturity." "He grew up," she wrote, "in a hothouse of intensive culture, and was one of the most complete examples I have ever known of the young genius before whom an adoring family unites in smoothing the way. This kept him out of the struggle of life, and consequently out of its experience, and to the end his intellectual precocity was combined with a boyishness of spirit at once delightful and pathetic." [24] Aestheticism in isolation or in a hothouse had equal difficulty rooting in American soil.

What this means as to the nature of the soil, even the long-fenced soil of Boston, remains an open question. George Santayana saw a tragic element in "the fate of a whole string of Harvard poets in the 1880's and 1890's," men who died young like Lodge and Stickney, "visibly killed by lack of air to breathe." They found individual appreciators but were otherwise ignored in America. "The system," wrote Santayana from Rome, "was deadly." They were not strong enough to stand alone and they had "no alternative tradition" to which they could turn, notably no established church aligned with the arts.[25] In *The Last Puritan* Santayana drew heavily on his Harvard experiences of the '90s, and images of Bigelow, Lodge, and Stickney swirl around his story of Oliver's struggle with ancestral attitudes. But these images reflect Santayana's own inclination to identify Protes-

24. Theodore Roosevelt, introduction to *Poems and Dramas of George Cabot Lodge* (2 vols. Boston, Houghton Mifflin, 1911), 1, xiii; Edith Wharton, *A Backward Glance*, p. 149. Lodge's family interest in the Far East was continued by George's younger brother, John Ellerton Lodge (1878–1942), who assisted Okakura, Fenollosa's former student and a successor at the Boston Museum of Fine Arts, in developing the Asiatic Art Dept. Lodge began work with Okakura in May 1911 and on Okakura's death became curator (1916). In 1920 Lodge became curator of the Freer Gallery of Art, which opened in 1923 (another Fenollosan collection; see below, Ch. 14), a position held until his death. Illness, which forced him to leave Harvard early in his sophomore year (1898), may have reduced family expectations. His productive career offers little evidence of his brother's mood of life denial.

25. Santayana to William Lyon Phelps, March 16, 1936, in Daniel Cory, ed., *The Letters of George Santayana* (New York, Scribner's, 1955), p. 306. Writing to Mrs. George Sturgis on Feb. 5, 1936, Santayana stated this view even more plainly: "American breeding can be perfect in form, but it is woefully thin in substance; so that if a man is born a poet or a mystic in America he simply starves, because what social life offers and presses upon him is offensive to him, and there is nothing else. He evaporates, he peters out." Ibid., p. 302.

tantism with fear of beauty, in exaggerated contrast to the aesthetic warmth and welcome of Roman Catholicism. Suspicion of the senses was traditional in New England, but by the turn of the century it was no longer socially coercive. This suspicion did not prevent enthusiastic response to Fenollosa's impassioned aesthetic embassies in the Puritan stronghold of Boston. Nor did it block the influential career of Fenollosa's teacher, Charles Eliot Norton, an apostle of the fine arts. The "genteel tradition" which Santayana pillories for its lack of vigor, its alien formalism, and its sense-denying preoccupation with sin, was certainly moral in aim, but its spiritual idealism did not preclude public appreciation of art. If the "last Puritans" failed, it was not so much because society rejected their sensitive perceptions but rather because they stood apart and failed to serve.

One of the dangers of Fenollosa's milieu of the early '90s was that he might be drawn toward a position apart from society at large, flattered in "a hothouse of intensive culture" out of touch with American life. Boston provided important support for Fenollosa's art missionary program; the museum afforded a firm base for scholarly research and for initiating public education in Far Eastern art. But if a new type of individuality nurtured through art were ever to be realized on a large scale in the United States, art would have to be experienced in a variety of ways, if not by everyone then not only by a few either. An aristocratic art revival had succeeded in Japan, but aristocrats, where they existed in America, were not likely to be leaders. Even in Boston, where upper class cultural leaders held considerable economic power, political power had slipped into other hands. One look at the polyglot, continental United States of 1895 was enough to show the thinness of aristocratic traditions and the absence of any cultural capital, such as Paris or London or Tokyo, from which new standards could be expected to radiate, assured of respect. Any American art revival, or rather art mission, would need its circuit riders and frontier evangelists; they were scarce among Boston's Brahmins of the '90s.

The one Brahmin who approached the role of art missionary in the early '90s was Charles Eliot Norton. But Norton was approaching seventy and his enthusiasm had softened as his tradition became more evidently genteel. Despite austere Calvinist forebears Norton made beauty a personal religion, and his social gospel proclaimed the tension between beauty and complacent American abundance. "The love of beauty," he insisted, "the service of it, the production of beautiful things are the test and measure of the true worth of the individual and of the nation." [26] Few could match his record of sustained service to arts and letters, a service aimed at informing national culture with the spirit of the best achieved by man.

In the ideal of service Norton found an appropriate way to fuse aestheticism with Puritan tradition and root a cosmopolitan inclination in native soil. Henry James, an aesthete impelled toward thicker soil, recognized in Norton's "distinction and value" the "advantage that they were to be virtues of American application, and were to draw their life from the signal American opportunity." In Norton, James saw the case of a Puritan fulfilled in an idiom both modern and American. "Nothing in fact," James wrote in London,

> *can* be more interesting to a haunter of other intellectual climes and a worshipper at the esthetic shrine *quand même* than to note once more how race and implanted quality and association always in the end come by their own; how for example a son of the Puritans the most intellectually transmuted, the most liberally emancipated and initiated possible, could still plead most for substance when proposing to plead for style, could still try to lose himself in the labyrinth of delight while keeping tight hold of the clue of duty, tangled even a little in his feet; could still address himself all consistently to the moral conscience while speaking as by his office for our imagination and our free curiosity.[27]

Yet even in the case of Norton's "transmuted Puritanism," perhaps because of it, his call to the labyrinth of delight did not carry

26. "A Portion of an Address Given in MDCCCLXXXVIII," *Knight Errant* 1 (April 1892), 6. Norton in the 1850s contributed frequently to the new *Atlantic Monthly*; after the Civil War he edited the *North American Review* and assisted in founding the *Nation*; in 1879 he became founder and first president of the Archaeological Institute of America; he pioneered in art history with writings on medieval art and architecture; he was American editor for his close friends, Ruskin and Carlyle, and became literary executor for both men; as a teacher for over twenty years he was, in the judgment of John Jay Chapman, more influential than any Harvard professor of his time. For Chapman's estimate and a perceptive analysis see Austin Warren, "C. E. Norton, Apostle to the Gentiles," *New England Saints* (Ann Arbor, University of Michigan Press, 1956), pp. 118–43. For a straightforward summary of Norton's career see Kermit Vanderbilt, *Charles Eliot Norton: Apostle of Culture in a Democracy* (Cambridge, Mass., The Belknap Press, 1959).
27. *Notes on Novelists* (London, J. M. Dent, 1914), p. 328.

beyond a limited range. Both his presence and his point of view were too refined; they lacked a robust and confident vigor to match an age of tycoons and explorers. More specifically, Norton's medievalism —his favorite centuries were the twelfth and thirteenth—had clear disadvantages as a vehicle for an American art missionary. The culture of the late Middle Ages attracted would-be aristocrats, who were drawn toward a "Golden Age" when artists were allegedly free from dependence on vulgar tastes.

The difficulties such a view faced in a democratic United States were evident in the rapid demise of *The Knight Errant*, an aristocratic Boston art journal which Norton helped inspire and to which Fenollosa and his museum assistant, Arthur Dow, both contributed. Using handmade paper and elegant typography, the editors attacked realism in art and materialism in life, raising their banner of idealism, by which they meant "the noble, sensuous, creative power of the Middle Ages." The architect Bertram Goodhue made the knights' position explicit when he called on those who would appreciate "the little true art we possess" to

> see through the dust of the crowd . . . until we can sweep away the galleries with their insane and incoherent collections of pictures and statues, can turn back the hands of the dial of time till we arrive at the period where art was not cosmopolitan and general, when aldermen and municipalities did not purchase pictures for the edification of the sovereign but unwashed public, and when World's Fairs were not established in the very midst of Philistia to confuse and finally annihilate the lingering artistic longings and perceptions of the people. . . . Art is not cosmopolitan, nor is it the property of the many.[28]

The Knight Errant's aristocratic exclusiveness indicated a limiting tendency present in Fenollosa's Boston milieu. Fenollosa was opposed temperamentally and philosophically to exclusions, whether medievalist, spiritualist, mystical, racist, or simply exclusions by aesthetes or insulated Brahmins. His principles were all inclusive; his inclination was to embrace all experience, to explore limitless possibilities. Yet his milieu might have drawn him toward elitist views. Adulation might have increased his self-regard to the point of dogmatism, a half step from prophecy. He might have become insulated or isolated; the nature of his work in Boston tended, at the least, to

28. "The Final Flowering of Age-End Art," *The Knight Errant*, 1 (1893), 107.

limit his audience. The Museum of Fine Arts was a private institution, its atmosphere rather rarefied; and the Japanese section on the second floor was specialized, somewhat remote for a missionary center.

It would be wrong, however, to exaggerate the limiting aspects of the Boston art world of the '90s. There was certainly no better place for Fenollosa to begin his American career. It was a question of emphasis, a question, as Henry Adams said, of "nuances." In Fenollosa's case, whatever nuances may have hedged his career were sharply realigned in 1895. Late in that year a series of events led him away from Boston so dramatically that he never returned.

> They come to look upon their most elevated subjects as unpractical, or, at least, too remote from realization to be more than a vision, or a theory. . . . A person of high intellect should never go into unintellectual society unless he can enter it as an apostle.
>
> We did not consider the ordinances of society binding on a subject so entirely personal. . . . In this . . . period . . . of my mental progress, which now went hand in hand with hers, my opinions gained equally in breadth and depth.
>
> John Stuart Mill, *Autobiography*

11 · AWAY FROM GENTILITY

Late in 1895 Fenollosa's career in Boston ended abruptly. In September his contract as curator of the Department of Japanese Art of the Boston Museum of Fine Arts was renewed for two years. Shortly afterward he applied for a six-month leave of absence; the executive committee granted him an indefinite leave. Fenollosa's resignation was accepted by the full board of trustees effective April 1896.[1]

Behind the trustees' action lay a scandal which was shocking to polite society in the '90s, and Boston's Museum of Fine Arts was a stronghold of conservative social attitudes. On October 2, 1895, in Minneapolis, Minnesota, where she was duly domiciled, Lizzie Millett Fenollosa was granted a decree of divorce from Ernest Fenollosa

1. The museum's financial records indicate Fenollosa received no salary for a considerable period previous to April 1896.

118

providing her substantial alimony, a property settlement, and custody of Brenda, now twelve.[2] In New York City a few weeks later, on December 28, Fenollosa married his former assistant at the Boston Museum of Fine Arts, Mary McNeil Scott of Mobile, Alabama. He was forty-two years old; she was thirty and very lovely, with dark hair, large dark eyes, and a handsome figure.

Fenollosa's divorce and swift remarriage were deeply disturbing to his friends. To many of them divorce was unforgivable on principle. This divorce was surprising as well. His old friends remembered his long courtship of Lizzie Millett through school and college and its romantic finale in a honeymoon voyage to Japan. Seventeen years of marriage seemed clear evidence of stability; their daughter Brenda seemed assured of a proper home. There is no record of indications of the coming breach in an outwardly harmonious marriage.

The minor poems, some of them love lyrics, which Fenollosa published late in 1893 along with *East and West* and "The Discovery of America," suggest that the happiest days of his marriage were past, but many of the sentiments were phrased conventionally, their tone shaped, possibly, by poetic fashion as much as by personal feeling. Together the poems reflect a restrained hedonism. Explicitly they celebrate a youthful love, lost, but not bitterly so. For the present

> Life hath her duties
> Stern and unchanged
> Moulding her beauties
> Sadly estranged.[3]

Nathan Dole, one of Fenollosa's oldest and closest friends, tried to understand the divorce, but he could not condone it. Dole's daughter, for example, never saw her godfather Fenollosa nor was his name mentioned in the household. Dole was none the less one of the few who tried to account for his friend's breach of the standards of the

2. The District Court of Hennepin County, Minnesota, decreed that Fenollosa pay alimony of $2,600 annually and, in addition, one half of any income in excess of $5,600 annually, all payments to cease on Lizzie Fenollosa's remarriage (she did not remarry). She received also, by decree, one half of a $50,000 annuity and "one half of the proceeds of the sale, when sold, of the Japanese prints and paintings possessed by defendant, or any part thereof." Lizzie G. Fenollosa, Plaintiff, against Ernest F. Fenollosa, Defendant. Judgment and Decree. October 2d, A.D. 1895.

3. "Reproach," in *East and West, The Discovery of America, and Other Poems,* pp. 78–80.

social world they both lived in, viewing Fenollosa as "perhaps too audaciously realizing his own unusual genius and therefore feeling justified in being a law unto himself . . . and suffering the inevitable consequences." [4] Fenollosa's love for Mary McNeil seems to have been a grand passion he would not resist; and he was willing to cut himself off from the Boston milieu which sustained his promising career. In this case love ran counter to prudent ambition.

When Mary McNeil Scott first met Ernest Fenollosa she had already been buffeted by the world enough to defeat a weaker, less talented woman. Born Mary McNeil she was raised in Wilcox County, Alabama, in the proud poverty of a family damaged by the Civil War. The McNeils had been moderately successful shippers; her mother's family were planters. In the '60s and '70s combined family resources, poor relations included, were barely enough to get along on. At seventeen Mary McNeil married Ludolph Chester, a handsome young man said to have danced beautifully. In an effort to make his fortune Chester went off to the Texas oil fields. He contracted pneumonia there and died, leaving his wife with an infant son, Alan, and no means of support. When the news that Mary McNeil had been widowed reached one of her former suitors, he wrote from his consular post in the Far East to propose marriage. Mary accepted. She had barely stepped off the ship in Japan in July 1890, when she was married to Ledyard Scott, consul in Kobe. Japan was a charming dream, Scott a harsh awakening. She was miserable, so her diary records in unhappy detail, unwilling to assent to his overbearing and self-righteous authority. Shortly after the Scotts' return from Japan they were divorced. Their daughter, Erwin Scott, stayed with her mother and her half-brother, Alan Chester. Not long afterward Ledyard Scott was killed, struck by lightning while sailing one afternoon on Mobile Bay.

Mary McNeil Scott—she retained her married name—survived these disasters and set out on a literary career, writing poetry for newspapers in Mobile and New Orleans. She hoped to make a place for herself among the literary ladies who wrote sentimental novels and practiced a higher journalism in lengthy notes on social and intellectual events. There was considerable demand for such writing in an era before gossip columns, and Boston was a center of this literary world. When Mary McNeil Scott heard from a friend of a

4. N. H. Dole, in *Ninth Report of the Secretary of the Class of 1874 of Harvard College*, p. 42.

job in Boston she applied quickly. The job involved assisting the curator of the Japanese Department at the Museum of Fine Arts. Fenollosa stopped in Mobile after a lecture in New Orleans and interviewed her. She knew some Japanese and was enthusiastic about Far Eastern culture; the curator was charmed.

In October 1894 a New Orleans newspaper reported through its Boston correspondent that Mary McNeil Scott had arrived and was beginning work at the Boston Museum of Fine Arts as an assistant curator in the Japanese Department.[5] She made friends with literary ladies and continued to write, mostly poems. A few were published and drew praise from Horace Scudder, then editing the *Atlantic Monthly*. She attended a number of artistic evenings, some of them spiritualist, and worked regularly in the Museum with Japanese paintings, enjoying their calm, sensuous elegance. She had known Fenollosa less than a year when his wife began divorce proceedings in September 1895. Mary McNeil Scott went to New York to await the court's decree, which was delivered in October. In December she became Mary McNeil Fenollosa.

Fenollosa's divorce, remarriage, and resignation from the Museum meant a sharp break with the entire aristocratic art milieu of Boston and a gentility which sanctified restraint and propriety. As it turned out he never returned to Boston, literally or figuratively. After leaving in 1896 he never again held an official position with a museum, university, or American school of any kind; nor did he write again for the *Atlantic Monthly*. This was not due simply to ostracism by Boston society; Boston's influence did not reach that far. But the official art world in the United States was very small in the '90s, and its respectability was zealously guarded, perhaps reflecting a competition for donors and patrons among institutions uncertain of their distinction. Fenollosa must have realized that the notoriety of divorce, even a quiet decree in Minnesota, would damage his career. At the least, official connections would be more difficult.

To make matters worse in the eyes of proper Bostonians, Fenollosa appeared to have few regrets. He made no apologies, entreated no one; he simply left Boston and his wife and daughter and turned away. He planned to support himself by lecturing and if necessary

5. Lilian Whiting, "Boston Days," *New Orleans Times-Democrat*, Oct. 23, 1894.

by selling some of his own collection of Japanese paintings and prints, the prints on a predictably rising market. At the same time he hoped to continue his work with Arthur Dow in art education at Pratt Institute in Brooklyn. And he counted on having more time for writing: poetry, novels, plays, history, philosophy—everything seemed possible. In the long view he planned to continue his efforts to alert the West to the significance of the Far East, this time from a center in New York rather than Boston.

The most encouraging prospects for reaching a wider audience than Boston had afforded were presented by the nationwide General Federation of Women's Clubs and its official journal, the *New Cycle*, which was published in New York. The General Federation had been organized in 1890 and four years later represented about 65,000 women in 375 clubs in every state and territory of the nation. The federation claimed to be organized "along the lines of general culture," with objectives "educational, ethical, and social," an example to the world of the great, untapped power of voluntary organizations cooperating in the name of common ends.[6] The cause of women's rights, despite official denials, lay at the center, but the rapid mushrooming of women's clubs of every variety and their consolidation under the banner of the General Federation preserved a base of broad cultural uplift. A typical year's program was that of The Women's Literary Club of Portsmouth, Ohio: "Our Club, Our Country, Social Question, Germany, Literature, Art, Progress of the World."[7] In its back pages the *New Cycle* recorded the rapid spread of voluntary association. The slogan, "Organization is the test as well as the sign of intelligence," ran across the title page of every issue, and a Maine woman hailed woman's discovery of herself through the power of organization as "the greatest discovery of the last quarter century."[8] Backing from the *New Cycle* provided a substantial asset for Fenollosa's prospective lecture career and his art missionary program.

Early in 1895 the *New Cycle* devoted an issue to art and archaeol-

6. For a statement on aims by the President of the General Federation of Women's Clubs, Mrs. Ellen M. Henrotin, see "Record of Clubs," *New Cycle*, 8 (July 1894), 19–22. Cf. the Massachusetts State Federation of Women's Clubs' discussion keynoted by Julia Ward Howe, ibid., pp. 40–42.

7. Ibid., p. 43.

8. Kate Clarke Estabrooke, "The Club Woman and Her Surroundings," *New Cycle*, 8 (Nov. 1894), 303.

ogy and featured Fenollosa's analysis of "Ancient Chinese Paintings." The associate editor, Mrs. Mary E. Boyce, herself a writer on archaeology, drew attention to Fenollosa's work and its "national importance." In a concise summary of his career she indicated his exceptional qualifications and abilities, "the acumen of a philosopher, the insight of a poet, and the enthusiasm born of exhaustive knowledge," all to be focused on the art life of America. Mrs. Boyce assured her readers that his historical studies were accompanied by concern for "the application of aesthetic principles to practical work." "He has developed from his researches in the art of both hemispheres," she declared, "a philosophy of aesthetics which . . . aims to adapt itself to the educational, the social, and the industrial needs of his day and country." [9]

Fenollosa's articles on the responsibilities of art museums to the people justified Mrs. Boyce's confidence that he sought to make art relevant. His position in 1896 indicated a respect for popular judgments, which had not been prominent in Boston. And he could not resist taking a slap at the pretensions of aesthetes who set works of art apart from the rest of life. "There has been a tendency in some professional quarters," he wrote, "to value art narrowly for art's sake, to claim the privilege for artists of a close communion, to deny the ability of the public to think, or write, or criticize, or take serious concern about matters of art. For these specialists art is technique, studio tradition is sacred; all speculation bearing on art's relation to things beyond itself, is twaddle." [10] Fenollosa opposed this current, which would make museums into display areas for unrelated aesthetic objects to be contemplated by an initiated elite. Such an approach to art smacked too much of aristocracies and authorities. The primary goal for art museums was to open ways of seeing to everyone. "There is no education," he insisted, "like intelligent seeing." [11]

During the winter of 1895–96 the *New Cycle* underwent reorganization and emerged as *The Lotos*, "a monthly magazine of literature, art, and education." Women's club news remained, but subordinated now to a more ambitious literary and artistic program. At the center of *The Lotos* stood the Fenollosas and their friends Mary Boyce

9. "The Work of Professor Fenollosa," *New Cycle*, 8 (March 1895), 568–70.

10. "Art Museums and Their Relation to The People," *The Lotos*, 9 (1896), 842.

11. Ibid., p. 933.

and her daughter Neith; Arthur Dow, Fenollosa's assistant curator in Boston, designed the new covers and supplied illustrations; from February until September *The Lotos* was run as a family affair. The pattern was clear at the outset. The first of five issues opened with Fenollosa discoursing on "The Symbolism of the Lotos" and Mary McNeil Scott discussing "Poetry in Its Relation to Life." Neith Boyce contributed a story and a regular column on books, and Arthur Dow examined "The Responsibility of the Artist as an Educator." Fenollosa's catalogue for a current New York exhibition of Japanese art came in for extended notice, followed by a regular column on the fine arts written from an unmistakably Fenollosan point of view. To the ladies in Dubuque it was evident that Art was at the helm.

The guiding artistic principles of *The Lotos* included a liberal amount of nationalism. Neith Boyce indicated with pride the superiority in current magazine fiction of "domestic" over "imported" and cried, "Let the eagle scream!" The "dawn of a national art" was carefully examined for signs of "fruition." The paintings of Arthur Davies ("an evolution from his own nature, just what true art is always") were closely scrutinized, and on his first return from Europe Davies was quoted in confirmation of the "heroic" possibilities for art in a land of true liberty.[12] Yet art criticism proceeded from Fenollosan principles, with attention to the primary aesthetic elements of line, color, and *notan*. The future of American art was tied to assimilation of these universal principles. Nationalism supported the cultural fusion of East and West.

In "The Symbolism of the Lotos" Fenollosa returned to his central theme of the evolution of a world culture. Individuality is to be the key characteristic of a new type of world man, and the symbol of that individuality is the lotus. For Fenollosa symbolism involves the imaginative grasp of "*life*, the unity and the order of related changes." The "truth of the world" lies not in sensations, or the receptive knowledge of classifications, but rather in the active creation of new values by ordering things otherwise "relatively inert." Creation demands all the resources of thought and of nature. Symbolism provides the medium through which the interplay of thought and nature can be glimpsed in its full vitality. Although any such glimpse soon dissolves, at best it can be focused into a momentary unity by the flash of

12. Neith Boyce, "Book Notes and News," *The Lotos*, 9 (Feb. 1896), 627. [EFF], "The Fine Arts," "Art Notes," "Lotos Leaves," *The Lotos*, 9 (1896), 637–41, 899, 811.

symbol. The special symbol of symbolism is the lotus, for the lotus symbolizes art. The lotus "lifts from the pool of sense," a "perfect harmony of individually curved petals in blossom." Through a like harmony art creates a value, "vital, transcendent, perfect in itself"; a work of art dares to exist outside of heaven as "a self-determined, self-harmonious individual." [13]

The lotus has an added value "for us in America to-day," according to Fenollosa, because it draws us to study the East. Americans must accept the fact that the East has come to stay. But more than that, we can recognize the germs of a new life of the world and assist the transmutation. We can transplant the lotus to western shores and at the same time build a bridge of science and industry and trade to assist Asian peoples in developing more abundant means of living.

> On our side we have to offer power over nature, logical analysis, personal self-assertion, cleverness at compromise, the equilibrium of compensation, a fitness to survive in a life of struggle. With the East comes insight into the soul, synthesis, the power of impersonality, harmony instead of compromise, harmony whose mutuality of helpfulness knows no competition. With us law is negative, a balance of mutual checks. With her law is positive, the conditions of harmonious living. So, too, art with us prides herself on being external, complex, competitive and popular. But with the Orientals art humbles herself to a search for the pregnant symbol, in lonely earnestness of self-expression. East and West are thus opposed in ideals which need each the other for complement. Each alone is beset with characteristic weakness. The West has a wonderful knowledge of means, but a poor conception of the worthiness of ends. It knows no value in itself upon which to expend its wealth. The East has a clearer conception of ends, of spiritual values; but an imperfect grasp of the means of attaining, of preserving them. The strength of the former is outward, arising from the balance of opposing wills. We may thus say that their respective symbols are the Lotos and the Arch.[14]

13. "The Symbolism of the Lotos," *The Lotos*, 9 (Feb. 1896), 578–79. Cf. Hegelian "Subjective Notion" above, Ch. 9, n. 16. The life of the lotus forms a dominant image in the ten progressive degrees of Shingon Buddhism. See E. Steinilber-Oberlin, *The Buddhist Sects of Japan*, pp. 97–101. And the lotus is central in Fenollosa's own Tendai Buddhism.

14. "The Symbolism of the Lotos," *The Lotos*, 9 (1896), 581.

After elaborating these Hegelian oppositions as the natal dialectic for a new type of world man, Fenollosa turned to the more specific question of "the relation of the symbolism of the lotos to the aims of this new magazine." The primary goal, as he saw it, was to reveal the spiritual unity of beauty and life. With due respect for advances in sanitation and longevity, in ease and wealth, *The Lotos* would serve rare individuality, not an altruism which took the pleasure of the greatest number as its highest goal. Fenollosa insisted that "Brotherhood" must recognize the claims of spontaneity if individual development is not to be crushed by the pressures of the average.

The magazine had a pronounced transcendental tone. Along with critical discussions of current painting, music, and literature went glowing appreciations of Hawthorne and Margaret Fuller. Stories by Mrs. Fenollosa and her young friend, Anne Dyer, vied in ideality. Articles discussed "Altruism" and "The Value of Impersonality." Occasional poems "after the Japanese" by the Fenollosas added a cosmopolitan note, but the spirit of the lotus seemed drawn toward Concord.

True to its anticommercial spirit *The Lotos* published no advertising. Subscriptions presented a continuing problem. Women's club news assured wide distribution as long as the *New Cycle* subscribers remained, and *The Lotos* put on a strong drive of its own to expand circulation. The General Federation now represented nearly 1,500 clubs, but even with its support *The Lotos* had difficulty providing a living wage for its staff. Despite increased coverage the September issue was the last.[15]

The Lotos made Fenollosa known along a potentially lucrative lecture circuit, and he filled a number of speaking engagements while he deliberated on future plans. The Japanese exhibit with his catalogue and Dow's posters had been successful in Cincinnati and Chicago, and interest in oriental art was increasing. His February lectures on Japanese art at the Metropolitan Museum had been well received, but friends in conservative educational and museum circles advised him that the scandal in Boston might impede an immediate lecture tour. Economical living in the peace and beauty of Japan until an extensive lecture tour could be assured seemed an ideal

15. By the fall of 1896 *The Lotos'* "Special Correspondents" (generally women's club officers) had increased their coverage from ten to twenty-three states, but at $.15 a copy and $1.00 a year a large circulation was necessary. The departure of the Fenollosas for Japan added the finishing touch.

solution. Another visit to Japan might also clarify the direction in which the new Asian man was developing.

Before sailing Fenollosa addressed the Liberal Club in Buffalo on "The Relations of China and Japan and Their Bearing on Western Civilization." His context was political. As Fenollosa saw it, the great danger to East-West fusion lay in Russian ambition for Asian domination.[16] The recent Japanese victory in her war with China had demonstrated Japan's role as guardian of the East and preserver of "the deepest and finest in Oriental principles." Only in alliance with Japan could China be saved. The tragedy of the present situation, according to Fenollosa, lay in China's refusal to accept reorganization by the Japanese and her rush into the arms of "barbarians" who sought only spoil. China's ruling officials had turned to Russia in a last attempt to preserve their corrupt power, while England, incredibly, had watched France and Germany join Russia in opposing Japan. Fenollosa pointed out that if Russia were allowed to control China her great Eurasian empire would dominate the world, and Asian civilization would be submerged in Mongol barbarism. The arrogance of England toward oriental civilization seemed most tragic of all. In alliance with England, Japan could foster China's great productivity with sympathy and insight. For Japan understands China, he asserted, since she has preserved in her own culture the best in Chinese ideals.

Fenollosa pictured the new generation of Japanese leaders as finally conscious of their mission to "develop from within" and to help the whole East develop herself, now that they had gathered from the West the force with which to protect themselves. Accordingly the West ought to respect this Japanese ambition, for the final type of the world's civilization depends on the conservation of all vital elements. Fenollosa asked that Eastern insights not be crowded out by the brute force of Western civilization "as if ours were right, as if ours were final . . . perfect, as if we had solved all the problems of the human soul and of man, and we could be their teacher and we could say that what they have to offer is of no importance." [17]

In outlining to his Buffalo audience the history of Sino-Japanese cultural relations and their contacts with the West, Fenollosa ampli-

16. The Russian threat to Asia had been suggested earlier by Fenollosa in "New Year's Eve, 1875," a poem published in 1893 in *East and West*.

17. "The Relations of China and Japan," p. 7, typewritten MS edited by Mary M. Fenollosa, in possession of Mrs. S. T. Whatley, Montrose, Ala.

fied one of the critical oppositions which he had indicated in the symbolic dialectic of the lotus, namely, opposing views of man's social organization. He pointed to the Eastern ideal of harmonious social relations and cited Confucius' recognition of the fundamental relations of art to character and to the state. "To keep in view the divine harmony," "to keep the soul free through art," this was the Confucian aim of social organization. Fenollosa maintained that such an ideal was not so much one of "impersonality," as Percival Lowell had claimed in *The Soul of the Far East* (1888), but rather one which encouraged individuality. Here Fenollosa returned to a theme developed in Boston. Lowell had confused the issue in describing Western individuality as "personality"; "excessive personality" would be a more accurate description. As Westerners, said Fenollosa,

> we constantly relate to matters with which we deal by having our own person at the center. We find it difficult to conceive of value in itself, of perfection in itself . . . to perceive an aim which is not connected in some way with personality and personal consciousness. And the strength of our institutions is that we derive them from the mutuality of this pressure of warring individuals upon all sides. This is contrary to the Oriental conception, which is that strength comes from harmony and not from warring interests until by neutralization a compromise is reached. This would seem to the East a negation of force, a certain amount of power lost. The Eastern conception is to establish harmony and further the full expression of every tendency conformably with every other.[18]

Since the art of harmonious living is too vital an element to brush aside in the scramble for spoils in China, Fenollosa concluded with a "definite proposition": "That Japan, in alliance with England, would be able to incorporate a distinctive Oriental element in the world's future civilization by reorganizing China with her own ideas providentially preserved, unless prevented by the ultimate triumph of Russian semi-barbarism."[19]

Fenollosa's high opinion of the wisdom of Japanese leadership and the benevolence of her ambitions in China reflected his talks with

18. Ibid., pp. 4–5. Where the rhetoric seems that of Mrs. Fenollosa as editor of the MS, I have followed the verbatim report printed in the *Buffalo Illustrated Express*, March 1, 1896.

19. "The Relations of China and Japan," pp. 24–25.

Japanese students and friends in the '80s. By 1896 many of these earlier hopes had become snarled in Japanese political conflicts, conflicts confused by oligarchic traditions, constitutional forms, and an imperial center—the whole further agitated by a rising militarism. The shapes of an emerging world civilization suggested by the lotus were already blurred by clouds of smoke in the valleys of Korea, smoke from Japan's Western guns. Fenollosa's belief in 1896 that "the final Asian man" would be Japanese seems curiously transcendental. His panoramic view of Far Eastern history seems closer to faith than to fact.

Fenollosa's vision of subjective developments ran the risk which Santayana saw as characteristic of American philosophers, the risk of losing contact with reality in order to preserve ideals. In this case the ideal was Fenollosa's lotus, symbol of a spontaneous individuality realizable in history through the fusion of whole cultures.

If Fenollosa were to avoid the deception of a "genteel" philosophical ideal, a possibly irrelevant transcendental myth about "final man," he would have to see whether, in Santayana's phrase, "the empirical world had become too hot for it." [20] Residence in Japan would avert the pressures of Boston's social gentility; it would put pressures of fact on Fenollosa's own philosophical gentility.

20. George Santayana, "The Genteel Tradition in American Philosophy," an address delivered in California, August 1911, published in *Winds of Doctrine* (New York, Scribner's, 1912), pp. 186–215.

He said: Study with the seasons
    winging past, is not this
    pleasant?
To have friends coming in from
    far quarters, not a delight?
Unruffled by men's ignoring him,
    also indicative of high breed.

Confucian Analects

12 · SPECULATIONS IN JAPAN

In April 1896 Fenollosa and his beautiful young wife set out for Japan, this time eastward, through England, France, and Italy. A visit to Japan would advance several matters. Fenollosa planned to purchase Japanese paintings, prints, and handicrafts for sale in the United States, with an eye to establishing some arrangement that might provide steady income. He was also anxious to renew old friendships and see how the art program he had helped develop was progressing; there might even be a chance of permanent employment in Japan. In any event the trip would allow time for gossip about the divorce to subside in eastern art circles. And the voyage itself was delightful with a bride who shared his enthusiasms for studios and galleries and the romance of travel.

From London and Paris the Fenollosas sent back material for the art columns of *The Lotos*. The Paris Salon was disappointing, but collections of Oriental art were always interesting, and they enjoyed a visit with Samuel Bing, connoisseur, art dealer, and publicist of Japanese art.[1] In Florence, Rome, and Naples they found nothing so

1. Bing's Paris art store was a center for collectors of Japanese art. Bing wrote the chapter on ceramics in Louis Gonse's pioneer study, *L'Art japonais* (1883) and formed an excellent collection of his own. From 1888 to 1891 Bing edited the six quarto volumes of *Le Japon Artistique*, a monthly periodical intended for artists, designers, and collectors, which appeared simultaneously in French, Ger-

exciting as the Turner paintings they had seen in London, but Fenollosa confirmed his admiration for the Florentine painter, Masaccio, one of the world's masters of line.[2]

From Cairo they steamed through Suez and the Red Sea and stopped at Colombo, Penang, and Singapore. All through the Middle East Fenollosa found agreement among the British that alliance with Japan was the best hope for Asia, but in Amoy and the treaty ports the tone shifted toward sympathy with "poor China" and a thinly concealed arrogance toward any Asiatic power that should threaten to interfere with the lucrative China trade or, worse, challenge the privileges and racial superiority of European concessionaires.

In July the Fenollosas arrived in Japan and settled temporarily in Kyoto, making trips to Tokyo as occasion offered. Okakura called as soon as he heard of his teacher's arrival and spoke enthusiastically of the continuing work of the Tokyo Fine Arts Academy and the success of the art movement. Fenollosa lectured in Osaka and Kyoto on Japanese art and again in Tokyo before officials of the Education and Commerce ministries; response was cordial. At Miidera Temple overlooking Lake Biwa he visited the Tendai shrine where he had passed through his Bosatsu degrees. With Mary by his side he prayed again, humbly invoking the guardian presence of Bodhisattvas. More than ever Buddhism seemed a key to all speculations. Tendai Buddhism offered a truly "synthetic" philosophy with all the color and texture which Hegel lacked.[3]

---

man, and English editions. Bing's reputation was further enhanced by exhibitions of his Japanese prints in the United States—Fenollosa had selected a Boston showing in 1894—and by Bing's 1897 sale catalogue of Edmond de Goncourt's Far Eastern collection. It was Bing's shop, "Art Nouveau," opened in 1896, which gave its name to that movement. Its English counterpart in Art Nouveau was the shop of A. Lasenby Liberty, another collector of Japanese art and a contributor to Bing's *Le Japon Artistique*. For the connection of Art Nouveau and Japanese art see below, Ch. 13.

2. Mary M. Fenollosa MSS, in possession of Mrs. S. T. Whatley, Montrose, Ala. Journals No. 2 and No. 3 recount the trip from New York to Yokohama, April 17 to July 6, 1896. Journals No. 2 through No. 20 run consecutively and cover the period from April 17, 1896, to Dec. 31, 1899. Hereafter cited as MMF MSS followed by journal no., page, and/or date.

3. MMF MSS, No. 7, Oct. 18, 1896. Affinities between the Hegelian synthesis of Being and Nonbeing and the Tendai Buddhist Middle Path were asserted forcefully by one of Fenollosa's former students, the influential Buddhist philosopher Enryo Inouye, notably in his *Bukkyo Katsu-ron* [To Invigorate Buddhism]

Fenollosa found Japan as stimulating as ever. The prospect of leisurely study and writing drew him to sound out his friends about a possible appointment as teacher or researcher. Official circles proved noticeably cool. His friends reported that all foreigners were regarded with suspicion. Any position would require prolonged negotiations, even on behalf of a former Imperial Commissioner of Fine Arts. In the six years since Fenollosa had left Tokyo, Japanese politics had taken a turn toward militarism and xenophobia. His welcome fell far short of what he had hoped.

He did succeed in establishing a business relationship, however; Bunshichi Kobayoshi agreed to have Fenollosa act as agent for the sale in New York of a large selection of prints, screens, paintings, stencils, and illustrated books. If this commercial venture succeeded and Fenollosa could establish an American outlet for Japanese goods on a stable footing, he would be able to live in Japan without the income from a government post. Accordingly, the Fenollosas returned to New York in November 1896. The lecture circuit in the United States could be appraised once again, and Professor Fenollosa might be able to settle a dispute with his former wife over personal property: paintings, prints, and books.

The Fenollosas stayed in New York on West Twenty-ninth Street, boarding with William H. Ketcham, the professor's associate in the sale of his own and Kobayoshi's art goods. The winter in New York proved financially disastrous. The first Mrs. Fenollosa undertook successful legal action to prevent her former husband's removing his private art collections from the United States, alleging failure on his part to supplement alimony payments in accordance with the divorce decree. Litigation dragged on for three years before a settlement returned a portion of his art works and books to him in Japan. Commercially, Ketcham turned out to be a bad choice for a New York agent. He appropriated much of Kobayoshi's goods, allegedly to avoid bankruptcy. The American marketing venture collapsed in a tangle of lawsuits which continued with transpacific complications after the Fenollosas returned to Japan in April 1897.

Fenollosa salvaged enough money to acquire his former Tokyo house on a semi-permanent basis. He settled down to study and write, living frugally in Japanese style with his wife Mary, stepdaughter

---

(1890); see Masanaru Anesaki, *History of Japanese Religion* (London, Kegan Paul, 1930), p. 362.

"Noshi" (Erwin Scott), stepson "Bochan" (Alan Chester), and a young southern writer and friend of Mary's, Anne Dyer. The household revolved around Fenollosa's own systematic program of study: a day each for philosophy, art, poetry, history, and science. Financial and legal worries were set aside, or at least met imaginatively, as in Fenollosa's draft novel of this period entitled "His Wife's Lawyer." Aside from this novel, drafts of a play, and necessary correspondence, Fenollosa stuck to his schedule, reading, reflecting, and writing.

Once again he felt drawn to Hegel. "In the evening had a gorgeous lesson in Hegel," his wife recorded in her diary; "were confronted for the first time by the stupendous statement that thought and being were the same. The way our studies tend to interweave," she added, "is one of the most wonderful things in the whole world." [4] On several evenings, for example, Fenollosa went over Wallace's edition of Hegel's *Logic* section by section, testing his own interpretations of this rigorous work on the two southern ladies of letters. Mary Fenollosa's response to her husband's ambitious program indicates the transcendental tenor of the household. "Philosophy," she wrote in her diary,

> is a sort of atmosphere and ozone to the intellect. Nothing stimulates one so. It is not perfumed like poetry, nor colored like history, but it moves in the colorless, odorless, intangible, divine and vital essences of thought itself. Surley [sic] man, who in his highest posibilities [sic] is as much creator of God as God was of him, should not be beaten down by externals. God is not less God if a star shatters. We are in the not-a of this incarnation. Heaven grant us strength to complete the trichotomy and free our spirit in a higher karma. I read a little of Emerson after coming up stairs last night. I am going to try and make it a rule to read a little of him and my dear Wordsworth every day. . . . In my best moments I almost exhult [sic] in all this trouble, feeling that the not-a of any mistakes or of selfishness has come so soon, and can be suffered out so soon. Emerson's law of compensation is only great and helpful in proportion to our recognition of the imperative necessity of the trichotomy. What a privilege to study and learn—not to hoard up in dusty piles but to use as daily nutriment and strength. Not mere abstract speculation, but concrete experiment. It is the difference between

4. MMF MSS, No. 8, p. 212, July 19, 1897. On Ralph Adams Cram's frequent visits see my "The Lotus and the Arch," Ph.D. thesis, Yale, 1957, pp. 198–206.

painted sunlight and the chemical effects of the real sunlight on plant growth, between a long description of a laboratory experiment and the vibrations of early spring sap. . . . At lunch E[rnest] was quite radiant and told us what a great constructive, intellectual and synthetic work he had been doing, planning out his whole philosophy of art in Hegelian trichotomies. . . . At night I begged E to read us in lieu of lesson or sermon, one of Emerson's essays. Then I selected at random one unfamiliar to me called Fate. As he read it we were almost carried away by its grandeur. It was a trichotomy embracing all eternity. It swept down to the abysses of despair, the nethermost hell, and then mounted in strong sweet curve to the throne of God. Anne was so overcome that she had to leave the room. E was irradiated— inspired—triumphant— Ah. What a soul is Emerson's.[5]

Despite his early enthusiasms for Herbert Spencer and his lifelong love of Hegelian trichotomies, Fenollosa never inclined toward a deterministic view of the world. Nor was his outlook ever noticeably pessimistic. The difficulties and rebuffs occasioned by his divorce do not seem to have reduced his sense of possibilities at all. On the contrary, his views of the world after 1895 were more sweepingly enthusiastic then ever. He was confident that modern humanity could, if it would, usher in a renaissance based not on aristocratic taste and leadership but on popular movements. Even though some of his own studies during this last Japanese sojourn were highly specialized, such as Chinese poetry and Japanese Noh drama, Fenollosa grew more profoundly democratic in his outlook. It was as though Boston's social ostracism had resolved ambiguities in his personal philosophy. His cool welcome by Japanese leaders and the confusions among elder statesmen at a national level in government, so evident in the '90s, added an Asian instance to strengthen the popular sympathies Fenollosa had expressed earlier in his youthful poetry.

For the moment, that is in the summer of 1897, it was enough for Fenollosa to study as though the seasons would wing past delightfully and forever. But as winter came on financial worries became more pressing. He and Kobayoshi finally concluded they had both been fleeced in their New York commercial venture and that little could be gained by further lawsuits. Prospects for a teaching

5. MMF MSS, No. 9, pp. 147–50, Aug. 30, 1897; No. 9, pp. 153–54, Aug. 31, 1897; No. 10, p. 114, Oct. 24, 1897.

post remained clouded by political rivalries and rampant anti-foreign feeling. Occasional lecture fees were helpful, but the winter brought little encouragement to hope for a permanent position. A lecture before Count Sano's influential art club was enthusiastically received, but factional rivalry in the government made support for any foreigner potentially dangerous, no matter how loyal that foreigner might be to Japanese national interest. Okakura was ostensibly forwarding Fenollosa's cause, as were the Kano family and Baron Kaneko, but as yet without result.[6] Nagao Ariga, one of Fenollosa's former pupils and a close friend, proposed that Fenollosa begin regular writing for Japanese publication, to start with a book on Confucian ethics, concise and artistic. Fenollosa agreed but work went slowly.[7]

In December 1897 Fenollosa's fortunes reached a low ebb. Money was gone. No official post had been offered to the former Imperial Commissioner. Even lectures were scarce. Friends were intriguing among themselves. None the less, the Fenollosa household maintained a rigorous study schedule, now stepped up to six days a week: "English, Aesthetics, History, Japanese, Philosophy, and Science; with Sunday for a rest!"[8]

A temporary job teaching English at the Tokyo Normal School opened up in January, the same month that Marquis Ito again became prime minister. In March Ariga was appointed confidential secretary to Ito, and on April 1 Fenollosa signed a one-year contract with the Education Department to teach English and English literature at the Tokyo Higher Normal School. In the meantime Okakura was forced to resign from directorships at the Tokyo Fine Arts Academy and the Imperial Museum, positions which he had held since the

6. Baron Kentaro Kaneko, a leading figure in several cabinets, had studied in the United States at Harvard in the mid '70s. He attended the Philadelphia Exposition in 1876, the Paris World's Fair of 1889, and assisted on the committee for the Columbian Exposition in Chicago in 1893, working there with Fenollosa. For his views on art and industry see his "Views Concerning the World's Great Exhibition at Paris," *Far East*, 2 (May 20, 1897), 189–95.

7. In 1885 Nagao Ariga published *Bungakuron* [On Literature], a work which interpreted literature and all art in terms of *hogo* or synthesis, in terms of the harmonious moral relations of man as outlined by Confucius. Fenollosa reread these essays in February 1898, as he was working on his own Confucian interpretations. Ariga's work is placed in the context of early Meiji literary theory in Okazaki Yoshie, ed., *Japanese Literature in the Meiji Era*, Eng. trans. V. H. Viglielmo (Tokyo, Obunsha, 1955), p. 688.

8. MMF MSS, No. 11, pp. 1 ff., Dec. 1, 1897; No. 11, p. 139, Jan. 11, 1898.

organization of the institutions. Anonymous circulars attacking Okakura mentioned Fenollosa as a "crazy foreigner," and a faction
headed by Baron Kuki campaigned quietly against Baron Kaneko.
Fenollosa managed to remain clear, probably because of the unim-
portance of his post at the Normal School. Toward the end of April
Baron Kaneko was appointed minister of agriculture and commerce,
an apparent victory over Kuki, but reorganization of the government
art program continued. In June, Jigoro Kano, one of the original
teachers of the Fenollosan system at the academy, was ousted, and
further shifts seemed likely with the resignation of Prime Minister
Ito and ensuing general changes.[9]

The tides of personal intrigue, political ambition, and xenophobia
which surged around Fenollosa qualified his earlier high regard for
the idealism of Japanese leaders. An article written that summer of
1898 for *Harper's* suggested, not surprisingly, that the Japanese might
not offer the worthiest prototype of the final Asian man. The occasion
for the article, characteristically entitled "The Coming Fusion of East
and West," was the birth of a new world power, the United States.

The crushing defeat administered to Spain that spring and summer
indicated to Fenollosa that the United States had finally overcome her
fear of foreign entanglements and would recognize her international
responsibilities. American victories had destroyed the European balance of power forever and had liberated the forces of a new century,
forces which were moving to concentrate "their whirling angry masses
over the focus of the China Sea." From Fenollosa's Tokyo vantage
point China seemed the key to the new century both economically
and culturally. The markets and productivity of China would give
world supremacy to their developer; let that developer be the United
States in conjunction with England. China, Fenollosa declared, is the
"worthiest candidate" for the culmination of civilization, the final
fusion of Eastern and Western cultures. Japan might properly act as
tutor; China offered the best possibility for an ideal synthesis.

Fenollosa saw the United States as a partner in a racial merger of

9. Japanese political intrigues as interpreted in detail by the Fenollosas and
their visitors in terms of day to day developments during the period from March
1 to July 1, 1898, are recounted in MMF MSS, Nos. 12, 13, and 14. For the
fullest account (although not altogether clear) of the "Art School Affair" see
Naoteru Uyeno's "The Cultural Background of Meiji Art, With an Outline of
Painting," in Uyeno, ed., *Japanese Arts and Crafts in the Meiji Era*, Eng. trans.
Richard Lane (Tokyo, Pan-Pacific Press, 1958), pp. 40 ff.

mutual benefit. American ideals were in sore need of Eastern insights; the best ends of living were ignored in deification of denial and desire. In America he saw puritan and epicurean extremes vying with one another. Americans in search of ideals were faced with either an unrelieved "desert of moral effort" directed toward accumulation, or personal pleasure considered as "sole relief from the chain of nature's means." Let America with her "rich germs of individual character and free institutions," her tolerance and humanity, join England in "race-sympathy" and merge lives and thoughts with the destiny of China. By a "true fusion of blood" Americans need no longer remain exotic, a "handful of bleaching foreigners." In conclusion, Fenollosa placed one foot on Wall Street and another in Miidera Temple to invoke American destiny and Columbus' dream of planting an Aryan banner "on the heights of an awakened East." [10]

For his own part he found in the study of Chinese philosophy and poetry added incentive to stay in Japan. His decision to remain was confirmed by a letter in November from a close friend who advised him to defer booking lectures in America for another two years in order to let the gossip of the divorce proceedings fade quietly away. In the meantime he met regularly with Nagao Ariga and Kainen Mori to study Chinese poetry; he accompanied Ariga on frequent visits to a Chinese philosopher; and he studied with Michiaki Nemoto, a leading authority on the *I Ching*, the most ancient of Chinese religious and magical texts.

At the same time, Fenollosa worked enthusiastically with Noh drama, beginning serious study in November 1898 by taking lessons on Noh acting and singing. He worked hard, building on his less systematic efforts in the early '80s. By late December he had made sufficient progress to call on the Noh patriarch, seventy-year-old Minoru Umewaka, the leading figure of the Meiji revival of Noh. "He was very affable," Fenollosa noted in his diary, "and talked with me for about 1½ hours. He asked me to sing, and I sang 'Hansakaba.' He praised me, said everything was exactly right and said that both he and Takeyo considered my progress wonderful; better than a Japanese could make. He said I was already advanced enough to sing in a Japanese company." [11]

10. "The Coming Fusion of East and West," *Harper's Monthly*, 98 (Dec. 1898), 115–22.

11. Fenollosa and Pound, *The Classic Noh Theatre of Japan* (New York, New Directions, 1959), p. 28. Minoru Umewaka carried on Noh traditions

The Fenollosas attended every Noh performance they could find. "E[rnest] thinks of nothing but Noh," Mary recorded in her diary.[12] He took copious notes on performances to supplement information from Umewaka and other actors. Many important traditions were passed down from father to son, noted only elliptically on the rolls of instruction, which served as texts for the players. As Umewaka pointed out to Fenollosa, according to the latter's notes:

> Such fine things as Matsukaze, the pose for looking at the moon, or at the dawn, or at the double reflection of the moon in two tubs, and all the details of business cannot be written down; at such places he [Umewaka] writes merely "kuden" (tradition), to show that this is something that can be learned only from a master. Sometimes his teacher used to beat him with a fan when he was learning. . . . Kuden, or this feeling for the traditional intensity, is not to be gained by mere teaching or mimicry, or by a hundred times trying; but it must be learned by a grasp of the inner spirit. In a place, for instance, where a father comes to his lost son, walks three steps forward, pats him twice on the head and balances his stick, it is very difficult to get all this into grace and harmony, and it certainly cannot be written down or talked into a man by word of mouth.
>
> Imitation must not be wholly external. . . . There is a tradition of a young actor who wished to learn Sekidera Komachi, the most secret and difficult of the three plays, which alone are so secret that they were told and taught only by father to eldest son. He followed a fine old woman, eighty years of age, in the street and watched her every step. After a while she was alarmed and asked him why he was following her. He said she was interesting. She replied that she was too old. Then he confessed that he was an ambitious Noh actor and wanted to play Komachi. An ordi-

despite considerable hardship during the unsettled years following the fall of the shogunate. The Umewaka family for three hundred years or more had played roles of *tsure*, or follower of the hero, for the Kanze family of lead actors. Minoru carried on the Kanze school traditions and collaborated with Kuro Hosho, head of the Hosho school, and later with Sakurama Bamba, an actor of the Komparu school. Bamba "was famed for his technical skill, as Kuro was for his nobility and Minoru for his intelligence." See Hisashi Furukawa, "The No," in Toyotaka Komiya, *Japanese Music and Drama in the Meiji Era*, Eng. trans. Keene and Seidensticker (Tokyo, Obunsha, 1956). Quotation on p. 102.

12. MMF MSS, No. 18, Jan. 12, 1899.

nary woman would have praised him, but she did not. She said it was bad for Noh, though it might be good for the common theatre, to imitate facts. For Noh he must feel the thing as a whole, from the inside. He would not get it copying facts point by point. All this is true.[13]

More than ever Fenollosa was attracted to an art that for all its sensuous rhythms and patterns was restrained and highly disciplined. Great performers were required to control their own lives so that the spirit of their acting would charge the dance forms with pure and intense emotion, not the emotion of imitated life but rather of spiritualized life. As in traditional Japanese painting, the aims were not realistic but ideal. And the sustained pauses of Noh dancing created effects analogous to the impact of empty spaces in painting. Fenollosa's own style of life with its disciplined pattern of meditation and action had something of this quality.

Stimulated by the variety of his studies Fenollosa enjoyed his teaching of English. Work on a textbook was coming along, and discussing Emerson with the eldest class was a special delight. Emerson, too, had been fascinated with hieroglyphics of nature and with the disciplines whereby the whole man might discover the unity of inner and outer worlds. Fenollosa was exhilarated by the affinities he kept finding in poetry, philosophy, painting, and the Noh. In the spring of 1899 he voiced the buoyant conviction that his work lay at the center of a new phase in world history. Asia, he proclaimed, will become the pivot for the twentieth century, and "the history of European races will have to be rewritten . . . Hang Chow shall be to them a second Athens, and Shanghai their London of the future." [14]

This sense of shifting historical perspectives gave a special quality to Fenollosa's speculations. As a professional philosopher turned art historian he saw his own unique opportunities and experiences projected against a large backdrop. The size of Fenollosa's stage kept a frame of events around his interpretations, and the shifts in his per-

13. *The Classic Noh Theatre of Japan*, pp. 30–31.

14. EFF to George P. Sanger, March 4, 1899, in *Seventh Report of the Secretary of the Class of 1874 of Harvard College* (Cambridge, Mass., 1899), p. 47. In this letter Fenollosa cited as support for his views Benjamin Ides Wheeler, "The Old World in the New," *Atlantic Monthly*, 82 (Aug. 1898), 145–53. Wheeler called for a historical perspective keyed to the "Great World," whose "agora" was now the outer ocean rather than the Mediterranean, and whose political organization would be not empire but self-government.

sonal fortunes gave him a certain detachment. In Japan he swung sympathetically toward Eastern ideals but stopped short of total absorption. Not so his good friend Lafcadio Hearn, whose career complements Fenollosa's in several ways and helps define the particular quality of Fenollosa's sympathy with Japan.

Hearn and Fenollosa not only loved many of the same beauties of Japanese life, they enjoyed each other's company. Before leaving Japan for Boston in 1890 Fenollosa had welcomed Hearn warmly, and they renewed their friendship during Fenollosa's return to Japan in the late '90s. To Fenollosa Hearn wrote of "the charm of old days (when I must confess you fascinated me not a little)"; [15] for his part Fenollosa was delighted with Hearn's sensitivity and love of beauty. A visit from Hearn in the spring of 1898 was described enthusiastically by Mrs. Fenollosa:

> He got here about 2:30. Anne and I of course kept out of the way. We heard E. greet him cordially. . . . About an hour later E. came bounding upstairs his face radiant and cried, "Oh, he is splendid. I love him as I do Okakura. He will see you. He *wants* to see you. It is a delight to see such a man!" Of course I hurried down. I had put on my Japanese kimono and tea gown thinking it would be a subtle compliment. As this was my first sight of him, I will try to describe the effect. A small man of a grey tone with delicate, slightly distorted features and with his entire personality warped, twisted a little to the right, the result, I suppose, of his semi-blindness and poor eyesight. He was thinner and smaller than I had thought, and his hair is very grey. The white, blind left eyeball is a terrible defect and one feels always his consciousness of this. . . . But his beautiful voice—sweet, vibrating —never loud nor piercing—has an irresistible charm—and as one knows him better and begins to feel that the shy spirit is creeping more and more from its fragile shell—one ceases to care for any-

15. Hearn to EFF, Dec. 1898, in Elizabeth Bisland, ed., *The Life and Letters of Lafcadio Hearn* (2 vols. Boston, Houghton Mifflin, 1906), 2, 413. For other letters from Hearn to the Fenollosas see 2, 381–84, 412–14, 401–03, 437, 440–42. Hearn and Fenollosa had a mutual sympathy with Latin warmth as opposed to "froid protestantisme"; for Hearn's Latin sympathy see 2, 310–13. The period of greatest intimacy between Hearn and Fenollosa during the latter's second visit to Japan was the spring of 1898; see MMF MSS, No. 12, esp. pp. 132–39, 217–19. Elizabeth Stevenson's account in her *Lafcadio Hearn* (New York, Macmillan, 1961), pp. 290–91, is misleading.

thing material. As Anne said, he carries his own environment with him. Many things he said were most beautiful and interesting. He spoke of the sympathy between Herbert Spencer and Buddhism. We don't agree to this but didn't contradict it. . . . As he stayed on he became more confidential, charming, and close. He told us of the book now in progress, a book of "Whys" which he calls *Retrospectives*, a series of ten essays trying to explain by science and Karma the subtle memories that attack us. . . . He stayed four hours. It was a wonderful afternoon. We talked of nothing else until bedtime. He has promised to send us a copy of Buddha-Fields. I hope he will do it.[16]

The legacy of Hearn's love affair with the island empire was an affectionate literary portrait, or, better, a landscape of old Japan, painted with sensuous imagery, delicate shades, and a flair for fantasy. For Hearn himself Japan offered a quiet home away from the ghosts of his past, a wild gallery sprung from a blood mixture of the world.

Patricio Lafcadio Tessima Carlos Hearn was born on a Mediterranean island to a Greek mother and an Anglo-Irish father. When he was two, his father, a British army surgeon-major, was transferred to the West Indies, leaving wife and child in Dublin. Before long his mother fled, leaving a great aunt to direct his education for the priesthood. After one eye was accidentally blinded, Hearn verged on a nervous breakdown; he was expelled from his English college and ran away from a Jesuit school in France. In the meantime his father had remarried and cut off financial support, so that his great aunt felt free to ship her young sinner to New York, where he arrived penniless and friendless in 1869, just turned nineteen.

Hearn drifted to Cincinnati, where he learned the printer's trade and began writing for newspapers. Soon he moved on to New Orleans, pulled toward the sensuous warmth of the tropics. He had already begun to explore the world's literature, pledged, as he put it, "to the worship of the Odd, the Queer, the Strange, the Exotic, the Monstrous," [17] wherever it might be, in Arabic, Indian, Persian, Congo and Creole, Greek and Latin, always returning to the French writers whose mood he modeled: Gautier, Flaubert, Baudelaire. A series of articles for *Harper's* sent him back to Martinique for two years amid

16. MMF MSS, No. 12, pp. 132–38, April 1, 1898. Later that week Hearn sent over an inscribed copy of *Gleanings in Buddha-Fields*.
17. Hearn to W. D. O'Connor, June 29, 1884, in *Life and Letters*, 1, 328.

the hot color of its flowers and women. The next winter in New York was unbearably damp and cold.[18] *Harper's* was willing to buy a series on Japan, so Hearn set off in the spring of 1890 for a new world which would be his final and happiest home.

Of Japan he knew little, but mystery was appealing. Pierre Loti's *Madame Chrysanthème* (1887) had piqued his interest; he had reported with mild enthusiasm on the Japanese exhibit at the New Orleans Exposition of 1885; and Buddhism made the prospect still more intriguing. In the *New Orleans Times-Democrat* he attacked the vogue of Theosophy and other neo-Buddhisms, but expressed sympathy for the "higher Buddhism" suggested by men like Emerson. "Buddhism," he wrote a friend in 1883, "only needs to be known to make its influence felt in America." [19] Buddhism, however, suggested wider areas than Japan. What focused Hearn's enthusiasm was a book by a cool and analytical Bostonian, Percival Lowell. "I have a book for you—an astounding book—a godlike book," wrote Hearn to his friend Gould. "But I want you to promise to read every single word of it. Every word is dynamic. It is the finest book on the East ever written; and though very small contains more than all my library of Oriental books. And an American(?) wrote it! It is called 'The Soul of the Far East.' It will astound you like Schopenhauer, the same profundity and lucidity." [20] Hearn was not equipped either to agree or disagree with Lowell's thesis. As he became familiar with Japan he grew more and more dubious about Lowell's theory of Japanese impersonality, but at the outset the broad outlook of *The Soul of the Far East* (1888) excited Hearn's imagination. Previous studies of Japan had been either

18. "Br-r-r-r-r-r-r-r-r-r! 'T is winter. My lizard blood freezes at the thought. In my room it is 71°: that is cold for us. New York in winter signifieth for such as me—Dissolution—eternal darkness and worms. Transformation of physical and vital forces of L. H. into the forces of innumerable myriads of worms." Hearn to H. E. Krehbiel, Oct., 1886, in *Life and Letters*, 1, 379.

19. Hearn to Wayland D. Ball, 1883, *Life and Letters*, 1, 265. Hearn commented frequently on spiritualist developments in Cincinnati and New Orleans newspapers. See esp. "The Buddhist Bugaboo!" and "Confused Orientalism," in *Oriental Articles*, Ichiro Nishizaki, ed. (Tokyo, Hokuseido, 1939), pp. 79–82, 101–03. From New Orleans Hearn wrote to W. D. Ball (in July 1885) on the subject of local hostility to "Eastern" ideas: "Even my editorials upon Sanskrit literature called out abuse of the paper from various N. O. pulpits, as 'A Buddhist Newspaper,' an 'Infidel Sheet,' etc.," in *Life and Letters*, 1, 346. For Hearn's reports on the Japanese exhibit at the New Orleans Exposition see *Occidental Gleanings* (New York, Dodd, Mead, 1925), 2, 209–40.

20. Hearn to George M. Gould, 1889, in *Life and Letters*, 1, 460.

slight books of travel and reminiscence or specialized monographs for a professional audience. Lowell was the first to attempt an analysis in depth for the general intelligent reader, and Hearn responded with quickened interest.

Hearn landed in Yokohama in 1890 at the end of March, the month of the cherry blossoms. From the beginning he was carried away. Soon after arriving he wrote:

> I feel indescribably towards Japan. Of course Nature here is not the Nature of the tropics, which is so splendid and savage and omnipotently beautiful that I feel at this very moment of writing the same pain in my heart I felt when leaving Martinique. This is a domesticated Nature, which loves man, and makes itself beautiful for him in a quiet grey-and-blue way like the Japanese women, and the trees seem to know what people say about them,—seem to have little human souls. What I love in Japan is the Japanese,—the poor simple humanity of the country. It is divine. There is nothing in this world approaching the naive, natural charm of them. No book ever written has reflected it. . . . And of course I am studying Buddhism with heart and soul.[21]

It was the spirit of old Japan, the spirit of the common people, with which Hearn fell in love. In the small town of Matsue, where he taught English after breaking with *Harper's*, many feudal customs survived, and Western ways had introduced only surface changes. In Matsue Hearn married the daughter of a local samurai and took her south to a post at the government college in Kumamoto. Contact there with Japanese officialdom dimmed his enthusiasm considerably, as did his experience as professor of English literature at Imperial University, Tokyo, from 1896 to 1903. The intrigues of official life and the steady tide of Westernization repelled him. He held many reservations about the future of Japan. But its past remained bright, and in a series of books published in rapid succession he sought to capture the elusive quality of *Kokoro*, the ebbing spirit of elder Japan. In *Glimpses of Unfamiliar Japan* (1894) and the ten books which followed in as many years, Hearn wrought for Western minds an image of Japan based for the first time on intimate sympathy and compelling imagination. The folklore and customs which filled Hearn's pages were strange, but in Japan Hearn found more than the purely exotic;

21. Hearn to Elizabeth Bisland, 1890, *Life and Letters*, 2, 3–4.

he found a "soft urbanity," an "ingenuous kindliness," a beautiful simplicity, a greater happiness than he had ever known. He became a Japanese citizen despite the severe financial loss incurred and adopted his wife's family name, Koizumi, meaning "little spring," taking also Yakumo, the poetic name for his new native province, Idzumo—"the place of the issuing of clouds." [22] As Yakumo Koizumi he lived in Tokyo apart from both Western teachers and Japanese officialdom in a small house with his wife and their four children, plunged into the enchantment of a world half real and half imagined, a land where family afforded shelter far back through Shinto ancestral time and where "the laughter of greeting voices, the bright smile and graceful bow, the kindly inquiry and wish to please, continue to make existence beautiful." [23]

Yet the charm of old Japan was tied to death:

> The mere sensation of the *milieu* is a placid happiness: it is like the sensation of a dream in which people greet us exactly as we like to be greeted, and say to us all that we like to hear, and do for us all that we wish to have done,—people moving soundlessly through spaces of perfect repose, all bathed in vapoury light. Yes—for no little time these fairy-folk can give you all the soft bliss of sleep. But sooner or later, if you dwell long with them, your contentment will prove to have much in common with the happiness of dreams. . . . But remember that here all is enchantment,—that you have fallen under the spell of the dead,—that the lights and the colours and the voices must fade away at last into emptiness and silence.[24]

During Hearn's first few months in Japan it was enough that the spell of the dead in the shrines of the gods was beautiful. To Fenollosa he wrote: "The intense delight of all this to me—the delicious ghostliness of it, is the sense of being in a world of mysteries and Gods all ALIVE, closer to you than neighbors, real, comprehensible, beautiful beyond description." [25] But the beauty of the

22. *Life and Letters*, 2, 293. "Yakumo" is also the first word in the sacred Japanese song, "Eight-fold Clouds," a song sung by a god-bridegroom at the dawn of Japanese history. K. K. Kawakami, "Yakumo Koizumi: The Interpreter of Japan," *Open Court*, 20 (1906), 624–32.

23. Hearn, *Japan: An Attempt at Interpretation* (New York, Macmillan, 1904), p. 16.

24. Ibid., p. 19.

25. Hearn to EFF, n.d. (c. spring 1890), MS in collection of George Matthews Adams, New York, N.Y.

144

dead did not satisfy Hearn's more speculative side. Part of the ideal of art to which he dedicated his life included science; "No romance equals it," he had written earlier. His final speculations attempted to fuse death with life, under the triple banners of Shinto, Buddha, and Herbert Spencer.

Spencer's "oceanic philosophy" had opened a "totally new intellectual life" for Hearn four years before he came to Japan,[26] giving him new respect for "all forms of faith" except Christianity, whose Jesuitical and other missionary forms remained deeply distasteful. Hearn's respect was principally directed toward faiths which could be gathered under Spencer's cosmic rubric—"the Unknowable." In Spencer's concept of "the Unknowable Reality," as the one thing permanent hidden under "all these changing shapes," Hearn found confirmation of the Buddhist accent on impermanence and flux. Equally plausible to Hearn as a scientific hypothesis was the idea "implied" by Buddhism of "an atomic spiritual ultimate," units of consciousness "permanently equal to every other and infinite in potentiality." At the heart of the phantom lives of everyday dwell individual Buddhas. These are the real selves, components of a multiform reality which undulates through time in "a psychical rhythm of motion." Hearn was convinced that the idea of the Self as an evolving composite was accepted throughout Japan, whether in its complex Buddhist form or in simpler Shinto beliefs, and that a Japanese *"thinks of himself as multiple."* [27] The pursuit of one's best Self was for Hearn the measure of the Orient's ethical superiority over the West.

Hearn granted Western intellectual superiority and admitted a close relation between intellectual accomplishment and individuality, in the sense outlined by Lowell and "proved" by Spencer, but he argued for the evolution of a higher individuality exemplified by Japanese morality. Much of Western "personality" and "force of character" seemed to Hearn to represent not evolutionary progress but merely "the survival and recognition of primitive aggressive tendencies, more or less disguised by culture." If evolutionary progress were to be made, the feeling of the uniqueness of self must be

26. Hearn to H. K. Krehbiel, 1886, in *Life and Letters*, 1, 374–75. "When one has read Spencer, one has digested the most nutritious portion of all human knowledge. Also the style is worth the labour,—puissant, compact, and melodious." Hearn to Elizabeth Bisland, April 14, 1887, ibid., 1, 392.

27. *Gleanings in Buddha-Fields* (Boston, Houghton Mifflin, 1897), pp. 211–66, esp. 225, 250.

decomposed, and in this task Hearn found strong allies. Science, religion, philosophy, and art by their tendency to reveal and magnify "cosmic emotion" would aid in the metamorphosis of Western notions of Self.[28]

Fenollosa was much in sympathy with Hearn's idea of a higher individuality. But he could not agree with Hearn's easy marriage of Herbert Spencer to the spirit of Japan. Spencer's airless system of inexorable external forces left little room for the spontaneity of the lotus, the growth of individuality from within outward. Hearn seemed to Fenollosa to be so intent on examining Spencer's "Unknowable" as to ignore the weight of dead materialism. Hearn expressed surprise that the Japanese could read Spencer "without a suspicion of the tremendous ghostly fact behind his whole system." [29] To Fenollosa it was clear that Hearn had supplied this ghost from the depths of his singular imagination.

In the field of Japanese art Hearn's attitudes remained curiously conventional. He may have been restrained by Herbert Spencer's view that Chinese paintings were grotesque in their "utter disregard of the laws of appearances—in their absurd linear perspective, and their want of aerial perspective." Hearn felt obliged to explain the lack of realism in Japanese art as the result of a concern for type or possibly for an ideal reality. His writings gave no hint of Fenollosa's speculations on the nature of visual language. Hearn's enthusiasm was directed toward the spirit of a particular painting in character-istically subjective fashion.[30]

Hearn's passionate identification with Japanese ideals points up the variety of American responses to Japan, responses keyed to the backgrounds of the individual interpreters. Edward Morse analyzed and classified Japanese life in meticulous detail, contributing to Japanese science a characteristic Western technique; to the American public he described Japan with the enthusiasm of a natural scientist for fresh areas to be explored. Henry Adams, obsessed with himself as the image of Western man's predicament, could not or would not

28. *Glimpses of Unfamiliar Japan* (2 vols. Boston, Houghton Mifflin, 1894), 2, 674–83, esp. 682–83; *Kokoro* (1896), pp. 243–51. Cf. *Japan*, pp. 494–96.

29. Hearn to B. H. Chamberlain, May 22, 1891, in Elizabeth Bisland, ed., *The Japanese Letters of Lafcadio Hearn* (Boston, Houghton Mifflin, 1910), p. 10.

30. *Gleanings in Buddha-Fields*, p. 107; *Kokoro*, p. 57. Spencer's comment is quoted in Houghton, *The Victorian Frame of Mind 1830–1870*, p. 149, from Spencer's *Education: Intellectual, Moral, and Physical* (1861).

project himself into an alien culture on its own terms. His companion, John LaFarge, observed Japan with sensitivity and measured appraisal, returning with the European center of his thinking unaffected. Sturgis Bigelow found confirmation in Japanese Buddhism of his own attenuated status apart from American life. Hearn identified himself with Japanese life almost completely, thereby avoiding both the cultural insulation of Adams and the objective analysis of Morse. Not that Hearn's response was any less subjective than Adams'; rather his personal needs were more readily satisfied by Far Eastern life, and intellectual analysis did not hamper romance. Among all the images of Japan projected by Fenollosa's American friends onto the screen of American thinking, Hearn's came closest to conveying the texture and spirit of Japanese life. Japan was the final enthusiasm of Hearn's restless career in search of a peace that his imagination could render beautiful.

By the late '90s Fenollosa's appreciation of plebeian art had quickened. So much so that he could agree with Hearn's sweeping tribute to Japan's "graces of arts and its senses of beauty, and its witchcraft to transform cheapness itself into luxury incomparable!" [31] As Fenollosa's mode of living drew him further from a milieu of aristocrats, he gave more attention to popular culture, to the prints and crafts which gave to the life of the whole Japanese people its singular aesthetic quality.

In his 1885 review of Gonse's *L'Art japonais,* Fenollosa had derided the Western vogue for Japanese prints as ignorant appreciation of an essentially vulgar and inferior art, an appreciation which mistook a shoddy realism for the highest spirit of Japanese art. Thirteen years later the art of commoners received more sympathetic appraisal. He asserted that in the Tokugawa period (1615–1868) popular culture, despite its "materialism and realism," for the first time in Japan's history absorbed "the truest vitalities of her soil." [32] In the spring of 1898 and again in the winter of 1900 Fenollosa wrote catalogues for print exhibitions in Tokyo, first an Ukiyoye show and then a special

31. Hearn to EFF, n.d., MS in collection of George Matthews Adams, New York, N.Y. Hearn's respect for craft had an ancestral aspect indicated by an old Japanese saying: " 'If we do not think, while using things, of the time and effort required to make them,—then our want of consideration puts us on a level with the beasts.' " *Kokoro,* p. 293.

32. "An Outline of Japanese Art," MS in possession of Mrs. S. T. Whatley, Montrose, Ala.

exhibit of Hokusai. They were the first exhibits of common prints ever held in Japan. At the same time he completed a draft of his pioneer book on Ukiyoye in which both Hokusai and the popular prints came in for praise. Ukiyoye, literally "the floating world," he contrasted to "a world of moral and intellectual fixity" sought by Confucian and Buddhist censors. And in Hokusai Fenollosa found the embodiment of the floating spirit of a common people newly aware of themselves. In encyclopedias and travel books and single sheet prints Hokusai mirrored the awakened interests of the people, and, said Fenollosa, "having faith in them, he sees more strength and beauty than they themselves see." In 1885 Fenollosa had scoffed at Gonse's "Hokusai-crowned pagoda," ignoring as it did the quality of more aristocratic art, and again in Boston, in his Hokusai exhibition catalogue Fenollosa had commented critically on the vulgarization of Hokusai's talents by low popular tastes. Now, as Fenollosa prepared to return to the United States, Hokusai took on the stature of a representative man. "The strength of the young nineteenth century was toward fact and scientific investigation; not so much a learned criticism as a riotous bath of the soul in the waters of realism." [33]

In April 1899 Fenollosa's teaching contract was renewed for another year, but he intended it to be the last and began preparations for leaving Japan. He hoped to recoup his fortunes by the sale in America of prints and handicraft of good quality, all to be produced by young Japanese artists and craftsmen of talent. Water color paintings and color prints formed the core of the ambitious project, and 600 were exhibited for sale under the auspices of the American Art Association in New York. The market became somewhat saturated—this proved to be Fenollosa's last commercial venture—but proceeds were sufficient to give some flexibility to his plans for return to the United States and a career as lecturer and writer.

The coolness of Fenollosa's welcome in Japan in the late '90s, contrasting so strongly with his triumphs a scant ten years before, impressed him with the facts of change. His own fortunes felt the bite of history in altered Japanese attitudes. As a result he had to look more carefully at the new Asian he had hypothesized. Ex-

---

33. EFF, *An Outline of the History of Ukiyoye* (Tokyo, 1901), pp. 17, 47. Fenollosa began the first draft of this pioneer work on Jan. 20, 1899, and finished the first draft Feb. 27, 1899; a final typescript was completed in Dec. 1899 with very few changes from first draft MS.

perience made his philosophizing more empirical. In particular the xenophobia and militarism now evident in Japan made him skeptical of the role of aristocratic leadership in moving toward cosmopolis. Wars of conquest and hatred for foreigners were both forms of exclusion. Fenollosa based his dialectic of civilization on inclusiveness rather than exclusiveness, on open selection rather than imposed rejection. His earlier work in Japan had drawn him into an aristocratic milieu; and the orientalism of Boston in the early '90s, if not aristocratic in the sense of Meiji Tokyo, had a certain exclusiveness about it. Fenollosa's fundamental sympathies were all inclusive, democratic in the spirit of Emerson and William James. For him the uncertain years from 1895 to 1900 served to bring out the ambiguities of his early successes and to strengthen his popular sympathies. The process was speeded by the indifference of his former friends in Japan and by the antagonisms provoked in genteel American art circles by his divorce. Most important, probably, his young wife's beauty and enthusiasms quickened his energies to a missionary ardor. The next stage in Fenollosa's long search for a cosmopolitan "passage to India" would be more democratic; the way led not through Tokyo or Boston but through Indiana.

PART 4 · *Art and Individuality*

Who are you indeed who would
talk or sing to America?
Have you studied out the land,
its idioms and men?
Have you learn'd the physiology,
phrenology, politics, geog-
raphy, pride, freedom,
friendship of the land? its
substratums and objects?

Walt Whitman, "By Blue On-
tario's Shore"

13 · PASSAGE TO INDIANA

On Fenollosa's final return to the United States he committed himself wholeheartedly to bringing to a wide audience of Americans
a sense of the radical relevance of beauty. If this relevance could
be really felt as an analogy to life, if a work of art could be experienced as incitement to attaining an art of living, then a new
golden age was possible. As Fenollosa toured a continental America
he contended eloquently that the question of the age was how to
make the lives of all of us "hot with beauty." His aim harked back
to Emerson's plea for "Man Thinking" to be man making his own
world; and it anticipated Ezra Pound's later dictum: "Man Reading
should be man intensely alive. The book should be a ball of light
in one's hand."

Fenollosa's lotus, his gospel of individuality through art, took
many forms after 1900 in its grass root passage to Indiana, to the
Chautauqua meetings at Winona Lake, the teachers associations of
Terre Haute, and the clubs of Indianapolis. The lotus could not
remain esoteric in Indiana, nor even exotic for long. The camp meeting enthusiasms of Winona Lake shook any fashionable oblivion
the lotus might once have suggested.

In the autumn of 1901, after a final shuttle between Japan and the United States, Fenollosa settled down to make a living as a public lecturer.[1] After speaking on the West Coast he swung on a tour through the upper Midwest. Three lectures delivered at the Detroit Museum of Fine Arts indicated that the lecture platform might provide a sound economic base for future intellectual speculations; "A Comparison of European and Asiatic Art" and "Japanese and Chinese Poetry" brought one hundred dollars each and "Problems of Art Education" fifty.[2]

Spring lectures at New York's Cooper Union and Detroit's Twentieth Century Club were a prelude to an intensive summer schedule. With Chicago as his base, Fenollosa toured the circuit of Chautauqua assemblies. In Bay View, Michigan, he spoke on "A Trip through Japan," "Buddhism," and "Principles of Art," and in Benton Harbor, Michigan, on "Japanese Life and Learning," before moving on for three lectures each at assemblies in Indiana at Winona Lake and Fountain Park.

The Winona assembly, in its eighth season, had become one of the most successful in the country under the astute management of the Reverend Solomon C. Dickey. In the summer of 1902 general attendance reached 80,000, with a special summer school enrollment of 1,100.[3] Dr. Dickey was delighted with Fenollosa's illustrated lectures and renewed his summer contracts annually, as well as assisting in winter bookings throughout the upper Midwest. For the next four years Fenollosa settled into a permanent lectureship for Winona's six-week season. Mary Fenollosa's description of Winona indicates the pattern of a successful assembly and the kind of setting which every summer attracted hundreds of thousands of Americans bent on self-improvement and cultural uplift.

> This place is, compared with Benton Harbor or even Bay View, like Coney Island and Monroe Park. Here all is prosperity,

1. Fenollosa left Japan in August 1900 and lectured during the following winter in the United States. He returned to Japan in April 1901 for a five-month visit in order to supervise publication of a folio edition of *An Outline History of Ukiyoye*, illustrated with twenty reproductions in Japanese wood engravings (Tokyo, 1901); at the same time he acquired additional paintings and prints for his own collection and possible sale.

2. C. L. Freer to EFF, Aug. 24, 1901, and Dec. 11, 1901, Freer Correspondence, MS vol. 8, pp. 229, 470, in Freer Gallery of Art, Washington, D.C.

3. For figures on attendance in Fountain Park and Winona see *The Chautauquan*, 36 (1902), 101, 221–22.

bright parks, flower-beds, vine trimmed cottages each with a name like "Fairview," "Idlewild," "Chicago," "Ghent," "Sunrise," "Swan Terrace," etc., a huge modern hotel, gymnasiums, and auditoriums, a second class hotel, The Inn, where Ernest nearly starved to death when here alone, and many other adjuncts of a thriving, well-managed summer resort. . . . Everything is exorbitantly high in price, the one exception being pads and writing material. The little town of Warsaw, near by, is not very much better. Winona Lake as it now stands is a tremendous monument to Yankee energy, enterprise, and judgment. About 8 years ago it was merely a small lake that needed dredging. Marshes bordered it. It has been carefully dredged now, and the work (itself a gift of the millionaire, Studebaker) will go on indefinitely. The rich lake mud has been used to fill up the marshes. This must be the chief reason for the extraordinary richness of growth in the flower-beds and vines. Every enterprise within the grounds is tributary to the great stock company which owns the place. No one can enter the grounds for any purpose whatever without showing a ticket at the gate and then being admitted by one of those automatic, revolving pig-stys that let in but one person at a time. The cottagers pay rent to the association, but also must have for each member of the household an entrance ticket. This is $5.00 each for the entire summer. Once within the grounds no other tickets are required.[4]

For the Fenollosas the "Swiss Terrace" in Winona Lake, Indiana, became a summer home; it was a relief not to have to haul boxes of lantern slides in and out of dusty trains and carriages. In the relative comfort of Winona Fenollosa polished his lectures and improved his slide collection, adding 400 high quality slides in 1905 and elaborating his historical comparisons of Eastern and Western art and life. He projected slides of Michelangelo and Kiyonaga side by side to illustrate mastery of line and contrasted Japanese studies of birds and flowers and clouds with photographs from nature in a continuing attack on the exclusive claims of realism. He drew charts of the historical development of Chinese and Japanese art and maps of cultural transmission routes. He arranged slides of the primitive art of Mexico and Easter Island to illustrate the evolution of art consciousness and to support the bold hypothesis of a widespread

4. MMF MSS, No. 21, pp. 88–92, Aug. 18–21, 1902.

Pacific school of design in which East and West had merged near the beginnings of history. More slides of Japanese stencils and textiles, lacquer and embroidery amplified the frequent examples of line, color, and *notan* which he projected onto the screen from the pages of Arthur Dow's book, *Composition*.[5] The response of audiences was enormously heartening. Fenollosa was elated at the quickening of interest in the Far East and its art and at the ready reception for his exposition of the basic principles of art and the relation of "harmonious spacing" to harmonious living.

The winter lecture season was equally active, and from 1902 to 1906 Fenollosa stumped the country in the name of the gospel of culture. Before women's clubs, teachers, and students, in museums, libraries, clubrooms, and schools Fenollosa interpreted the art and culture of the Far East and expounded his theories of art education. In 1903 he spoke in Minneapolis and St. Paul, Philadelphia, New York, and New Haven. In Washington he lectured at the White House as the guest of Theodore Roosevelt.[6]

The Washington series of seven lectures gave Fenollosa a chance to continue work on a history of East Asian design that would throw Far Eastern civilization into a new light. In the course of outlining the phases of Chinese and Japanese artistic development, he attacked the prevailing notion of a static Chinese society that lacked any history in the Western sense of change. Hegel had been completely wrong in this respect. A true history of China must account for the extraordinary peaks of artistic achievement in T'ang and Sung times, peaks which matched anything in the record of the West. "When Alfred was battling with savage Danes," Fenollosa informed his Washington audience, "Chinese poets and painters were pouring out their souls to catch the spirit of morning dew upon bamboo groves or of white herons upon a snow bough." He went on to introduce his listeners to the essay on landscape painting by the great Sung artist,

5. The slide collection was bought by Freer from Mrs. Fenollosa after Fenollosa's death and is now in the slide collection of the Freer Gallery in Washington, available to interested groups on application, in accordance with the wishes of Freer and the probable wishes of Fenollosa. On Dow's *Composition* see below, Ch. 15.

6. On the White House talk see MMF MSS, No. 21, pp. 124, 126, March 21 and 27, 1903. Erwin Scott Whatley (Mrs. S. T. Whatley), Fenollosa's stepdaughter, recalls that Fenollosa joined Roosevelt after dinner in a dual recital of a mutual favorite, Longfellow's "Skeleton in Armor." Conversations held with the author during Sept. 14–21, 1955.

Kuo Hsi. Kuo Hsi's reflections, then completely unknown in the West, appealed strongly to Fenollosa; he quoted them often and to good effect. "The sages wrote that poetry is formless painting, and painting is word-less poetry," he told his listeners in the words of Kuo Hsi. "So I pass my leisure in reading good poems of the masters. But, if I did not dwell in a quiet house, or seat myself in a retired room with windows open, tables dusted, incense burnt, and the thousand thoughts of the world crushed and sunk, I could form no true ideas like these poets, nor create the feeling of deep mystery and inspired taste."

On painting mountains Kuo Hsi's words were poetry:

> Shape ought to be high and steep, freely disposing itself like a man at ease, or standing up with haughtiness, or crouching down like a farmer's basket; depressed like a disc, or thick and solid, brave and grand, possessed of soul, solemn looking, gazing askance as in the attitude attending one's superior; or again as having a cover over it, or a chariot below it, seeming as if it had some support in front to lean over, or a thing behind to face against. Such are the great form aspects of mountains. Water is a living thing; hence its form is deep and quiet, or soft and smooth, or broad and oceanlike, circling like wings, or plump like flesh, or jetting and slender, violent and rapid like an arrow, bubbling in springs, leaping far down in cascades, weaving itself against the sky, burrowing itself below the earth, with grass and trees on its banks, looking joyous like fishermen at their ease, under the ornament of mist and cloud seeming fair like beautiful ladies; everywhere gay and brilliant under the sun that shines in the valleys. Such are the living aspects of water. Mountains make water their blood, grass and trees their hair, mist and cloud their divine coloring. Water makes mountains its face, huts and hedges its brow and eyes, fishermen its soul.[7]

From Washington Fenollosa went on to Dayton and Detroit, and in the next season, 1904, he toured the upper Midwest again, lecturing in Toledo, Columbus, and Indianapolis, speaking in Grand

7. "Landscape Painting and Poetry in Medieval China" (Lecture VI in Course of Seven Lectures, Washington, March 17th, 1903, notebook pages 101–77), quotations from pp. 164, 174–75, in possession of Ezra Pound, Brunnenburg, Tirolo, Italy. Extracts from Kuo Hsi's essay were published in Fenollosa's *Epochs of Chinese and Japanese Art* (1912), 2, 12–19.

Rapids and Detroit. He introduced new material on "Russo-Japanese Relations" and interpreted "The Meaning of the Orient for the United States" in terms which reaffirmed Japan's politically crucial role as guardian of the East and mediator of East and West, each to each.[8]

By 1905 Fenollosa's platform reputation was established, and he hoped to be able to give more time to writing and less to traveling. A successful lecture series at the University of Chicago and another at Drexel Institute in Philadelphia offered an opportunity for extended investigation and scholarly presentation that was lacking in his one-night stands. The hinterlands remained both stimulating and lucrative, however, and in January and February of both 1905 and 1906 he traveled through Ohio, Indiana, and Michigan, and down to Kentucky. The content of his lectures was becoming increasingly systematic as his own philosophical and historical thinking crystallized under the pressure to complete a series of manuscripts on which he was working in New York.

A Terre Haute, Indiana, program indicated Fenollosa's high level of approach as well as the strength of the urge for culture in Indiana. A month before the program was officially announced local newspapers hailed the efforts of the Civic League to obtain his services. The "brilliant Professor Fenollosa" would crown a season which had been noteworthy for its cultural features, as every winter should. For in Terre Haute, proclaimed the *Star*, "There is enough of culture, enough interest in literature, music, and art to make them not only desirable but almost necessary." In February the *Gazette* announced success.

> Mr. Ernest Fenollosa will give three illustrated lectures on "The Foundation of Criticism and Education in Art" at Normal

8. Fenollosa's excitement over Russian moves in Manchuria and a proposed set of articles are indicated in MMF MSS, No. 21, p. 146, May 11, 1903. Fenollosa's lectures on Russo-Japanese affairs were evidently going well (see EFF to C. L. Freer, Oct. 20, 1903, in Freer Correspondence). Continued Russian penetration of northern Korea and failure to withdraw from Manchuria together with breakdown of Russo-Japanese negotiations led to Japanese severance of diplomatic relations with Russia on Feb. 6, 1904, and the attack two days later by the Japanese on Port Arthur, bottling up the Russian fleet. Successive Japanese victories led up to the peace treaty signed Sept. 5, 1905. Japanese military successes amazed the Western world and created increased interest in all things Japanese.

Hall under the auspices of the Terre Haute Normal Alumni Club, the Art Section of the Civic League, and the city teachers.

I. The Structural Basis of Art
II. A Direct Comparison of European and Oriental Arts
III. Semi-Universal Principles of Structure and Use in Art Especially as Applied to Art in Education.[9]

Despite Fenollosa's formidably abstract language, he was a great success in Terre Haute and throughout the Lyceum and Chautauqua circuits. His virtuoso performances and distinguished appearance surely helped. But his success owed something to the reform spirit which flourished nationally during his touring years. Fenollosa's artistic road to utopia seemed more possible because of the well-traveled roads of other spirited reformers and orators. Terre Haute, for example, was the home of Eugene Debs, and the town had welcomed a variety of crusaders since the early days of Robert Ingersoll and Susan B. Anthony. During the Progressive era civic boosting traditions combined with moral energy, optimism, and a fashionable respect for high culture to create an atmosphere receptive to an art missionary. The growth of industrial blight and baffling city problems increased the nostalgia of a generally prosperous people for pastoral pleasures easily associated with art, and easily confused with art.

The enthusiasm Fenollosa often encountered raised real difficulties. Art appreciation could easily remain merely a ladies' club flutter, in the mood of excited yearnings and vague aspirations which kept Browning clubs active. This kind of enthusiasm bore little relation to the "mobility and daring" of imagination which Fenollosa felt was necessary if the tone of national life were to shift away from timid conventions toward genuine individuality. Yet there were signs that individual experience with art was multiplying, that many people were for the first time grappling with the problems of making some beautiful thing. Despite inevitable amateurishness the Arts and Crafts movement was an important sign. It involved the effort of creation; would-be artists had to select from among possibilities

9. *Terre Haute Star*, Jan. 15, 1905; *Terre Haute Gazette*, Feb. 19, 1905. The lectures took place on Feb. 21, March 2, and March 10. Fenollosa's eloquence and effectiveness as a lecturer is further attested to by Moncure Biddle (1882–1960), who recalled that one of his father's law partners in Philadelphia regarded Fenollosa as the best platform lecturer he had ever heard, even in an age of great lecturers. Conversation with the author in June 1955.

variously glimpsed that single order felt as most appropriate. Fenollosa's audiences were more responsive because they had in some cases discovered how difficult it is to bring a fit order to anything.

In the United States support for Arts and Crafts grew from a coterie enthusiasm in the '90s to a national movement which flourished up to the first World War. The progress of the movement helps account for Fenollosa's success; its aims and achievements suggest some of the ambiguities inherent in Fenollosa's vision of artistic individuality in a democracy.

The American Arts and Crafts movement took many of its cues from its British counterpart but developed different emphases. William Morris was its leading English exemplar and John Ruskin a major prophet, but in the United States the medievalism of the English movement tended to be submerged in an eclectic swirl of Hopi rugs, Colonial silver, and mission furniture. Ruskin's nostalgia for the hierarchies of church and aristocracy was lost, for the most part, in transatlantic voyage, and Morris' socialism led not to active working men's organizations but rather to the beginnings of city planning and the call for a democratic and national art and architecture. Arts and Crafts in the United States tended to be eclectic rather than doctrinaire and individualist rather than collectivist.

An American Pre-Raphaelite Brotherhood had been established in New York in 1863 but had proven too exotic, as Emerson, for one, had sensed, and the program to revive "true Art" in America met with little success.[10] Not until the Centennial Exposition of 1876 did the movement to reunite art and craft gather momentum. The exhibits in Philadelphia stimulated the development of schools and museums aimed at training commercial designers and art teachers. And these new professionals leavened the mass of amateurs who provided the main support for Arts and Crafts activities at the turn of the century.

The specific aesthetic canons of American Arts and Crafts varied considerably, and experiments led in many directions. In the visual

10. " 'We like our own period and what is vital in these days about us, especially in poetry, but the Rossetti work is not touching us—it is exotic.' " Recounted as Emerson's view by William Bell Scott, recalling two meetings with Emerson on Emerson's last visit to England. William B. Scott to Moncure Conway, May 11, 1883, in Janet C. Troxell, ed., *Three Rossettis: Unpublished Letters to and from Dante Gabriel, Christina, William* (Cambridge, Mass., Harvard University Press, 1937), pp. 48–49.

arts, with which Fenollosa was primarily concerned, Arts and Crafts merged with Art Nouveau [11] to produce a novel emphasis on curvilinear elements in opposition to traditional geometric standards. The organic, horticultural patterns of Morris with their flowing tendrils and fanciful medieval lines added their stimulus to experimental photography and lithography. Japanese book illustrations and the single-sheet prints of Ukiyoye helped unsettle conventional symmetries of design and framing; in this Japanese "floating world" the basic grammar of artistic construction was made visible, "lavishly poured out," Fenollosa commented, "on every object that a yeomanry of taste might handle." New forms enlivened Arts and Crafts by making conventionally trained eyes more alert to new ways of seeing.

The variety of artistic impulses which stimulated Arts and Crafts was especially evident in Chicago, the center of one of Fenollosa's most successful lecturing areas. Fenollosa had become familiar with Chicago in 1893 while he was working with the Fine Arts jury of the World's Exposition, and he had been active in Chicago again in 1895 before leaving for Japan. During his stay in Japan his Boston assistant, Arthur Dow, remained in close touch with the Chicago scene. Dow's influential book, *Composition*, containing the first extended outline of the Fenollosa-Dow theory of art education, was published in 1899, and the Prang Educational Company featured the book in its displays in the Midwest. *Composition's* Chicago debut aroused considerable interest and was covered extensively in the Chicago art journal, *Brush and Pencil*.[12]

From Chicago offices *Brush and Pencil*, "An Illustrated Magazine

11. For a discussion of the extensive international roots of Art Nouveau and its relation to other contemporary artistic developments see Nikolaus Pevsner, *Pioneers of Modern Design* (New York, Museum of Modern Art, 1949), and Stephan T. Madsen, *Sources of Art Nouveau* (Oslo, 1956). Two excellent articles with extensive bibliographies focus on oriental connections: Clay Lancaster, "Oriental Contributions to Art Nouveau," *Art Bulletin*, 34 (Dec. 1952), 297–310; and Ernst Scheyer, "Far Eastern Art and French Impressionism," *Art Quarterly*, 6 (Spring 1943), 116–43. Art Nouveau was publicized by a series of new European illustrated art magazines (date first published in parentheses): *Studio* (1893), *Pan* (1895), *Jugend* (1896), *Simplicissimus* (1897), *Deutsche Kunst und Dekoration* (1897), *Art et Décoration* (1897), *L'Art Decoratif* (1897), and *Ver Sacrum* (1898).

12. See Mabel Key, "A New System of Art Education," *Brush and Pencil*, 4 (Aug. 1899), 258–71. A Fenollosan approach is evident in her later *Brush and Pencil* articles on "Artistic Lithography: Its Present Possibilities," 5 (Oct. 1899),

of the Arts and Crafts," chronicled the art activities of the upper Midwest from 1897 to 1905. A regular Boston column accompanied notices of New York and European art shows, but the focus was on Chicago and Indianapolis and Minneapolis, on Western painters, Colonial crafts, and Burbank's colorful Indian portraits. Of Pre-Raphaelitism *Brush and Pencil*'s editor wrote in 1899:

> This movement was decidedly English and insular. It could never have developed under our skies and our boundless horizons. The poetry of this movement is based on legend and fairy tale; ours rings with no uncertain sound for freedom and truth. Walt Whitman alone can put to rout the whole group. His word rings true, is of the soil, is native, sanguine, and original.[13]

Many of the writers in *Brush and Pencil* felt that Chicago offered a natural center for "sanguine and original" work, notably by the architect, Louis Sullivan, who proclaimed passionately that "the power of imagination and the science of expression become limitless when we open our hearts to nature and to our people as the source of inspiration." Illustrations of the designs of Sullivan and Frank Lloyd Wright accompanied discussions of outdoor advertising, Indian paintings, and photography shows, illustration, poster work, and

31–44; "The Power of Line in Illustration," 5, 200–17. Cf. "The Passing of the Poster," 4 (April 1899), 12–19.

Louis Prang of Boston's Prang & Co. pioneered in the promotion of art educational materials and in color printing; he worked closely with Frederick Pratt of Pratt Institute in early experiments. For a sidelight on Prang from a leading lady of Arts and Crafts see Candace Wheeler, *Yesterdays in a Busy Life* (New York, Harper, 1918), pp. 248–52. Dow's warm reception in Minneapolis in the spring of 1900, several months before Fenollosa's return from Japan, was indicative of growing interest in art. He was a guest of honor at the First Annual Exhibition of the Work of American Artists, held by the Minneapolis Society of Fine Arts, and spoke on successive nights at the Teachers' Club, the Minnesota School of Fine Arts, and the University of Minnesota. See *Brush and Pencil*, 6 (May 1900), 86. For an account of the development of the Fenollosa-Dow theory of art education see below, Ch. 15.

13. Charles F. Browne, "The Editor," *Brush and Pencil*, 3 (Jan. 1899), 256. For a comparison of the Boston and Chicago Arts and Crafts Societies (both established 1897) see Oscar Lovell Triggs, "Arts and Crafts," *Brush and Pencil*, 1 (Dec. 1897), 47–48, and Henry L. Johnson (Secretary of the Boston Society), "Exhibition of the Society of Arts and Crafts, Boston, Mass.," *Brush and Pencil*, 4 (June 1899), 165–73. The national flavor of Chicago Arts and Crafts went beyond editorial pronouncements in articles in *Brush and Pencil* (1900–01) on historical periods, art industries, and Western Americana.

general craft activities. An influential clubwoman surveyed the rapid multiplication of clubs studying art and art history and credited Chicago's Columbian Exposition with stimulating developments in Omaha, Nashville, and Atlanta. Another survey of "The Arts and Crafts Movement at Home and Abroad" in 1900 concluded that "no art movement of any sort whatsoever has been so widespread, so popular, so practical." [14]

Interest in Japanese art kept pace with the upswing of Arts and Crafts, for Japanese art harmonized with many of the same contemporary art currents. It blended with Pre-Raphaelite interest in nature and curvilinear ornament, with the flowing experiments of Art Nouveau, the flat exuberance of posters, the linear suggestions of lithographers and engravers, and the "accidental" composition of photography. Its visual grammar provided an answer to the search for basic design principles to apply to art industry and art education. And above all, Japanese art represented a popular culture in which craftsmen were artists and the whole people an appreciative audience.

Ironically, Japanese military successes seemed to add to America's appreciation of art. Japanese victory over Russia in 1904–05 was cited in many quarters as evidence of the virility of artistic refinement. President Eliot of Harvard put it succinctly when he gave public praise to the "extraordinary artistic qualities of the Japanese as a race, qualities they exhibit in conjunction with great industrial efficiency, remarkable sanitary wisdom, and an unparalleled energy and devotion in war." "We ought never to have imagined," he continued, "that the sense of beauty harmonized only with softness, fineness, or frailty in the human being. . . . It is undeniable that the American democracy, which found its strongest and most durable springs in the ideals of New England puritanism, has thus far failed to take proper account of the sense of beauty as means of happiness and to provide for the training of that sense." [15] Although the

14. Louis Sullivan, *Brush and Pencil*, 4 (April 1899), 25–26; Adelaide S. Hall, "The Demand for Art in America," *Brush and Pencil*, 5 (March 1900), 248–53 (Mrs. Hall was Chairman of the General Federation of Women's Clubs as well as Chairman of the Art Committee of the Illinois State Federation of Women's Clubs.); "The Arts and Crafts Movement at Home and Abroad" (unsigned), *Brush and Pencil*, 6 (June 1900), 110–21.

15. Excerpts from an address by Charles W. Eliot delivered at the dedication of the Albright Art Gallery, Buffalo, N.Y., reprinted in *Brush and Pencil*, 16 (July 1905), 30–33.

Harvard President's remarks may have given undue importance, characteristically, to New England puritanism, they drew attention to a popular American misconception which continued to obscure the radical relevance of art to individual experience of all kinds. There were indications, then, of a new sense of the energizing possibilities of art, but prospects were by no means sure. Individuality in Fenollosa's sense lay below the affable surfaces of self-improvement.

The culture of Chautauquan meetings and the art clubs of the Midwest was often surprisingly intellectual and devoted to self-improvement with some passion. Nor was it confined to women. But its sweetness and light lacked dark edges which might have clarified a cheerful atmosphere of success; and this culture was too communal to have intellectual bite. William James commented after visiting Chautauqua that he was "held spell-bound by the charm and ease of everything, by the middle-class paradise," by kindness, cheapness, equality, but that in the triumph of orderliness and ideality over disorder and sin, life was lost. Not surprisingly, Fenollosa looked beyond the lecture platform. It served as a pleasant livelihood, but the search for wider audiences led him in other directions. Along the way he continued to reformulate his gospel of individuality through art more precisely and more radically. He would have to discover a passage to more than Indiana.

> How to give all access to the mas-
> terpieces of art and nature, is the
> problem of civilization.
>
> Ralph Waldo Emerson, *Conduct*
> *of Life*

14 · A NEW JOURNAL AND A BOLD GIFT

Journalism offered Fenollosa a chance to reach an audience which
might never come to Chautauquan meetings or join an Arts and
Crafts Society. And writing would help clarify his ideas. In 1906 a
promising opening developed. He assumed direction of what
amounted to a new journal, aptly if hopefully titled *The Golden Age.*
The Golden Age had run into financial difficulties as a children's
magazine. Fenollosa's new format was aimed at the general public,
especially parents of school children and professional people connected with education. It became clear that the "golden age" referred
not to childhood or to the imagined glories of some past age but to
the American people's present progress toward a broader humanity
animated by beauty.

In the first of a series of articles on "The Bases of Art Education"
Fenollosa keynoted the new editorial policy. "The future of this
country," he wrote, "the cast of its culture, will depend largely upon
how we deflect the minds of our youth toward appreciating beauty.
And we cannot shirk the responsibility. Silence passively lends
strength to the Philistine." [1] Fenollosa declared that in his own youth
there had been a time when he had hated art because the poor and
the hungry of the world could not be fed on images, but that he
now recognized the necessity of beauty if life were to be worth while.
To that end "this magazine" entered the arena of the "mass opinion
of the hardworking public."

1. "The Bases of Art Education: I. The Roots of Art," *The Golden Age,* 1
(April 1906), 160.

The opening editorial announced a broadening of scope to include coverage of "world federalism," "alien peoples" (particularly China and Japan), and "Socialism and Individuality." In the early issues Hayne Davis, secretary of the American delegation to the Inter-parliamentary Union, urged federation of the world; Professor George Krapp of Columbia contributed articles on philology; and natural history was covered by Gustave Straubenmuller, superintendent of the New York City public schools, and C. W. Beebe, curator of birds at the New York Zoological Park. Mary Fenollosa reviewed Maude Adams' *Peter Pan* and found in the East Indian dances of Ruth St. Denis a fusion of art and music at a level above mere "personality." Gaylord Wilshire of *Wilshire's Magazine* presented a socialist view-point in "The Trust and Socialism." Individualism was to be fully discussed in future issues along with anarchy and art and such economic issues of the day as protectionism and the single tax. But *The Golden Age*, after a bow to the muckrakers, set out to pass beyond corruption to a new synthesis, declaring its faith in "humanity and in American institutions and ideals." Its aims were advanced but not radical, well suited to the rising spirit of Progressivism.

The new synthesis was provided in Fenollosa's conception of individuality. Once again he focused on popular attitudes toward art. Appreciation of freely ordered artistic possibilities stimulates a general freedom of the mind. The "art-process" illustrates the exercise of originality; the true work of art presents individuality achieved. All of us, if we would, asserts Fenollosa, could achieve this kind of "brain-freedom" through contact with art, but we keep "the infinitely volatile colors" of our mind "weighted like prisoners in our conventional souls." "It is only the rare one of us who makes of his mind a revolving flashlight that can free all the elements for their specific combinations. Yet this dullness is our own fault; for we all share the faculty; we might all become tolerable individuals if we would." What Americans can learn from art is that all great creations are utterly unlike, that they are individuals because of their glimpse of a unity which was the artist's to see and is ours to understand. But this rare glimpse of unity, this sense of the right relations among the complex elements in a work of art, can only be attained through originality, not through imitation. In the art of life, therefore, conformity presents a similar obstacle to achievement of those right relations which constitute one's own individuality. "Given two souls of equal mobility and daring, it does not follow that they will roam over the fields of possibility in the same order, rejecting the same by-ways, following the same skein of clues. The chances are infinitely that they will be sucked into diverging currents." [2] And so they must if a new synthesis is to be created and if the rigidity of formalism is to be avoided.

In arguing for fluidity of mind and for "mental variability" Fenollosa found support in Burbank's work in crossbreeding plants. The superior performance of hybrids suggested that human mixing might lead to analogous social gains.

> As you break up stagnation of race types, of clan groups, or of village families who have intermarried for centuries; as you disturb brain cells and currents that have become accustomed to fixed channels; as war and cataclysm and discovery demand readjustment of all tissues;—in short whether the mixing be due to physical or mental impregnation,—it is all analogous to the crossing of varieties among the most stubborn plants. What we call the fixity of species in nature is probably nothing but the same sort of stubborn habit with which the mechanical or the savage mind clings to its narrow traditions. [3]

As a historian Fenollosa considered art "the most sensitive barometer to measure mental variability," and he found the level of popular appreciation significant. "In all creative eras," he wrote in his opening article, "as of Athens, Florence, and Kyoto, the masses of the people have understood art, art has been democratic—a baker could vote intelligently on civic commissions. It ought to be so in America today but it isn't." Today artistic judgments are handed down like "a Grand Duke's ukase" from New York, Boston, and Chicago, while the mass of men remain oblivious of art. [4]

As Fenollosa saw it in 1906, the main obstacle to the free life of art was the assumption that the goals of life were only two—longevity and pleasure. In the dominant laissez-faire economics, with its "automatic adjustment of supply and demand," he saw consumption deified as productive, consumption become the "apotheosis of practicality." Yet, he went on to ask, is it "practical" to overlook food

2. "The Bases of Art Education: III. The Individuality of the Artist," *The Golden Age*, 1 (June 1906), 281.

3. Ibid., 282.

4. "The Bases of Art Education: I. The Roots of Art," *The Golden Age*, 1 (April 1906), 161.

adulteration, child labor, and sweat shops? Are the ideals of "a bald living-wage" and "nerve-tickling" fit ends for a man's life? We slave in offices without sun and light, competing with each other for what? That we may "roar at buffoons" and gorge ourselves? That we may bellow at each other across exchanges so that we can "suffocate in gaudily hung drawing-rooms amid furniture that flashes a thousand garish lights from gilt excrescences"? [5]

The root of these empty ideals lay in what Fenollosa termed "over-personality," a word recalling his earlier critiques of Percival Lowell's views and his own prophecies of East-West fusion. Now he focused on American education and found encouraging signs that appeals by teachers to pride and wealth and rivalry might be replaced by goals of self-development. The spread of kindergartens and the success of the Chicago Laboratory School indicated a hopeful future for the ideal of growth from within, an ideal which seemed to Fenollosa to link the natural self-expression of a developing child with the universal principles of history and art. By means of "sympathy" the child, the artist, and the historian can "project their minds out into the object, and not only know it but feel with it." "The real process of thought," he wrote, "does not merely label things, like so many apothecary's jars on a shelf. A thought grows like a living tissue. . . . A keen historian's reasoning is the key to all reasoning, since its test of truth, of reality, is just the organic interplay of all the facts." The idea of "organic interplay" united his educational, historical, and aesthetic thinking, and in *The Golden Age*, although there was scant consideration of East-West fusion, the image of the lotus inevitably returned, this time modified by a strain of empiricism. "Thinking is *thinging*," declared Fenollosa, "to follow the buds of fact as they open, and see thought folded away within thought like so many petals." [6]

Fenollosa's organicism was more than metaphorical. He had little respect for mechanistic philosophy or for machines; both placed man in a groove mired in a rut of the average. Fenollosa embraced possibility and change. Like William James he relished the challenge of novelty and uncertainty. "In war, in politics, in society, in daily life a thousand new situations arise; that is part of the fun," wrote

5. Editorial in *The Golden Age*, 1 (May 1906), 189–92. Fenollosa made similar points in "The Coming Fusion of East and West," *Harper's Monthly*, 98 (Dec. 1898), 115–22.
6. Editorial in *The Golden Age*, 1 (June 1906), 263–64.

Fenollosa. "The problem never repeats itself. A machine can do only one thing, but man can do a million things, and things which he has never tried before." This was the root of Fenollosa's optimistic commitment to education and art. "Social and educational conditions," he concluded, "are partly under man's control"; individuality of mind can be encouraged and trained by the creation and appreciation of art. The question of our age and every age is how to make the lives of all of us "hot with beauty." [7]

The Golden Age faded out of sight in the summer of 1906,[8] this final question largely ignored by the American public. But several months earlier a substantial step had been taken toward realizing Fenollosa's ambitious program in a permanent institutional form, an especially satisfying complement to his inevitably fleeting lecture work. On January 24, 1906, at 5:45 P.M., Charles L. Freer cabled to Fenollosa at the Hotel Barstow in New York: "Smithsonian Regents accepted unanimously today." [9] The United States government had agreed to accept Freer's art collection on his terms, and the future of the Freer Gallery was thereby assured.

Freer's collection had been acquired with Fenollosa's careful advice; federal acceptance gave form to a unique conception of the educational possibilities of an art museum. The philosophy of selection was assured preservation under terms of the gift and remains as fruitful evidence of Fenollosa's close association with a man of rare discernment.

When Fenollosa first sailed for Japan in 1878, Charles Lang Freer had been working for eight years in Kingston, New York, first in a cement factory and then as a clerk in the offices of the local railroad superintendent, Colonel Frank Hecker. With Hecker, Freer went to Detroit in 1880 and became assistant treasurer of the newly organized Peninsula Car Works. He worked with Peninsula and its successors until merger with the American Car and Foundry Co. Freer had grown up in poverty; he became a millionaire. In 1900, at the age of forty-four, Freer retired from business and devoted his energies to the development of his art collection. A bachelor of

7. "The Bases of Art Education: III. The Individuality of the Artist," *The Golden Age*, 1 (June 1906), 283–84.

8. *The Golden Age's* demise was probably hastened by the San Francisco earthquake, which collapsed elaborate promotional schemes for "The Golden Age Trip to the Golden Gate," a railroad ride to a convention of the National Education Association.

9. Freer Correspondence, MS vol. 19, in Freer Gallery, Washington, D.C.

refined tastes, Freer became a passionate collector. He had purchased a few things in the '80s, including some Whistler etchings, and in the '90s had begun to collect Japanese prints. Very few of these early acquisitions remained in his collection. He wanted only the best, and not until after his retirement from business did he have time to develop his own artistic judgment and to acquire works which could stand up to his increasingly discriminating appraisal.[10]

Freer met Fenollosa in the early '90s, but their friendship did not develop until he had returned for good from Japan and Freer had retired. To Freer, Fenollosa brought a scholar's integrity and a connoisseur's enthusiasm as well as an unequaled knowledge of Far Eastern art. To Fenollosa, Freer gave loyal and continued support both financial and personal. Freer's home in Detroit offered a calm luxury in which Fenollosa could enjoy at leisure the beautiful paintings which both men loved. Freer was immaculate in his dress, his habits, and his business ledgers. He was attracted by the delicate intensity of Japanese paintings, the elegant harmonies of Whistler, the purity of ancient Eastern pottery. If Fenollosa's enthusiasms stirred Freer, as the sensuous gold screens of Koyetsu must have, the record points to restraint, to responses controlled and concentrated. Next to Freer the scholarly Fenollosa seems flamboyant.

At the start of Fenollosa's lecture campaigns Detroit offered ready bookings, largely at Freer's urging. In the first few years when Fenollosa's income from lectures was small, Freer bought several fine paintings and a batch of prints from his adviser, all at good prices (but never without checking the market). Fenollosa's critical advice over the years saved Freer many thousands of dollars and brought Fenollosa welcome fees. They met regularly in New York and Detroit from February 1901 up to the time of Fenollosa's death, and their frequent correspondence records Fenollosa's key role in acquisition of the oriental part of Freer's collection.

Freer made a point of not buying European art and of patronizing live American artists.[11] This attitude distinguished him from most

10. A high regard for quality was maintained by Freer in his business dealings as well as in his artistic activities. "I agree fully with your prophecies as to the future use of cement. The one great aim of Michigan cement manufacturers should be quality. With this secured and adhered to, the consumption will, in my opinion, at the end of five years fully equal all that you have said." Freer to A. C. Raymond, Feb. 7, 1901, Freer Correspondence, MS vol. 7.

11. Freer made the point explicit in a brusque letter: "My collection does not include paintings by European artists." Freer to J. F. Wyckoff, Jan. 26, 1906, Freer Correspondence, MS vol. 19.

wealthy art patrons of the day. He bought from F. S. Church because he was an old friend and from Tryon, Dewing, and Thayer, because he thought their work stood at the head of American contemporary painting. Their muted palettes and refined subjects—Thayer's virgins were famous—must have caught his eye. But his passion was for Whistler, and Fenollosa supported Freer's natural inclination by indicating Whistler's close relationship to Far Eastern art. Fenollosa assured Freer that to future historians of world art Whistler would represent a decisive moment in the fusion of Eastern and Western insights and techniques.

Freer had few illusions about the place currently accorded art in American life, but he was hopeful for the future, and it was toward the next generation that both he and Fenollosa were building. To a critic of American indifference to fine art he wrote in rebuttal that New York was no more selfish than the rest of the world, that encouragement and appreciation of art have always been rare, flowering only for brief moments in Renaissance Italy and in China and Japan.[12] And Freer saw signs of a growing appreciation of fine things, especially among the new millionaires, even though they regarded art as another field for competition and conquest. These men boomed the market for paintings as Freer indicated in a letter to an old friend:

> Thoroughly fine paintings by first class men are advancing rapidly in price, and the number of buyers in this country are rapidly increasing. When Morgan, Whitney, Yerkes, Clark and other giants get their real fighting blood up, and it seems to be nearing the boiling point, we little fellows will have to go to bed and stay there.[13]

Freer competed by specializing and by developing his own taste apart from the urging of dealers. Even the inflation of art prices seemed a hopeful sign that "a tremendous interest in fine things is surely rapidly growing in America." [14]

Freer's ace in the game with the "giants" was Fenollosa, whose advice kept dealers in line. But at heart Freer was playing a different game.[15] The giants vied for prestige through art ownership, and high

12. Freer to Augustus Koopman, Dec. 12, 1901, Freer Correspondence, MS vol. 8.

13. Freer to W. K. Bixby, Feb. 7, 1902, Freer Correspondence, MS vol. 9.

14. Freer to Charles J. Morse, Feb. 4, 1903, Freer Correspondence, MS vol. 10.

15. For dealers who regarded art in purely commercial terms Freer had little respect. Of T. E. Kirby, a prominent art dealer and auctioneer, Freer wrote that

prices often reflected their desire for "conspicuous consumption." Freer combined personal appreciation with public responsibility, and he considered the educational value of his collection crucial. On both counts, appreciation and education, Freer shared Fenollosa's central concerns. As he phrased it, Fenollosa was a man "thoroughly intelligent" with "remarkable appreciation of beauty." [16] And Freer felt the power of Fenollosa's eloquent interpretations of the significance of Eastern civilization. Freer wrote to an English correspondent that

> He [Fenollosa] has done more than any other person to advance the interest in the art of Japan and China. He is also deeply interested in the literature and civilization of these countries, and is doing very forceful work in connection therewith. His training, experience, high scholarship, and gift of oratory peculiarly fit him as a lecturer. . . . My excuse [for writing], if one is needed, is to be found in the interest I have in spreading of reliable information everywhere concerning the beauty of the art and civilization of the East.[17]

In Whistler, Freer found an artist who was both American and Far Eastern and who stood at the forefront of the world's contemporary artists, but when Freer tried to exhibit Whistler's paintings in the United States he met repeated opposition. Whistler was still considered too bold and eccentric in many circles to receive official approval. His bout with Ruskin and his proclamation of the superiority of the artist's eyes over the vision of academy and society alike seemed arrogance to many. Whistler had broken the rules, never recanted, and that ended it. Freer insisted that art ignores rules, but juries and exhibition officials resisted firmly.[18]

Controversy continued after Whistler's death, although Freer managed to persuade the Copley Society of Boston to present a memorial exhibition in February 1904. For the occasion *Lotus*, a new magazine

if he continues to treat artists roughly, "he will soon place himself on a level with Pepsin Gum and Paine's Celery Compound." Freer to T. W. Dewing, March 11, 1903, Freer Correspondence, MS vol. 11.

16. Freer to D. W. Tryon, Feb. 10, 1903, Freer Correspondence, MS vol. 10.
17. Freer to J. M. White, Oct. 31, 1904, Freer Correspondence, MS vol. 15.
18. For Freer's opposition to rules see esp. Freer to Abbot H. Thayer, Nov. 10, 1906, Freer Correspondence, MS vol. 21. Freer was particularly aroused by the attitude of Sir Purdom Clarke of New York's Metropolitan Museum, a noted opponent of all artistic innovation. See Freer to Mary M. Fenollosa, Feb. 9, 1910, Freer Correspondence, MS vol. 29.

published in Boston by a friend of Freer's, issued a special Whistler memorial number in which Fenollosa assessed "The Place in History of Mr. Whistler's Art." [19] Fenollosa approached Whistler from the historical perspective of world art rather than from the usual base for Western criticism—"the brief fortunes of Academic Art between the fifteenth and nineteenth centuries." Whistler's significance, as Fenollosa saw it, lay in his creative response to the fresh stream of Far Eastern art which flowed into Europe in the '60s and '70s, particularly the Japanese prints which supplemented more familiar porcelain designs. By assimilating the Japanese spirit Whistler succeeded in

> throwing himself into the universal current, in making his individual feeling the sole test of his constructive schemes, reaching new power in dramatic movement and poignancy of line, in subtle contrapuntal marshalling of his silvery grays, and in cooler and more normal ranges of color harmony, like translucent films of glaze in pottery. The simple truth is that he is the first great master who comes after the union of East and West, the first who creates naturally and without affectation in their mingled terms.[20]

This is what made Whistler a "pioneer of the Future" for Fenollosa and what gave Freer's collection its unique historical importance and educational potential.

In describing "The Collection of Mr. Charles L. Freer" in *Pacific Era* for November 1907, Fenollosa reaffirmed Whistler's significance and provided a clear expression of Freer's guiding principles. The three parts of the collection represented an aesthetic unity "destined to play a great part in developing the future art of America": a selection of Chinese and Japanese painting second only to Fenollosa's own in the Boston Museum of Fine Arts, a superb collection of ancient glazed pottery, and the world's best collection of the works of Whistler. These three sections combined to demonstrate a fundamental visual language free from the tradition of narrow realism and suggesting a future fruitful interplay between East and West. "As a whole," wrote Fenollosa,

19. *Lotus* was published at 380 Boylston St., Boston, Mass., by Bunkio Matsuki, a Japanese art dealer. The Whistler Memorial issue, vol. I, no. 1, appears to have been the first and last published, although future plans were announced. (*Lotus* bore no direct relation to *The Lotos* of 1896, Fenollosa's journal.)

20. "The Place in History of Mr. Whistler's Art," *Lotus*, 1 (Dec. 1903), 16.

this collection strikingly illustrates the most conspicuous fact in the history of art, that the two great streams of European and Asiatic practice, held apart for so many thousand years, have, at the close of the nineteenth century, been brought together in a fertile and final union. The future historian will look back to the year 1860 as a nodule, a starting point in the whole subsequent course in the world's art. . . . Whistler thus stands forever at the meeting point of the two great continental streams; he is the nodule, the universalizer, the interpreter of East to West and West to East.[21]

When Freer offered this imaginative (and immensely valuable) collection to the Smithsonian Institution as a gift to the national government, the regents were reluctant to accept even when prodded by President Roosevelt. They were mostly scientific men with conventional tastes and openly skeptical about "impressionist art," as they called it. Freer would pay for building a suitable gallery, but the government would have to maintain it in perpetuity. Negotiations dragged on for a year. Final acceptance, which Freer cabled to Fenollosa, meant none the less that a novel educational ideal was assured a permanent future.[22] Freer was not a scholar himself, but his gift

21. "The Collection of Mr. Charles L. Freer," *Pacific Era*, 1 (Nov. 1907), 59, 61. Fenollosa developed a number of affinities among the three parts of the collection. For example, he noted that the under clays of the pottery and the undertones of Whistler's paintings diffused light in an analogous fashion; that similar translucent films gave depth alike to the rough grounds of pottery and the coarse, hand-laid paper, whose clay-like shadows Whistler overtouched "with light, swift scumblings from a broad, dry brush . . . half-concealing, half-revealing"; that Koyetsu's shower of cool, opaque greens hurled against varnished gold leaf struck the same note as Whistler's Peacock Room decorations; that Whistler's middle-tone color harmonies were reminiscent of a Chinese view of color as "a flower growing out of a soil of grays" filled with subtle *notan* relationships; that Japanese prints had helped free Whistler's eye to unexpected beauties, breaking into the primary canvas-rectangle with a part of a horse, a slice of a man, of a hanging cloth (pp. 57–66).

22. In a 1904 letter offering his collection to the Smithsonian, Freer stated his own views explicitly: "No attempt has been made to secure specimens from unsympathetic sources my collecting having been confined to American and Asiatic schools. My great desire has been to unite modern work with masterpieces of certain periods of high civilization harmonious in spiritual suggestion, having the power to broaden esthetic culture and the grace to elevate the human mind." Quoted in *Catalogue of a Selection of Art Objects from the Freer Collection*, Smithsonian Institution Bulletin 78 (1912), p. 5.

made liberal provision for continued study of Far Eastern civilization. The collection was to be available for first-hand study and for public lectures; and Fenollosa's slides formed the nucleus of an expanding loan service for schools and educational groups.[23]

The Freer Collection's distinction lay in combining aesthetic discrimination with historical interpretation toward an educational end. As such it approached those ideal relations of an art museum to the people which Fenollosa had set down in *The Lotos* in 1896 and had stressed consistently. The proposition that beauty is a necessary cornerstone of public welfare seemed to Fenollosa to follow clearly from the premise that art can free men's minds. He reasoned thus: society exists so that men may lead fit lives; fit lives require free minds; minds are freed by art; therefore society needs art. The beautiful things in a people's museum—the Smithsonian was that—exemplified a union of freedom and public welfare.

There remained the question of a museum's necessarily historical consciousness. Considering art and freedom historically, that is in relation to change, Fenollosa saw mobility of response as the key to great art as well as to the accelerated changes through which society was passing. The history of art, then, demonstrated in its succession of momentary harmonies a unity in the midst of flux, the unity of the free imagination in its historical encounter with change. In the modern world it is "this very multiplicity of our consciousness" that makes us "study and digest the work of all mankind." "The only unity in art," wrote Fenollosa in *The Lotos*, "is the thread of its history," a history of individual free resolutions of possibilities forever changing.[24] The art museum affords the best opportunity for the transmission of this insight. Accordingly, policies of acquisition and preservation should provide full opportunity for scholarly research and should focus on a museum's "highest 'raison d'être,' " educational service. The challenge to museums is simple but sweeping: to intro-

23. The Freer Gallery director (from 1920–42), the man who gave shape to many of Fenollosa's educational plans, was John Ellerton Lodge, who had been trained under Fenollosa's successor at the Boston Museum of Fine Arts—a doubly ironic touch in view of the virtual ban on Fenollosa in Boston following his departure in 1895. For John Lodge was a younger brother of George Cabot Lodge, and he, too, was probably introduced to Japan through Sturgis Bigelow, an archibishop of Fenollosa's social excommunication. On John Lodge's career see above, Ch. 10, n. 24.

24. "Art Museums and Their Relation to the People," *The Lotos*, 9 (1896), 846, 934.

duce the power of beauty into the lives of men and thereby educate in them a sense of the relations of freedom and change to individuality.

Fenollosa's hopes for museums and art journals, even for the Freer Gallery and *The Golden Age,* were clearly extravagant. They were part of his wider optimistic faith in man's capacity to live freely and to develop an individual style of life in which the risks of novelty and uncertainty could be tolerated. Uncertainties might even be celebrated, as Kuo Hsi had suggested, through play in the sphere of art. This was the center of Fenollosa's dream of a lotus blossoming in America as a model for an emerging world culture.

The dream would surely dissolve along with the insubstantial stuff of so many nineteenth-century utopias if it failed to take on form and substance in the life of some historical society, in this case the life of an expansive continental United States. Fenollosa's lectures and writings, his journalistic ventures and museum work, for all their vigor barely touched the surfaces of national life. The lotus needed roots in the institutional fabric of society if it were to thrive or even survive amid the gusts of change sweeping across America.

If a man keep alive what is old
and recognize novelty, he can,
eventually, teach.

Confucian Analects

15 · TOWARD INTELLIGENT SEEING:
THE FENOLLOSA-DOW SYSTEM OF
ART EDUCATION

"There is no education like intelligent seeing," Fenollosa maintained. Man seeing was man alive, man learning to be free by sensing the risks undertaken by artists in their free sightings of chaos. In his essays in *The Golden Age* he had tried to drive home the relevance of these views, but *The Golden Age* was short lived. Fenollosa's call to artistic subversion of conventions was heard by only a tiny segment of "the hard-working public" he set out to alert and educate. More hopeful were prospects for his theories in the field of education. If American schools could be persuaded to re-educate children's eyes radically, a new generation might approach Fenollosa's utopian society where free individuals lived beautiful lives.

All utopias, however, must compete with a variety of other dreams. Fenollosa's plans for the future confronted a sprawling educational system that was really many systems pulling in different directions at once. American schools in 1900 felt the pressures of an urbanizing, industrializing society in the throes of a population explosion that was literally polyglot. New buildings were rising. The curriculum was changing. Disputes about educational philosophies were lively. There was general agreement that education was a key to national progress but its tasks were prodigious. Education meant training for citizenship as it had since the early days of the Republic; in 1900 citizenship also meant Americanization of millions of recent immigrants and their children, a training in morals and manners as well as political traditions. Education meant a means of getting ahead in the world; it should be practical and useful. At the same time it should be democratic in the sense of providing equal opportunities for all. And there was growing support for the idea that one of the most important opportunities schools should provide was the opportunity for self-development, a chance for each individual to discover and develop his unique potentialities as a human being.

Fenollosa's proposals to reform art education developed amid controversies which reflected the varied goals of American schools. Fenollosa's emphasis on "harmonious spacing" as the key to all design and his stress on artistic individuality drew opposition from influential quarters: from tax-conscious school boards who opposed all art in education as an unnecessary frill; from moralists who saw art education as properly didactic, its role to illustrate divine love, ethical conduct, and virtuous suffering; from utilitarians who wanted only manual training and mechanical drawing (precursors of "vocational arts"); and finally, from academic art teachers and their publishers and suppliers who felt their traditional methods threatened. On the other hand, the new kindergarten theories which Francis Parker and John Dewey were extending throughout the lower grades offered welcome encouragement. To "progressive" educators artistic activity seemed especially suited to self-expression and a pattern of child development keyed to spontaneity and free experiment.

Education in America has attracted utopians because of its flexibility and variety; but it has baffled attempts at sweeping reforms by its stubborn localism, decentralized and pluralistic. The enormous expansion of American schools in the years after 1900 preserved this localism, even compounded it by abandoning such standard texts as *McGuffey's Readers*, but centralizing counterforces were developing at the same time, notably a national center for teacher training in New York, Teachers College, Columbia University. Without the national influence of this center Fenollosa's utopia might have been interred quietly with *The Golden Age*.

The story of how Fenollosa's theories of art education were established and spread across the country is the story of ideas which live anew in institutions. In the schools of America Fenollosa's lotus blossomed as the progressive unfolding of a sense of design. How Fenollosa's philosophical responses to Far Eastern art were transformed

into a working guide for school teachers is the story primarily of
Arthur Wesley Dow. Fenollosa was himself too independent to fit
smoothly into any institutional framework; Emerson and Li Po were
too close to his heart. Fenollosa was basically a philosopher and historian and spent his last years in the limbo of a private scholar. Arthur
Dow was a painter and a teacher. Judging by results he must have
been an excellent administrator as well. In the course of Dow's thirty
years of teaching he converted a generation of art teachers to Fenollosan principles, thereby re-educating the eyes of students from California to Maine, from Michigan to New Mexico. In Dow's classes in
Boston, in his courses at Pratt Institute in Brooklyn, and most important, for eighteen years as director of the Fine Arts Department at
Teachers College, Columbia, he carried on a vigorous and sustained
program of persuasion which was in effect revolutionary. Dow's first
meeting with Fenollosa in the Boston Museum of Fine Arts in 1891
proved decisive in the "Americanization" of Fenollosa's lotus.

Arthur Dow was thirty-four when he met Fenollosa. His career as
an artist had developed along conventional lines, and prospects were
promising. His work had been well placed at three Paris Salons, and
one painting had been selected for the Paris Universal Exposition of
1889. But he was restless under the rules of academic painting and
commercial pressures toward prosaic genre scenes and crayon portraits. At the heart of his interest in art lay a desire to render "the
poetry and mystery" of nature.[1] From the beginning his concern with
the spiritual quality of art was nearly as pronounced as that of his
mentor, Fenollosa.

Dow grew up in Ipswich, Massachusetts, not far from Salem, in a
community indifferent to art and suspicious of artists. Although his
parents had little money, the support of relatives enabled him to finish
Newburyport High School. Further education was out of reach. For
several years after graduation Dow supported himself by teaching at a
one room school in a rural Ipswich parish. At the same time he became interested in local history and began sketching historic houses,
encouraged by a local Methodist minister and antiquarian, Augustine
Caldwell. It was Caldwell who requested Dow to translate for publication the meditations of Madame Guyon and who introduced him to
Mrs. Sarah Farmer. Mrs. Farmer was deeply stirred by Madame
Guyon's spiritual exercises and became interested in the career of the

1. A. W. Dow to Minnie E. Pearson, June 12, 1883, in Dow MSS in possession of Ralph Ladd, Cambridge, Mass.

young Ipswich translator. Dow had been drawing and painting for several years, and Mrs. Farmer offered encouragement and financial help.[2]

By 1881 Dow had sold several pictures, and he ventured to Boston for further art training. He was interested primarily in landscape and decided against the school at the Boston Museum of Fine Arts in favor of classes with James Stone, an artist who had taken French lessons from Dow the previous summer in Ipswich. Dow lived in Stone's studio, and the congenial atmosphere confirmed his decision to make a career of art. For three years he studied in Boston and gave classes of his own in neighboring towns as occasion offered. In the shadow of Beacon Hill he read Whitman for the first time and felt the pull of another "lover of nature" who refused to be constricted by the rules of art. Dow voiced the conviction that he, too, would cut loose from all rules and paint "just as I see and feel, gathering what is good from all sources." [3]

The primary source of artistic inspiration for a young painter in the '80s lay across the Atlantic, and in the summer of 1884 Dow sailed for Europe. In Paris he studied for three winters at the Julian Academy. In the summers he went to Pont Aven in Brittany to indulge his passion for landscape. Finisterre was almost as beautiful as the marshes and meadows of Ipswich and the colony of artists was delightful.[4] The Paris Salon of 1887 accepted one of Dow's landscapes, and that spring he returned to the United States to replenish his finances. He painted scores of Ipswich sunsets and moonrises and cleared $660 from a one-man show in Boston, enough to return to France the following April. A summer in Pont Aven and a productive winter in Paris, culminating in two paintings in the Salon and one in the Uni-

2. Sarah Farmer was led through Caldwell to Madame Guyon; after the Chicago Parliament of Religions of 1893, Mrs. Farmer became the leading light at Greenacre, a religious colony in Eliot, Maine, at which the Dows were frequent visitors. The colony worshipped alternately at the feet of Madame Blavatsky, Abdul Bahai, Ole Bull and Mrs. Bull, Kola the Parsee, and divers swamis while maintaining itself as a Protestant retreat. Dow was interested in spiritualism throughout his life, but in his early years he was more orthodox and inclined toward Anglican liturgy. He was disgusted by Romanism in Paris, but for a considerable period in Boston he prayed regularly in the evening before a candle and crucifix.

3. Dow to M. E. Pearson, July 7, 1883, in Dow MSS.

4. Gauguin was painting at Pont Aven at the time, but I have found no evidence of contact between the two men.

versal Exposition's show of the decade's best, convinced him that his period of apprenticeship was over.

Returned from Paris in August 1889 Dow settled down to make a living as an American artist, with Ipswich as his base. He painted industriously, exhibited in Boston, Rochester, Chicago, and New York, and sold some canvases, but only a few. Eighteen months persuaded him that sales were largely a matter of contacts and that residence in Ipswich was too big a barrier, even for a thoroughly American artist. In January 1891 he moved to studios in the Mechanics Building in Boston and began to study painting intensively from every angle—contemporary, old masters, history of art and artists—looking for some way out of mediocrity, searching for freedom from artistic standards established by academic and social fiat. In the Boston Public Library he came across a book of Hokusai sketches; they were exciting. "It is now plain to me," he wrote to his fiancée, "that Whistler and Pennell whom I have admired as great originals are only copying the Japanese. One evening with Hokusai gave me more light on composition and decorative effect than years of study of pictures. I surely ought to compose in an entirely different manner and paint better." [5]

He had heard about the new Department of Japanese Art at the Museum of Fine Arts, and a week later he sought out the new curator to see if there were more books on Hokusai which he might examine. Fenollosa opened the storeroom door and, threading carefully through crates and packing boxes, led Dow into a new world—the soft ink studies of Sesshu, the brilliant colors of Korin, the sensuous detail of Okyo. It was Madame Guyon wrapped in an Ipswich sunset. Dow never recovered. He returned regularly and soon agreed with Fenollosa that "pictorial" and "decorative" art are properly considered in terms of the same principles. By June he was writing that "line, notan, and colour" are "the trinity of power." [6]

Dow worked on these new theories and techniques that summer in Ipswich, continuing experiments through the next winter with his Boston art classes. He grew even more enthusiastic as Fenollosa began to give historical order to the mass of paintings. The following spring Dow sent out a circular for his summer class in landscape painting which announced a crucial shift in his thinking.

5. Dow to M. E. Pearson, Feb. 27, 1891, in Dow MSS.
6. Dow to M. E. Pearson, June 19, 1891, in Dow MSS. For a dramatic account of Dow's meeting with Fenollosa see "Arthur W. Dow," *The Lotos,* 9 (March 1896), 709–10.

> The method of instruction will be changed from that heretofore
> pursued, in that there will be included a special study of line, dark
> and light, and color, as synthetic principles; with reference to the
> works of Japanese masters, of early Italians, and of the modern
> French school; the aim being to develop creative grasp in the
> rendering of subject, rather than any narrow line of abstract tech-
> nique.[7]

From the outset Dow used historical examples to illustrate and support his new theories and to develop in his students the key artistic
quality of appreciation. The Japanese led the way closely followed by
the Barbizon landscapists, Corot and Millet (in whose work Fenollosa
pointed to Japanese affinities), and the Italian painters of primitives,
those masters of flat arrangement whom Jarves and LaFarge appreciated earlier. In his class in Ipswich that summer of 1892 Dow introduced the Japanese brush to his students, and in subsequent classes in
Boston he gave more and more attention to the brush as the basic instrument with which to develop power of expression and a sense of
the subtle relationships of line and *notan*. At the same time he began
his own pioneer experiments with wood-block printing.

   "The thought is taking shape in my mind," Dow confided to his
fiancée,

> that as I am living in an atmosphere of the highest art, and best
> thoughts upon art, it should soon bear fruit in a substantial way
> —not only in my regular landscapes but in screens and panels
> and decorations, and in water color and prints—not that I am to
> divide up into all these, but thoughts of these things ought to
> come and be put down as they come. I shall try my hand at them
> and see if I can't do something that shall be fine and also of
> financial value. I feel as if I had the power now to compose and
> to know when a thing is good.[8]

   In March 1893 Dow lectured at the Unity Club in Boston on syn-
thetic art principles and contributed "A Note on Japanese Art and
What the American Artist May Learn Therefrom" to *The Knight
Errant*. In this article, his first published statement on art education,
Dow pointed to the universality of the grammar of Japanese art and
launched his attack on the narrowly representational criteria of the

7. Circular for Ipswich painting class, Summer 1892, in Dow MSS.
8. Dow to M. E. Pearson, Feb. 7, 1893, in Dow MSS.

academies. In Fenollosan language Dow maintained that beauty was a matter not of accurate description but of ideal synthesis.[9]

Fenollosa continued the attack on realism at Chicago in the summer of 1893, this time in the name of individualism and originality. The occasion was a meeting of the art department of the International Congress of Education at the World's Columbian Exposition. Asked to discuss the question of the value of copying and modeling in training an artist, Fenollosa replied that an artist must turn to art rather than to nature for his instruction, that great works of the past constitute a valuable aid in developing originality so long as art is not frozen to past standards. The artist inherits "unlimited possibility" and should recast the possibilities of line and light into new relations.[10] The revolutionary implications of Fenollosa's remarks were largely ignored, judging by published accounts of the Congress. The ensuing addresses and discussions assumed that art should represent noble themes and that the higher forms of painting, namely figure and landscape, required the traditional studies of anatomy, perspective, lighting, and costume.

That autumn Dow began regular work at the museum as Fenollosa's assistant.[11] He continued to paint but devoted more and more time to working with Fenollosa toward a system of art instruction suitable for American schools. Fenollosa had developed his system in Japan to mesh with traditional methods and he could rely on his students' early training in brush and "sumi" and in calligraphy. Dow had done enough teaching to be acutely aware of the lack of such background in American art students, and he tried to work out a practical approach that would make sense to students whose previous training, if any, ran along traditional academic lines. The idea of composition

9. The tone of Dow's article was as aristocratic as the rest of the magazine and linked Japan effectively with medievalism: "Japanese art is the expression of a people's devotion to the beautiful. It is an art which exists for beauty only, in lofty isolation from science and mechanism, from realism and commercialism, from all that has befogged and debased other art." In "A Note on Japanese Art and What the American Artist May Learn Therefrom," *The Knight Errant,* 1 (1893), 114.

10. EFF, "Studying Art—Discussion," *Proceedings of the International Congress of Education of the World's Columbian Exposition, Chicago, 1893* (New York, National Educational Association, 1894), p. 472.

11. Dow had been paid $1 per hour for his earlier help. In the fall of 1893 he was hired at an annual salary of $800. On Oct. 24, 1893, Dow married Minnie Eleanor Pearson of Lowell, Mass.

seemed to offer the best bridge for an American understanding of synthetic principles.

When Dow talked on composition before the Boston Art Students' Association in February 1894, he stated in simple terms the distinction between composition and study which formed his basic point of departure from current methods:

> Let me now draw a sharp distinction between *composition* and *studying*. In making accurate, truthful paintings from nature, we are learning to *represent* objects with the idea of ultimately combining them in a composition, but a pictorial composition is not merely an assemblage of objects truthfully represented, it is the *expression of an idea,* and all the parts must be so related as to form a harmonious *whole*. It cannot be a work of *art* unless it has this quality of wholeness. A study must be accurate; a composition must be beautiful. Painting "what you see, and as you see it" is only studying; it is not creating; it is not composing. Long continued study is a needed discipline, but let it have its proper place and not be misnamed.
>
> By painting from nature, aided by drawing, perspective, and other sciences, we learn much about forms, textures, and colours of things and how to represent them in different mediums, as oil or water-colour, but when we try to combine various objects, as for instance, hills, trees, and a river, into a picture, we feel the need of a new faculty which is but imperfectly developed, in short, the ability to *compose,* the *creative* faculty, not the imitative.[12]

It is this creative faculty which orders line, *notan*, and color into harmonious wholes.

The pattern of the relationship between Dow and Fenollosa was established at the outset of their public campaigning. Their positions were very close; their emphases were complementary. Dow's talks were geared to studio practice and the fundamentals of art apprecia-

12. For this quotation and for a summary of missing Dow correspondence, I am indebted to the notes of the late Arthur Warren Johnson, of Ipswich, Mass. (in possession of Ralph Ladd, Cambridge, Mass.), on which Johnson based his "Arthur Wesley Dow," *Ipswich Historical Society Publications*, no. 28 (Ipswich, 1934). In this memoir Johnson's focus on Dow's Ipswich locale is helpful, but other aspects of Dow's career are handled too loosely to be uniformly reliable.

tion. Fenollosa, more of a theorist, provided support with philosophical and historical arguments.

When Fenollosa addressed the Boston Art Students' Association on "Imagination in Art," he stressed man's capacity to explore possible combinations and to select felt wholes.

> If we admire imagination for its power of construction, that is the deeper cause of the pleasure, and defines it. And such construction underlies all great art, not merely successful ornament. . . . In art, imagination is the faculty of thinking and feeling in terms of a single image. It implies the integrity, the wholeness and purity of the image.
>
> Imagination comes from the word "image"; not a fancy, not a dream, not a vague blur of consciousness, but a clear, unbroken image. It is a visible integer. . . . Visual art is to be distinguished from ordinary sight, from vague revery, and from imperfect phantasy, in this, that the artistic image has persistence, congruity, natural limits, a kind of organization within itself. In strong imagination it is singular and complete, a group of parts, lines, and proportions, which lacks nothing essential to make its wholeness clear, which admits nothing which tends to distort the image, or disturb its integrity.[13]

Imagination should not be confused with thought. "At best a thought can be only a very partial image." The thought of a painting's subject does not produce of itself an image in Fenollosa's sense of the word. The image is created and appreciated by "this quick power of the imagination which seems in a moment to explore a million possible combinations and to seize upon the right one." This power is what art education can train. "We have educated our children," claimed Fenollosa, "too much to think, too little to see and feel wholes."

Dow's work in Boston and at his Ipswich summer school was satisfying, but training a small number of budding artists began to seem less important than the more general goal of widespread public education. On this score Dow's faith in progress, like Fenollosa's, was unassailable. Art appreciation, he contended, could never be lost once developed; it was "a step on a track which leads forever upward." "It is certain," he declared, "that Art is to be a great force in the social system in the near future. We are learning that art means more than drawing and painting pictures—that the appreciation of art means

13. *Imagination in Art* (Boston, 1894) pp. 5, 6.

more than buying oil paintings—that the effect of art on *life* is something that we cannot do without. Beauty is a blessing that we have a right to *demand*." If the public taste were suddenly made aware of beauty, "what an upheaval would result—the laws would be changed —business relations would change—the whole life of the nation would be revolutionized." Public indifference to art was formidable, but education could change the situation radically.

> Our greatest hope is the public school. Teach the child to know beauty when he sees it, to *create it*, to love it, and when he grows up he will not tolerate the ugly. In the relations of lines to each other he may learn the relation of lives to each other; as he perceives color harmonies, he may so perceive the fitness of things that when he becomes a business man he will not build artists' studios around a boiler shop. He will not take some waste room over a freight yard and make it into studios because fit for no other use—nor would he associate studios with a skating rink and a dog show. . . .[14]

This belief in the total revolutionary power of art appreciation echoed the enthusiastic vision at the heart of Fenollosa's career. Fenollosa and Dow shared this sense of mission, and it was the power of this conviction which gave Dow's career as educator its particular quality and effectiveness.

The decision to commit himself completely to teaching was a difficult one for Dow to make. He considered carefully in the early months of 1895. If he did so there would be time for only occasional painting of his own and little for the wide variety of artistic activity which intrigued him. His work in wood-block prints was particularly successful. The Boston Museum of Fine Arts held a special exhibition of these color prints; and for the catalogue Fenollosa wrote a glowing introduction in which he hailed Dow's application of Japanese techniques to Western expression as "an epoch-making event." Once the blocks were cut the artist could concentrate attention on the subtleties of color relationships made possible by varied hand pressure, paper texture, and pigment. Colored prints from wood blocks offered an art in which multiple tonal possibilities could be explored and executed.[15]

14. Untitled notes in Dow MSS.
15. "Pigment washed upon the wood, and allowed to press the sheet with touch as delicate as a hand's caress, clings shyly only to the outer fibres, the hills of its new world, leaving the deep wells of light in the valleys, the whiteness of

During the summer of 1895, soon after his wood-block show, Dow accepted an offer from Pratt Institute in Brooklyn to join its faculty as an instructor in composition; it was a step toward a teaching career. Pratt Institute, founded in 1887, had already established a reputation for its pioneering spirit. Its goal was to make practical training in the arts available to the public at large, and its early classes contained many prospective teachers. Methods were experimental. A kindergarten had been established several years earlier, and new theories of education were hospitably received. The head of Pratt's Department of Fine Arts, Walter Scott Perry, was conservative; he maintained the traditional distinctions between construction, representation, and decoration and focused on the instructional value of geometric forms, nature, and historic ornament.[16] But he let Dow advocate heresy, and soon Dow's classes were filled with enthusiastic students.

Dow secured a studio in New York for his own work and lectured at the Art Students League as well as Pratt. Fenollosa served as visiting lecturer at Pratt during Dow's first year. When Fenollosa sailed for Japan in April 1896, Dow was firmly established and at work on a book which would make the new synthetic system of art instruction widely available.

The four years of Fenollosa's Japanese sojourn were busy ones for Dow. He visited Italy with the particular aim of examining Italian primitives in the light of synthetic principles. In 1898 he served as curator of Japanese prints at the Boston Museum of Fine Arts. At the same time he continued his teaching at Pratt. Most important, he concentrated work on a book which might serve to spread the gospel of composition. It was published early in 1899 and was titled, simply, *Composition*, with the subtitle, "A Series of Exercises Selected from a New System of Art Education." Dow paid tribute to Fenollosa's key role in the formulation of the new system and launched a frontal attack on the orthodoxies of realistic drawing.

The new system's principles were stated clearly and were maintained through nineteen subsequent editions. "The first step in the

the paper's inner heart, to glow up through it, and dilute its solid color with a medium of pure luminosity." EFF, introduction to *Special Exhibition of Color Prints, Designed, Engraved, and Printed by Arthur W. Dow* (Boston, Museum of Fine Arts, 1895), p. 5. See also Arthur Dow, "Painting with Wooden Blocks," *Modern Art*, 4 (Summer 1896), 85–90.

16. See esp. W. S. Perry, "Art Education in Relation to Public Education," *NEA Addresses and Proceedings*, 1896, pp. 694–701.

Art of Painting," wrote Dow, "is the drawing of lines as the boundaries of shapes." [17] The exercises started with the simplest line arrangements and proceeded toward more complex relations of line and *notan*. In this first edition color was barely mentioned.[18] Dow stressed that the exercises outlined were to be considered as the first part of a more fully developed course. They were a guide to principles rather than a set pattern. But the drift was clear. Training must proceed from the simple to the more complex, and at every turn the work of Japanese masters illustrated the line of development.[19]

Dow leaned heavily on Japanese elements in his universal theory. The monochromatic ideals of Japanese art, the emphasis on the brush, and the predominance of Japanese illustrations indicated the extent of Far Eastern influence, or, better, the importance of Japanese examples for a cosmopolitan art. To illustrate line composition Michelangelo appeared alongside the Kanos; Giotto's tower faced a Japanese room; and Piero della Francesca joined Hiroshige (see Illustrations). To demonstrate composition in dark-and-light there were sketches from Whistler, Puvis de Chavannes, and Dow's own work, as well as from Sesshu and Kakei.

Although the emblem on the title page read "synthesis," Dow's contribution was to analyse the multiple elements into single components whose arrangement could lead to appreciation of beauty at the very beginning of art instruction. To show how readily synthetic principles could be understood he printed examples of work done in his classes at Pratt.

17. *Composition* (Boston, J. M. Bowles, 1899), p. 7.

18. Fenollosa's comments on color written early in 1899 indicated a similar reluctance, still influenced by *sumi* ideals: "Color is practically inconceivable without the support of the other two. Its differentiations must have shape-boundary however blurred, and derive their force largely from variations of depth; and these color affinities of even a few areas become so complex and subtle, that there is almost no hope for any unity among them unless every element of their force be kept pure and distinct." In "Outline History of Ukiyoye," p. 38, MS in possession of Mrs. S. T. Whatley, Montrose, Ala. Fenollosa maintained that Hogai Kano could pick out the best Western paintings on the basis of photographs, without previous familiarity, that an eye for *notan* and line was fundamental. Cf. Picasso's confirming remarks in Brewster Ghiselin, ed., *The Creative Process* (New York, Mentor, 1955), pp. 56–57.

19. That simple sense experiences should precede complex ones was a Pestalozzian "law" of learning. Fenollosa also pointed out that in musical education "we begin with the simpler problems and advance to the more complex." "Outline History of Ukiyoye," p. 36.

Composition ran through three editions in its first year of publication, and by the time of Fenollosa's final return to the United States in 1901 the new system was spreading rapidly. The Prang Educational Company of Boston, manufacturers of art educational materials, keyed a traveling promotional exhibit to Dow's book with considerable success. And *Composition* rode along on a wave of interest in art education, in arts and crafts, and in Japanese art and life—the same complex of currents which contributed to Fenollosa's successful lecture tours.

In the minds of many educators Japanese art stood for liberation from colorless pencil drawing and from drab schoolroom walls. A Massachusetts observer noted that "the coming of color from Japan has transformed our schoolroom," bringing fresh life to "deserts of black, white, and gray." [20] And at the National Educational Association meeting in 1900 a Minneapolis drawing supervisor commented on the new trend. "There has been during the last two or three years," she said, "a great wave of enthusiasm for the use of the brush and color, which has swept over the educational world and whose influence has been felt in nearly every city and town where drawing is included in the public-school course of study." [21]

20. Henry Turner Bailey, "Japanese Influence in American Schools," *Lotus*, 1 (1903), 35–38. Bailey's remarks are suggestive: "Down to about 1890 . . . the schoolrooms from the seaboard to the slope and from Texas to the Canada line were deserts of black, white, and gray, except for the rosy faces of the children and a girl's dress here and there. Not only were the walls untinted, and pictures unknown, flowers never thought of, and ornaments of every kind non-existent, but every means of expression was colorless. Blackboards and white chalk, gray slates and gray pencils, white paper and black ink, these, and these alone, were used. I was punished for using a vermilion pencil the first day of a new year. . . ." Bailey, at one time Massachusetts State Supervisor of Drawing and editor of *School Arts*, was a leading art educator who published extensively.

21. Bonnie Snow, "The Relative Value of Brush and Pencil as Mediums of Expression," *NEA Addresses and Proceedings*, 1900, p. 516. Miss Snow went on to support the brush as a valuable addition to art education when combined with existing media, noting that objections to the brush "come mainly from those interested in the publication of drawing-books and from the manufacturers of pencils." H. T. Bailey described the situation as follows: "Somewhere about the year 1890 the influence of Japanese art began to be discernible in the exhibition of drawings of public school children. Just how or where it first began leavening, just who was the first to introduce an element so potent, is hard to say. . . . People everywhere were dissatisfied with the old, colorless, mechanical, drypoint mediums, and were anxious for something better. Just at this juncture Japanese art appeared. Japanese art was not unknown in America before 1890, but Jap-

Color was the third basic category of Dow's system and was intended to be introduced after line and *notan* relationships were adequately appreciated. Response to color training was so enthusiastic, particularly in kindergartens and early grades, that Dow's system was modified rapidly to place color on an equal footing with line and *notan*. The manufacturers of colored paper joined the Froebelians in urging creative color expression, and the revised editions of *Composition* reflected this strong demand. The monochromatic ideal of *sumi* paintings was supplemented by expanded comments on the Venetian masters of color. As Dow's former teacher, James Stone, remarked acidly, "Just now some of the drawing teachers are recovering from a severe attack of Japanese notan." [22]

While Dow was busy teaching, Fenollosa continued to lecture on the basic principles of art education. In Detroit and Terre Haute and at his regular summer course at Winona Lake, Fenollosa balanced his historical and cultural lectures with educational material. And he continued the campaign at meetings of teachers whenever his schedule permitted. At the Minneapolis meeting of the National Educational Association in 1902, for example, he addressed a joint session of the departments of art and manual training. He urged the union of art education and manual training on the grounds of their common base in structure and design. At the same time he renewed his attack on representational canons of art and advocated that the term "structural" be adopted in place of such artificial terms as "decorative," "conventional," and "mechanical." "An important practical law in all art work," asserted Fenollosa, "is that all line and color systems should utilize, spring from, carry out, enrich but never obscure, the structural elements given in the uses, forms, and materials of things." "Art," he continued, "consists in the positive value given to each

---

anese art in a usable form was not to be had until about that time. The print, the novel book with its quaint drawings, the fabrics of dainty patterns, and of an excellence all out of proportion to their cost, the good-sized brushes with such point, such snap, and so much better than the moppy 'camel's hair' in quills, so much cheaper than the red sables in their nickeled ferrules,—all these came in abundance just when they could be appreciated by a thousand waiting teachers." In "Japanese Influence in American Schools," *Lotus*, 1 (1903), 36–37.

22. Accurate observation of nature was Stone's central criterion. See his "The Relation of Nature Study to Drawing in the Public Schools," NEA *Addresses and Proceedings*, 1900, pp. 524–30.

other by a group of contiguous visual areas," a principle as true in architecture and basket-weaving as in painting.[23]

Again at Chicago Fenollosa attacked representational criteria before an audience of educators. The occasion was the dedication of Blaine Hall at the University of Chicago's School of Education in May 1904. This time Fenollosa's argument was placed in the context of the culture epoch theory:

> It was about a year ago that Professor Dewey and I were discussing the question whether it is possible to demonstrate that the order of progress in getting the power for an artistic creation in the mind of a single individual—and therefore the psychological order of development of the artist's powers—is practically identical with the historical order of the development of the art powers in the human race. If that could be shown . . . we should then get the broadest possible inductive basis for something like a scientific view of education.[24]

He went on to demonstrate that the historical development of artistic power indicated a growth in the ability to create space relations rather than in the ability to represent nature accurately. And he suggested that realism itself was a natural product of the desire for finer and finer space relations and line relations, turning the tables completely on theorists who brushed aside decoration as pleasant superfluity. If the historical development of art power hinged on the "single impression" which unifies space relations, then a similar development should be the aim of art education for the individual.

The culture epoch theory stirred much speculation among educators, and its implications for the problem of sequence of elements in a curriculum were thoroughly examined and re-examined in the '90s and the following decade in the light of new studies in child psychology.[25] At the Laboratory School at the University of Chicago, a

23. "Possibilities of Art Education in Relation to Manual Training," NEA *Addresses and Proceedings*, 1902, pp. 564–70.

24. "The Fine Arts," *Elementary School Teacher*, 5 (Sept. 1904), 15.

25. For a lucid summary of culture epoch theory in relation to education see C. C. VanLiew, "The Educational Theory of the Culture Epochs Viewed Historically and Critically," *First Yearbook of the National Herbart Society* (1895), reprinted in *Publications of the National Herbart Society 1895–1900* (Chicago, 1908), pp. 67–114. A symposium based on Van Liew's article was published in *Second Yearbook of the National Herbart Society* (Bloomington, Ill., 1896),

center of psychological experiment, the Fenollosa-Dow theories were merged with Dewey's own penchant for stories from life. As a result Laboratory School children up to the age of thirteen drew pictures as stories and developed their decorative capacities in such craft activities as bookbinding and textile work. At thirteen they were introduced to Dow's *Composition* in order that structural beauty might provide the base for any further drawing. Despite Dewey's relegation of synthetic principles to craft work and adolescent drawing, Dow and Fenollosa remained convinced that their principles applied with equal validity throughout the educational process. In his classes at Pratt Dow stressed to prospective art teachers the universal relevance of a synthetic approach.

Dow's classes at Pratt were growing, but the impact of his teaching was geographically limited by a preponderance of students from New York. The year 1904 marked a turning point in his career. Columbia's Teachers College had indicated earlier that they might offer him a position as director of their Department of Fine Arts, with full authority to introduce his system throughout their extensive courses of training. Such a job offered a tremendous opportunity to reform art education on a national scale, but it would mean the end of Dow's own career as an artist. The administrative responsibilities as well as the teaching would demand a full-scale commitment. He obtained a year's leave of absence from Pratt and set off around the world to examine at first hand the arts and crafts of all known civilization.[26] The trip would give him time to decide on future plans, and the chance for a year's travel might not come soon again.

His interest focused on Japan, and Tokyo highlighted his trip. Bearing letters of introduction from Fenollosa, Dow started westward through Canada and sailed out through the Golden Gate in September 1903. Japan presented a whirl of beauty; for Dow the whole countryside was a demonstration of composition at its best. From the first long, dark coastline and the emergent mass of Fuji to the last pine-dotted hillside Dow's impressions were overlaid with images from

---

pp. 56–140; see also John Dewey, "Interpretation of the Culture-Epoch Theory," *Public School Journal*, 15 (1895–96), 233–36.

26. Dow was interested in handicraft throughout his life and pioneered in many fields. Reference to Dow's application of "natural" educational methods to textiles, metal, and press work is made in Rho Fisk Zueblin, "The Arts and Crafts Movements—The Education of the Producer and the Consumer," *Chautauquan*, 37 (May 1903), 174.

Hokusai and Hiroshige, Okyo and Korin. At Tokyo University and the Imperial Museum he watched and studied. He went to performances of Noh plays, visited printmakers and craftsmen, and was instructed in painting by Tomonobu Kano. It was in Tokyo that Dow received a definite invitation to head the Teachers College Fine Arts Department. He accepted before he left Japan and received final confirmation in India, whence he headed westward through Cairo and Athens back to New York.[27]

Dow took up his new duties at Columbia with enthusiasm. His basic course in art structure stressed the cardinal principles of synthesis at every turn of an extensive historical investigation of the arts and crafts of the world. Japanese examples retained an important position, and Fenollosa's writings provided texts and references throughout the seventeen years that Dow taught at Columbia.[28] As the art program grew, the synthetic approach as outlined in *Composition* was amplified in a variety of activities. The Department of Fine Arts in cooperation with the School of Education offered courses for training teachers, supervisors, and directors of art; in cooperation with the School of Practical Arts, courses for professional workers in design, painting, sculpture, industrial arts, and house decoration; in cooperation with model and practice schools, courses for children from kindergarten through high school. All these activities were vitalized by Dow's innovating approach and his personal dedication. He advocated highly personal teaching and kept up with his former students as they fanned out across the country, always ready with advice when asked, or even a visit when it would help.

Dow and Fenollosa maintained close contact in New York, and Fenollosa's articles in *The Golden Age* and his lecturing gave additional support to Dow's frontal campaign. Charles Freer, who had met Dow in 1901, was always helpful. To a supervisor of drawing in the Detroit Public Schools Freer wrote: "Professor Dow is unquestionably the foremost American in art education and his graduates now

27. In India Dow was particularly impressed by the Dravidian art of Madura, the cloth manufacturing of Madras, and the Madras School of Arts, where the finest traditional arts were combined with current crafts; and he was deeply moved by the Taj Mahal. Through Sarah Farmer and Mrs. Ole Bull he contacted several religious sects in Calcutta.

28. As late as 1922 assigned reading for Dow's course, Fine Arts 69, included Fenollosa's *Review of the Chapter on Painting in Gonse's L'Art japonais* (1885), *Outline of the History of Ukiyoye* (1901), and *Epochs of Chinese and Japanese Art* (1912).

working in public and private schools throughout America are accomplishing great good. If your sister is permitted to aid you in properly establishing Professor Dow's methods in Detroit's Public Schools, every intelligent citizen of our city will eventually approve. . . . Make any use of this letter to you appropriate." [29] Detroit was soon in the Dow camp.

Many Europeans were interested in Dow's system from the beginning. *Composition* was translated into French in 1900; foreign students appeared at Dow's 1903 summer school in Ipswich; and that same summer an exhibition of his students' work reached Fribourg in Switzerland. By 1908 controversy was widespread, and at the London International Congress for the Advancement of Drawing and Art Teaching, Fenollosa and Dow found both vocal opposition and warm encouragement. Once more Fenollosa gave eloquent support to the exhibit of work by Dow's students. Dow drew battle lines sharply by declaring to the Congress that there were really only two kinds of art instruction.

> These systems radically different in character . . . I shall call . . . The Academic (Analytic) and The Structural (Synthetic). The Academic method is a reflection of the professional art school. Its origin may be traced to the late Renaissance. Its method is traditional and scientific, making the acquirement of knowledge of nature's facts the first step and the foundation of all progress. The pupil learns to draw, but defers expression until he has attained proficiency in representation. The process is imitative and the standard external.
>
> The structural is a return to the natural method of pre-academic days. It was the method practiced in Europe from ancient times down to the Renaissance, is still used by the Orientals and by all who are independent of scientific domination . . . the purpose is the development of power in the individual. Self expression begins at once, involving all forms of drawing and leads to appreciation. The process is creative and the standard is individual judgment of fine relations. . . . Instead of setting up external nature as the standard, the action of the human mind in harmony-building becomes the foundation for study.[30]

29. C. L. Freer to Miss Alice V. Guysi, July 21, 1906, in Freer Correspondence, MS vol. 20. Miss Guysi's sister was duly appointed and in Sept., 1906, began duties as asst. supervisor of drawing in Detroit's public schools.

30. "Summary of Views Presented," in Dow MSS. Fenollosa was an honorary vice-president of the American Committee to the London Congress.

Dow's position at Columbia assured a strong institutional base for the future spread of the "structural" principles that he and Fenollosa supported so staunchly. The goal of developing "power in the individual" by a focus on "the action of the human mind in harmony-building" recalled Fenollosa's writings in *The Golden Age*. In particular it reflected a psychological side of Fenollosa's philosophy of art, a psychological concern which developed during Fenollosa's later years in New York.

Fenollosa's psychological theories of harmony-building linked the unique work of art with the free individual in an aesthetics of radical individualism. To the extent that this individualism jibed with the ethos of Progressive America it helps account further for the success of the Fenollosa-Dow system. Yet the question remains as to what kinds of personal and social harmony Fenollosa had in mind. His entire career and especially his last years in New York suggest that Fenollosa's aesthetics was part of a personal style of life.

Given two souls of equal mobility and daring, it does not follow
that they will roam over the
fields of possibility in the same
order, rejecting the same by-ways,
following the same skein of clues.
The chances are infinitely that
they will be sucked into diverging currents.

Ernest Fenollosa, "The Bases of
Art Education"

16 · THE INDIVIDUALIST

Fenollosa remained on the fringes of the official worlds of art and
education during his last years. His reputation as a lecturer was secure
and he was well known in educational circles, but his only continuous
affiliation was with the Winona Lake summer meetings. He lived as
an independent scholar. At times he moved more than he might have
wished, as lecture demands had to be met. But generally he moved
freely, following his inclination. Most important, he was able to set
aside substantial stretches of time for concentrating on his own work
—literary, philosophical, and historical.

During his last years there was a quality of marked independence
in Fenollosa's speculations and in his style of life. Thinking and living were alike removed from conventional attitudes and established
forms. Throughout his life Fenollosa was something of an outsider.
He was not alienated. It was not a question of rejection and *anomie*
or even disenchantment; Fenollosa remained buoyantly optimistic,
energetically pursuing wide ambitions. Rather he maintained a certain detachment from habitual forms and institutions. The freely
roaming, sometimes playful quality of his speculations owed something to his separation from widespread American preoccupations

with success and respectability. The breadth of his reference stemmed certainly from wide travel and study; his extraordinary career in Japan and his continuing efforts to mediate between alien cultures and to explain each to each forced his thinking outside common frames. But there remained in his writing and living a note of defiant reserve beginning, possibly, with his mother's death when he was still a boy, a note clear in his youthful poetry, implicit in the special intellectuality of his Harvard career, echoed darkly in his father's suicide, muted during the precocious successes in Japan and Boston, then sounded dramatically in divorce and elopement to a Japan already estranged from its former Imperial Commissioner of Fine Arts. The years from 1896 to 1908 were years of movement and change for Fenollosa, although the pattern was not one of restless wandering. The family household if shifting was still stable and a restful center. These years were rootless in a cosmopolitan sense, a sense of futures not tied to particular past places. Fenollosa had little contact with his relatives in Salem, his former friends, or even his daughter Brenda.[1] His own uprootedness may have emboldened his speculations on the roots of art.

For a time he settled with his wife and stepchildren in Alabama just outside of Mobile in a rambling frame house they called "Kobinata" ("Little Sunshine Hill") after their Tokyo villa. They designed a garden in Alabama style, harmoniously spaced around a winding driveway. Inside Kobinata the walls were hung with familiar kakemonos, and the rooms were made flexible by a few large, elegant Japanese screens. Living in Alabama was inexpensive and the household was leisurely and relaxed. Fenollosa customarily wore loose Japanese robes and slippers around the house, in sharp contrast to the meticulous formal dress of his lecture appearances. Kobinata served as a quiet, congenial home where he could meditate before paintings, undisturbed for hours, and where he could talk freely to

1. A younger brother, William Silsbee Fenollosa (1854–1941), after a few years teaching music in Boston, married and returned to Salem to live; he had no children. No letters or evidence of close contacts between the brothers survive. Nor is there evidence of contact with his stepmother, Annie E. (Kinsman) Fenollosa (d. 1911), or with his much younger half-brothers, Clarence, Sidney, and Manuel Fenollosa. Clarence and Manuel died before 1900. Brenda Fenollosa (1883–1959) lived with her mother until Brenda married (July 11, 1906) Howard Morris Johnson. Brenda was remarried (June 30, 1913) to Moncure Biddle (1882–1960). Lizzie Goodhue Millett, the first Mrs. Ernest Fenollosa, never remarried.

Mary and the children of the many projects he was carrying forward.

The lecture circuit ran well north of Kobinata, however, and Fenollosa made New York a second base of operations. In 1903 he took an apartment on Morningside Heights, and that winter and the next, when he was not on the road lecturing, he worked at Columbia University, studying Chinese literature, history, and art and helping Professor Friedrich Hirth inaugurate the systematic study of Far Eastern civilization at Columbia.[2] After 1905 Fenollosa stayed in an apartment at the Hotel Barstow on West Twenty-third Street, a location which was more convenient for city life. Along with his scholarly writing he worked on fiction and on several plays. His wife Mary continued to work on her own novels, some of which were quite successful. *Truth Dexter* (1901) was followed by *The Breath of the Gods* (1905) and *The Dragon Painter* (1906), the first two under the pen name Sidney McCall. A book of verse, *Out of the Nest* (1899), and an essay, *Hiroshige, the Artist of Mist, Snow, and Rain* (1901), added to her reputation as a writer. Her work was conventional in its style but warm and imaginative, and it showed a serious professional concern.

Ernest and Mary Fenollosa were both somewhat romantic figures; they were a striking couple—handsome, accomplished, articulate, widely traveled, curious about everything. They could have cultivated an extensive social life. They seem rather to have preferred their own work and a small group of friends, usually people of some seriousness. There was George Krapp, a pioneer philologist at Columbia, Horace Fletcher, a prolific writer on "menticulture," George Jay Smith, a former Columbia professor of English, now a supervisor of teacher examinations for New York schools, and, of course, Arthur Wesley Dow. Fenollosa was well aware of the reform "isms" which swirled around him in New York—*The Golden Age* argued socialism, modern dance, and women's rights—and his own art reforms rode some of these currents, but he kept his distance. His enthusiasms remained those of the scholar: solitude for reading and independent work, the stimulus of serious talk, the delights of music, painting, and the theater.

The tone of Fenollosa's New York milieu is preserved in an outline of one of the plays that he was working on during his last winter at the Barstow on Twenty-third Street. It was to be "a modern morality

2. Hirth held the first appointment to the Dean Lung Chair of Oriental Languages, endowed in 1902 by Horace Walpole Carpentier.

play" with "the Individualist" as the central figure opposed by "the forces which, in our society today, are tending to crush individualism." His notes made the theme explicit; its variations recalled the strictures on over-personality framed in Boston fifteen years earlier. "The solid value, the dire need of true individuality, must be clearly distinguished from crankhood, mere idiosyncrasy, mere personality. These may be embodied in minor characters."

These minor characters indicate the distance Fenollosa had traveled from Boston. Aligned with the Individualist are:

The Subjectivist—Bohemian, idiosyncratic
The Honest Crank—objective, but hasty
The Socialist Reformer—an anarchist
The Aesthetic Idealist

In the opposition are:

The Social Leader, who fears what may be "talked"
The Puritan Tyrant
The Employer of Labor, who dictates political views of his laborers
The Bromide by nature and education
The Newspaper Man, who deifies the average
The Educationalist, who grafts
The Scientific Pedant

"The individualist is the center of a Bohemian group, therefore might suppose him to be a great young inspired preacher in New York, a sort of modern and wiser Savonarola, a better Dr. Parkhurst . . . not bound to the church. Yet he is not an evangelist of ordinary method. His windmills are conformists and conformism." [3]

The outline was evidently dashed off quickly, sandwiched between notes on paintings, and laid aside along with a mass of works in progress.

The Individualist is a familiar figure in Fenollosa's writings. An "inspired preacher . . . not bound to the church" tilting at conform-

3. "Notes Taken Before Mr. Freer's Collection in Detroit," MS in Freer Gallery of Art, Washington, D.C.; a six-page outline dated Nov. 12, 1907, is written in this notebook, otherwise concerned with paintings. Of Fenollosa's other plays and novels none remain save as they were incorporated in his wife's published novels. Of these *The Breath of the Gods* (Boston, Little, Brown, 1905) and *The Dragon Painter* (Boston, Little, Brown, 1906) have Fenollosan touches.

ism by new methods; the description fits the evangelist of Fenollosa's art gospel preaching the continual renewal of life through art. Through art men can be edged out of the ruts of habit by a glimpse of new possibilities significantly ordered, limitless possibilities risked by a single man. The intense focus of a work of art in its permanent achievement of individuality reminds men that in their own lives they might be individuals, if only for a moment. Music and poetry, with their sequential order, provide analogies for a man's coping with a sequence of moments over the duration of his lifetime. Fenollosa insisted again and again—which is why this view must be stressed —that the analogy of art with life was crucial and that since such an analogy is always individual its impact is rarely conformist.

The sketchiness of his outline underscores a major difficulty. This reiterated theme of individuality remained vague, easily dismissed as a well-meant plea for sweetness and light. The characters in Fenollosa's morality play help define the kinds of conformity which reduce possibilities and the kinds of single-mindedness which tend to avoid conformity, but the quality of the individualist's own life remains obscure. The individuality of the "great young inspired preacher" might lie simply in his being inspired. The individualist's ideal aspiration might be to remain always aspiring as, for example, in Tennyson's "Ulysses," where the voyaging itself replaces any attained objective, where "some work of noble note" is sought after but remains "evermore unseen." [4] Fenollosa's pile of projects begun but unfinished suggests his delight in grand visions and in the high excitement of the first vivid imaginings of a great work. The question of completed achievement, which confronts any would-be individualist, confronts him. His philosophy asserts the radical relevance of achieved order to individual life, including, certainly, his own. What evidence of creation, then, during these years of his independence supports his recurrent advocacy of individuality?

In 1906 there was direct evidence of attained order in a fresh statement of Fenollosa's aesthetic theory and in the completion of a monumental history of Chinese and Japanese artistic civilization. Both statements, the aesthetics terse and intense, the history sweeping and eloquent, rested on thirty years of experience and speculation, lecturing and writing.

Fenollosa's philosophy of art reflected a widening of his aesthetic

4. See W. E. Houghton's excellent discussion of "Enthusiasm" in his *Victorian Frame of Mind*, esp. pp. 291–97.

experience and a gradual fusion of Western and Eastern theories. Its emphasis of attention shifted as the role of art in his own life changed in the course of his long journey from Salem to the Hotel Barstow on Twenty-third Street. His final view, which linked beauty with freedom, change, and individuality, was a philosophy of life which mirrored the varied possibilities he had himself glimpsed and ordered. In a sense his aesthetics explains the quality of his career. Throughout Fenollosa's life his experiences with art—whether music, painting, poetry, theater, or philosophy—drew him outside of himself, away from the shy self-concern of his youth and, later, out from an inward mysticism. In philosophical terms the objective reality of the work of art insistently modified both solipsist and idealist tendencies. The work of art was clearly itself the stage where tentative solutions were discovered, where ordered selections existed; beauty could not be simply an idea or response in the mind of its maker or appreciator, nor could it exist at some non-sensible level of reality.

Yet Fenollosa had been swept away by Hegel at first. In his early efforts to revive Japanese national art he gave a formal Hegelian interpretation to traditional Sino-Japanese artistic canons. In the '90s in Boston his philosophizing retained an idealistic emphasis and a rhetoric which was often florid. Not until he left Boston and thereby, symbolically, left mysticism, aestheticism, and aristocracy did his artistic theories become individualized and more empirical and his language more vernacular. As his activities involved him increasingly in the pragmatic controversies of American education, "Idea," as a philosophical category, tended to disappear, perhaps because art teachers who talked idealism often practiced academic methods limited to "moral" themes. Fenollosa kept the term "synthesis" to describe aesthetic experience as a whole, but his attention gradually focused on the psychological processes of creation and appreciation, the flashing glimpse of possibilities uniquely ordered. The direction of his thinking shifted from rationalistic categories toward a vitalist gestalt.

In a series of articles in *The Golden Age* Fenollosa offered what was described as "the most authoritative statement of his principles and methods yet printed." The series was entitled "The Bases of Art Education," and the second article on "The Logic of Art" brought his analysis of aesthetic experience into a fresh stage worth considering at length. His approach was logical but with a pronounced psychological and organic accent; his language was idiomatic, his examples calculated to persuade that idol of Progressive reformers, the average man, to make distinctly unusual efforts.

Reason works through the bee's hexagonal cells and the beaver's primitive engineering. Much more does it work in an artist's brain, much more through the ways in which colors—and sounds, too—pull and strain and transform and irradiate each other. See how the simple lines of a fine building demand their rights down to the infinitesimal fraction of an inch; how, if we redraw them, trying a thousand specious changes, they strain and chatter—even swear—and finally change back in smart protest to their original positions. It isn't that you do it; it's the thing itself that defends its own integrity. The proportions, the transitions from rectangle to curve, the accent and color of the massed reliefs, the orchestration of the shadows—all these are features, as sharp as in an individual face, which the successful artist seems rather to have discovered than created, as if he found them somewhere in space where they had lain concealed, awaiting him, since the foundation of things.

But there is reason and reason. Anybody can make conventional classifications, quote definitions, and then learn to read the labels on the bundles which nature hands us. . . . The living soul is an individual who moulds its face into a unique mask. It cannot be labeled, because no one feature can stand for the whole. Change one line a hair's breadth, and the whole is gone. The force lies in the interplay of the parts, in which all are of equal value. . . .

Here I lay a spot of red paint down on my canvas. Next I choose a green which I dot near it. The red is immediately changed, and so is the green. In contrast to the green the red has taken fire, and the green now glows inwardly like an emerald. The reaction is mutual. . . .

So I might go on creating, that is, finding added colors, each one of which would modify all the previous reactions in the way of making them all finer. The process will grow progressively harder, until somewhere in the increasing complexity we are likely—nay, all but the color-master is *sure*—to make a misstep, a mischoice, that is, to add a color, which, in forcing the inevitable combination, weakens, dulls, disturbs the old balances, and instead of piling up glories, stains all with mud. Such a process followed at random inevitably leads to mud;—most color attempts of ordinary artists *are* mud,—confused, jarring, self-obliterating color passages, like the jumble of sounds rising from a crowded street—no clear tone, but chaos. If, however, the magic has been accomplished,—as may happen now and then in real art,—and ten colors, say (a modest allowance), have been mutually juxtaposed so that their multiple cross relations have only clarified and irradiated each other, then no one is cause and no one effect, for all is cause and all effect. The color effect may be called a color individual which has no definition, no possible existence, except in that one stable equation. There it lies, created or discovered, whichever you like, out of ordinary dead pigments. When Nature plays this game for us, as in some sunset pageant, we cry "How beautiful!"—admitting that the reason of it, the wonderful cross harmony, is in things too. . . .

An entirely new set of mental powers must be brought into play, a new calculus, to sweep like a lightning flash through these billions and trillions of possibilities of which the infinitely larger part produce mutually disturbing effects; to throw these away instantaneously in great blocks; and to seize by instinct upon the few scattered regions where hope of success may lie. It really is done, as the psychology of art shows,—as every truly creative artist knows,—by being almost superhumanly sensitive to the mutual pulls of all possible colors upon each other and of all possible lines; to feel their several tensions vibrating in a microscopic balance; to rush along the criss-cross paths of their subtle affinities and actually see them displaying the secret process of their crystallization. . . . We see the results, and we can describe the nature of the process; but the process is so incredibly rapid that we must experience it, follow it, on its own terms, in order to believe in its magic efficacy.

But, wonderful though it may be, I am ready to assert,—and this is the outcome of many experiments in both hemispheres, —that this magnificent faculty is possessed in a considerable degree by every one of us. Every child born into this world is endowed with it as part of his humanity; but the trouble is that we ordinarily lose it in early childhood just because a medieval bigotry for the *barbaracelarent* logic—an obsession quite as fatal as Confucian classics—forces it into disuse and atrophy. The chief condition under which we might enjoy and develop it is merely that we exercise it. Whatever else art education may be, it must at least involve the constant exercise of this peculiar faculty of feeling tensions and seeing wholes in groups of color and line,—just as surely as we learn to walk by walking. . . .

The self that we here find is something far deeper than the froth of personality, something that belongs to all free spirit, as to nature. In short, the trained soul of the artist, while not itself the principle of crystallization, is just the peculiar solvent or medium in which the crystallization occurs. The real crystallization is in the units of the art itself; and thus I may close by repeating the half humorous definition which I once gave off-hand at a symposium of sages. "Art is a saturated solution of all the involved elements in terms of each other." [5]

This was Fenollosa's final analysis of aesthetic experience, and it reiterated his faith in a root order in the midst of flux as well as his faith in the individual man's ability to create significant orderings of his own. The metaphors of this compressed philosophical statement made it clear that the individualist could not simply aspire, he must act. Forces continually in tension and collision demanded an active ordering. The seminal quality of Fenollosa's idea of "a saturated solution" would become evident later in avant-garde poetry and painting. At the moment, in 1906, the "golden age" seemed to lie not far ahead. The drama of history was entering a new and perhaps final act, in which the cultures of East and West would merge into a single world culture whose rich variety would provide the setting for a new culmination of individual life. An important step for Westerners led away from parochial thinking in the direction of increased understanding of the civilization of the Far East. To this end Fenollosa concentrated during the spring and early summer of 1906 on completing his interpretation of the historical development of Far Eastern art.

Several months earlier in a *Golden Age* article on "The Roots of Art" he suggested an extensive context for his art historical writing. Art was rooted in society; its creative eras were linked to mass participation and democratic judgments. It was intimately bound up with intellectual currents, with the level of technical knowledge, with the usefulness for a particular way of living of "solid things appropriately placed," and with the trained minds of creators and apprecia-

5. "The Logic of Art," *The Golden Age*, 1 (May 1906), 230–35.

tors. All these roots of art and their interrelations entered Fenollosa's history, and in nearly every direction he broke new ground, aided immensely by the scholarship of his Japanese friends and colleagues.[6]

In *Epochs of Chinese and Japanese Art* Fenollosa departed radically from those historians who classified art work according to materials used, literary descriptions, representational facility, or decorative qualities. No attempt had yet been made to relate artistic achievements to the historical development of Sino-Japanese civilization. "Art," wrote Fenollosa,

> is the power of the imagination to transform materials—to transfigure them—and the history of Art should be the history of this power rather than the history of the materials through which it works. At creative periods all forms of Art will be found to interact. From the building of a great temple to the outline of a bowl which the potter turns upon his wheel, all effort is transfused with a single style. Thus classification should be epochal, and in attempting thus to treat it for the first time it becomes possible partially to trace style back to its social and spiritual roots.[7]

Most Western critics and historians either dismissed Far Eastern art on the grounds of its inaccurate drawing or else set it apart from the mainstream of European art and praised its decorative qualities. Fenollosa insisted that common aesthetic qualities united the art of East and West. "We are approaching the time," he wrote,

> when the art work of all the world of man may be looked upon as one, as infinite variations in a single kind of mental and social

6. "The Roots of Art," *The Golden Age*, 1 (April 1906), 160–63. Particularly helpful were Kainen Mori on Chinese literature, Nagao Ariga on Chinese and Japanese philosophy and history, and the Kano painters. Throughout his seventeen years in Japan Fenollosa made extensive notes on all his studies, on literature, the theater, history, philosophy as well as art. One such MS, "The Outline Sketch of the History of Doctrines in China," runs to 763 pages in a detailed account of the period from the prehistoric emperors to the 12th-century reign of the Sung emperor and artist, Hui Tsung (or Kiso Kotei as Fenollosa calls him).

7. *Epochs*, 1, xxvii. Some twenty years later Langdon Warner confirmed Fenollosa's claim to priority: "Though Western knowledge of Oriental art has progressed since his death, it has followed the path blazed by him. While his information was derived from his Japanese friends, his conclusions were his own and they were formed at a time when there was no background of Western appreciation." "Ernest Francisco Fenollosa," *Dictionary of American Biography* (New York, Scribner's, 1930), 3, 326.

effort. . . . If we come to see that classification is only a convenience, valuable chiefly for chronological grouping, and that
the real variations are as infinite as the human spirit, though
educed by social and spiritual changes, we come to grasp the
real and larger unity of effort that underlies the vast number of
technical varieties. A universal scheme or logic of art unfolds,
which as easily subsumes all forms of Asiatic and of savage art
and the efforts of children as it does accepted European schools.
We find that all art is harmonious spacing, under special technical conditions that vary.[8]

On this logical foundation Fenollosa sought to build an artistic
whole of his own. In method *Epochs* was admittedly "a single, personal life-impression," an attempt to create a unified interpretation
by means of proportion, an effort to give to history the structural relations of art. The historian was concerned with interpreting relations in time analogous to a painter's creation of relations in space.
The historian's creation was confined to a finished past, but in reconstruction he had also to order cultural space. The historian of art
must consider the relations of moments of achieved beauty to the
cultural conditions in which these moments occurred. By concentrating on moments of high artistic achievement and passing lightly
over the intervening years of mediocrity, Fenollosa hoped to pene-
trate to the cultural roots of aesthetic imagination and to create at
the same time a "crystallization" of historical possibilities which
would convey the "essential humanity" of Far Eastern peoples. Accordingly, he complemented his aesthetic principle of harmonious
spacing with an exploration of art's relation to free individuality. His
findings confirmed his belief that artistic creativity depends upon a
free society in which individuality is unfettered by formalism. He
set out to write art history as "a record of the causes that have produced unique individuals," and in each of the peak epochs of Far
Eastern art he found a climate of intellectual freedom.[9]

8. *Epochs,* 1, xxiv.
9. *Epochs,* 1, 72. Much of Fenollosa's historical material was drawn from his
own MS, "The Outline Sketch of the History of Doctrines in China," which
focused on intellectual history, on the fortunes of Taoist, Buddhist, and Confucian ideas projected against a background of military, political, and economic
events. Each chapter of the MS includes a section on the "acts and lives" of
"leading Chinese personages," for the most part philosophers, artists, and literary
men. There is little discussion of economic or political freedom in this MS or in
Epochs.

The central movement in Fenollosa's historical drama stemmed from the dialectical struggle between Confucian socialism and an individualism associated with Taoist and Buddhist beliefs and practices. Opposing Chinese attitudes were set early, when Confucius formulated the common ends for which individual freedom was to be curbed and Laotse, in the South, "the land of freedom and natural beauty," advocated the absolute freedom of the Ego as a base for "a more internal morality than can be mechanically deduced from utilitarian ends." [10] In considering the Han period (208 B.C.– A.D. 221), with its military expansion, general prosperity, and wide geographic contacts, Fenollosa traced the best art to non-Confucian sources. The great artistic flowerings of the T'ang and Sung periods he traced directly to widespread encouragement of free individuality. In the confident national unity of T'ang China (618–907 A.D.) "the lordly Confucians of the North" joined their Buddhist and Taoist brothers from the South in an atmosphere of religious liberty, and an eclectic individuality thrived. Of Li Po, laureate for a time and champion of personal freedom, Fenollosa wrote: "Nature, man, ethics, Taoist fancies, and Buddhist devotion, all enter his verses as natural friends." [11] T'ang painting he considered to have reached its height in association with the mystical Buddhism of Tendai, a sect of "positive, optimistic Northern Buddhism," in which by "self-directed illumination" and "loving work" in the real world man strives to evolve salvation.[12] In the later art of Sung (960–1280), especially in Southern Sung (1127–1280), the spirit of Ch'an (Zen) Buddhism, with its artistic worship of nature, carried Chinese civilization to heights unequaled in human history, and again Fenollosa found the ideal of individuality at the center of the illumination. The decline of Sung art, as with all artistic declines in China, was attributed to the "puritan" Confucian formalists, who stifled personal freedom and aligned themselves readily with ruling hierarchies, whether Mongol, Ming, or Manchu. It was in Japan that the ideals of Sung culture were preserved during their continued Chinese eclipse. At the base

10. *Epochs*, 1, 15. Fenollosa moved quickly over the Empire-inaugurating reign of Shih Huang Ti (247 B.C.–210 B.C.) without considering its sweeping reorganizations. In his historic burning of the books the Ch'in tyrant broke with the past in the spirit of a "Nietzscheism backing raw freedom and force against formalism." *Epochs*, 1, 16.

11. *Epochs*, 1, 119.

12. *Epochs*, 1, 121–23. Fenollosa was confirmed into Tendai Buddhism in 1885. See above, Ch. 10, for the progressive and aesthetic aspects of his interpretation of Tendai.

of the artistic peak of Ashikaga Japan (1392–1568) Fenollosa found
Zen ideals of free individual speculation, intellectual and artistic.
Subsequent summits of Japanese art he interpreted as reflexes of
the historical alternation between a socially extensive artistic freedom and the imposition of formal rules by a static elite. In every
case artistic vitality was found to depend on the freedom of artists.

The kind of cosmopolitan tone which marked Fenollosa's writing
is evident in a passage from *Epochs* in which he explains the failure
of any Ming renaissance in terms of the decision as early as 1421 to
shift China's capital from the Yangtse valley to the far northeast
Tartar capital of Peking. Peking, with its scant artistic traditions, little more than a taste for material splendor, offered a prize for conservative Confucian literati, who "leaped unchecked to the head of
the Tartar horses" and guided their alien masters in statecraft. "It
is strange," wrote Fenollosa,

> that both Mongols and Manchus should have lent ready ear to
> the repressive propaganda of both Confucian atheists and Chris-
> tian scholars, but should have thrown down between them all
> that poetic Taoist and Buddhist idealism which has been the
> core of Chinese imaginative life. Of the more honest of those
> Confucians, it was no doubt a definite desire to make China into
> a moral machine, where every rite, ceremony, industry, and even
> thought should be conducted along pre-established formulae.
> Their ideal is uniformity; their standard is not insight but au-
> thority; their conception of literature is bounded by the dic-
> tionary; what they hate most is any manifestation of human
> freedom. . . . Of the less honest, the motive was doubtless to
> further that method of absorbing all local official patronage by
> which tax lists became legitimate prey for extortion. The modern
> Confucian government of China is a government of corrupt
> Puritans; a ring more closely monopolistic than Tammany's, and
> worse than Tammany's because of its moral hypocrisy. . . . The
> Mandarin class is China's Old Man of the Sea, a parasitic
> growth that chokes the life out of any effort at readaptation.[13]

Fenollosa's analogies are wide, perhaps, but his argument sticks
in the mind, a prelude to his savage attack on what he saw as the
specious formalism and imitative narrowness of *bunjingwa* painting.
On amateur calligraphy Fenollosa remained a Kano.

13. *Epochs*, 2, 142–43.

Fenollosa's panoramic history was weakened, like most bold general hypotheses, by overstatement. His sweeping account of Sino-Japanese development was seriously flawed by lack of information on the art of post-Sung China, notably Ming painting. As a result the decline of Chinese civilization was overdrawn. Some of Fenollosa's specific attributions have been corrected by later research. But his work stands as a major imaginative act, a pioneering effort to order the shape and flow of a great civilization while respecting its unique moments and beauties—the whole narrated in vivid language. References to Western art and history seldom intrude; rather they suggest affinities within a world historical evolution still in process. Despite its often impassioned rhetoric, possibly because of it, Fenollosa's *Epochs of Chinese and Japanese Art* challenged world scholarship to view history and philosophy as well as art from a cosmopolitan perspective. Fenollosa wrote as a passionate cosmopolitan, and it colored his history, but it is that tone which sets *Epochs* apart from parochial nationalist writings, and even from no less parochial regional, that is Western, standards of judgment. Fenollosa's ways of proceeding, evolutionary and cosmopolitan, are, of course, Western; the point is that these particular Western ideas were less limiting than most and rarely have they been matched so effectively by experience and grasp. As a result *Epochs* marks an important gateway for genuinely international scholarship.

Fenollosa had scarcely finished the major work on his history when he was called back to Winona Lake for lectures and to Detroit for a pleasant visit with Charles Freer and Gaston Migeon, art director of the Louvre, who was touring the world's collections of Far Eastern art. This was typical of the fast pace which Fenollosa set for himself. The next winter in New York, for example, his schedule included a series of twenty-four lectures on world art at Miss Kearney's School and a twelve-lecture series on Far Eastern art at American Institute Hall. When he went abroad in 1908 for what turned out to be his last trip, he had lecture bookings for the next five years, most of them in series long enough so that he could organize and refine portions for written works in progress.[14]

14. Freer supervised Migeon's tour of the United States and set up his itinerary to focus on the centers of Far Eastern Art—New York, Boston, Chicago, Detroit, and Montreal, where Sir William Van Horne's collection was of the first rank. Migeon recognized the value of Fenollosa's work and supervised a French edition of *Epochs*, entitled *L'Art en Chine et au Japon*, adaptation et préface par Gaston

Fenollosa enjoyed excellent health, aside from an occasional bout with influenza, and there was no letup in his activities during his last winter. Particularly interesting were plans for a noncommercial exhibition tour of Chinese and Japanese art which Freer, among others, was promoting. Freer had followed Migeon to Japan, both men armed with letters from Fenollosa, and after a delightful visit Freer returned to the United States enthusiastic about international understanding. Formal plans were made at a Nippon Club meeting in New York in February 1908. The proposed show of works on loan from the Japanese government would start in New York and tour Boston, Philadelphia, Washington, Buffalo, Chicago, and St. Louis. Freer obtained President Roosevelt's approval and the support of art leaders in key cities. The Japanese government was cooperative, and Freer's offer of a permanent pavilion in New York improved prospects. Fenollosa guided the executive committee in New York, but negotiations proceeded slowly.

That same winter Fenollosa gave a lecture series in the Hall of the National Society of Craftsmen and contributed to Gustav Stickley's widely circulated journal, the *Craftsman*. The lectures covered Far Eastern art from painting through architecture and landscape gardening. Tanyu had designed gardens, as had the great Kanawoka, a painter of legendary talent who was "a *spacer* and chief among landscape gardeners of Engi." [15] Fenollosa had shaped his own garden at Kobinata in sweeping curves, and he maintained that garden design, like all art, was a matter of harmonious spacing.

The *Craftsman* gave full coverage to Fenollosa's activities and published several of Mary's poems. Editor Stickley had started in 1901 to spread the gospel of Morris and Ruskin but had developed on his own a bungalow socialism which replaced Gothic arches with logs, Morris chairs with mission furniture, and medieval masons with do-it-yourself rock-studded cement. Fenollosa suspected the easy mediocrity of amateur craftsmen but supported the craft revival as evidence of a broadening art consciousness in America.

Fenollosa sailed for Europe in the spring of 1908 with Mary and young Erwin Scott ("Noshi"), his sixteen-year-old stepdaughter. In

---

Migeon (Paris, Hachette, 1913). A letter from Fenollosa to Freer, March 12, 1907, indicates attendance at the American Institute lectures averaged 75 persons at $2 per person. The lectures were sponsored by Yamanaka, the art dealer.

15. *Epochs*, 1, 158. Note also: "To treat landscape as if it were a very serious way of building, and a splendid way of building, with the Japanese is centuries old." EFF, "The Fine Arts," *Elementary School Teacher*, 5 (1904), 25.

London he attended the International Congress for the Advancement of Drawing and Art Teaching. (He was respectable enough by then to be made an honorary vice-president of the American committee.) Touring the Low Countries, Germany, and France, he guided a special group of students around the galleries and enjoyed the added delights of music and the theater. In Munich a magnificent performance of Goethe's *Faust* stirred him deeply. In Paris, while waiting for new lantern slides to be made up, he surveyed the contemporary art scene, reporting critically in the September *Craftsman* on the imitative "decadence of French influence" in the Paris Salon. His only kind words in this article, which was the last he wrote, were for the liveliness of a few Spanish paintings; ironically, it was his first published appreciation of the artistic possibilities of his father's native Spain.

In September 1908 Fenollosa was back in London, working at the British Museum and greatly excited over the discovery that Alaskan walrus tusk carvings tended to confirm his theory that a single school of design extending to the rim of the Pacific had united East and West at the dawn of history. If this were so, America's artistic merger with the Far East would be a reunion of the separated threads of world history. One morning—it was September 21, the day before the Fenollosas were due to sail for home—Fenollosa had a sharp heart attack. The doctor put him to bed and prescribed complete quiet but felt that his recovery was so complete that plans for sailing could go forward. Resting in bed Fenollosa listened to his stepdaughter read aloud several of his favorite poems from *The Oxford Book of English Verse*. He asked for Rossetti's "Blessed Damozel," and as she was reading it, he cried out, "Mary," and died from a final attack.

Fenollosa's ashes remained in London's Highgate cemetery until, as he had wished, they were transported to Japan to the hills overlooking Lake Biwa and the gardens of Miidera temple.[16] There, on the first anniversary of his death, his ashes were reburied; the chief

16. The question is complicated as to who transported Fenollosa's ashes and how. Mary Fenollosa, in her preface to *Epochs*, refers to the removal as a "unique and beautiful tribute paid to Professor Fenollosa by the Japanese government." Ezra Pound, in his introduction to 'Noh' (1916), states, "the Japanese government sent a warship for his body." Aline Saarinen, in *The Proud Possessors* (1958), asserts that Charles Freer paid for the removal of Fenollosa's ashes. Mrs. S. T. Whatley, Fenollosa's stepdaughter, stated to the author in November 1961 that no warship was involved and that expenses were paid by Yamanaka, the New York art dealer and friend of Fenollosa.

priest chanted the familiar prayers of Fenollosa's Buddhist order and cast many-colored paper lotus leaves on the fresh grave. Within a year the site for mourning ceremonies was marked by an open pagoda with five stone memorials: a Fujiwara type of granite monument erected by the Japanese government, two stone lanterns, a stone flower vase, and a stone incense burner, dedicated by Arthur Wesley Dow and Charles Freer of the United States, Gaston Migeon of France, and Laurence Binyon of Great Britain. It was a cosmopolitan memorial.

Mourning ceremonies have been held annually in Homei Chapel at Miidera. Cakes and flowers and poems are placed before a portrait of Fenollosa which hangs in the center rear of the main hall. One such poem, written by Baron Tsuji, reads: "Hence becoming a part of Japan's earth you may rest nearer the Buddha." In the graveyard the pagoda around the five memorial pieces is covered on three sides with white cloth. In front are apples and persimmons. On the twelfth anniversary of his death a twelve-foot stone monument was dedicated in Uyeno Park on the grounds of the Tokyo Art School, which Fenollosa had helped found thirty-three years earlier. On the monument a carved portrait of Fenollosa heads an extensive calligraphic inscription recounting his career.[17]

At the end of the second World War the United States State Department and the Art Commission for Protection of Monuments sent to Japan Langdon Warner, one of America's leading art historians and connoisseurs, a scholar and teacher trained at the Boston Museum of Fine Arts. On landing Warner went directly to Miidera and placed a wreath on Fenollosa's grave.[18]

17. A picture of the monument and a translation of the inscription appeared in the *Boston Evening Transcript*, Dec. 24, 1920, under the heading "Japan's Tribute to Fenollosa," with an accompanying tribute by William Sturgis Bigelow. When Bigelow died in 1926, his ashes were sent to Japan in accordance with his wishes and placed in a grave on the slope below Fenollosa's pagoda in the grounds of Miidera Temple.

18. Lamont Moore, former director of the Yale Art Gallery, drew my attention to Langdon Warner's fine act.

PART 5 · *Metamorphoses*

The etymologist finds the dead-
est word to have been once a brilliant picture. Language is fossil
poetry.

Ralph Waldo Emerson, *The
Poet*

17 · A POETICS FOR COSMOPOLIS

In his efforts to renew the individuality of art and the art of individuality, Fenollosa worked primarily toward the development and communication of a visual language, a grammar by means of which all
men could share the liberating experience of an artist's ordering of
limitless possibilities. He advocated artistic fusion with the Far East
as a prelude to more general cultural fusion, and Japanese art offered a promising medium of merger. It had already demonstrated
its seminal force in Western painting and design; it was available for
broad distribution in the form of prints and books and brushes; and
it embodied the ideals of Far Eastern civilization in a persuasive and
communicative form. Yet Fenollosa's philosophy of aesthetic possibilities carried implications for all the arts, and in poetry, especially,
his Far Eastern researches and speculations supported Western developments of continuing significance, pointing the way toward a
modern world culture. In the poetry of Ezra Pound, Fenollosa's lotus
was reborn and its aesthetic and historical implications further clarified. Pound did not discover Fenollosa's writings until 1912. When
he did his excitement over his "treasures," as he called them, was intense. Fenollosa's papers were a "ball of light" in Pound's hand, leading directly to *Cathay* and 'Noh' and on into *The Cantos*. In *The
Cantos* Fenollosa's ideas became part of a poetic vision of cosmopolis
that is also cosmopolitan in its challenge to readers to follow the
many skeins from the world's literatures which Pound has woven
together.

Fenollosa's poetics, the most important of his literary legacies, developed within a framework of philosophical speculations, study of Far Eastern poetry, and, most important, Fenollosa's own visual experience, in which painting, calligraphy, and Noh theatrical tableaus all coalesced. His own poetry did not bear out his radical poetics; it remained conventional for the most part. Of Fenollosa's favorite poets—Emerson, Longfellow, Shakespeare, Keats, Browning, and Rossetti—only Shakespeare and, to a lesser extent, Keats bear out Fenollosa's theory that since poetic language mirrors nature's process it demands verbs which transfer forces from concrete image to concrete image. Even though Fenollosa knew his Shakespeare well, it was the Far East which stimulated his speculations. In terms of these Far Eastern stimuli it is clear that his work with Chinese and Japanese poetry began well after his visual aesthetics had taken shape.

As early as 1894 Fenollosa suggested the focus of his later poetics. Talking to a group of art students in Boston he emphasized the role of the image in imagination. The very word "imagination" derives from "image" and refers, he declared, to the "faculty" of thinking and feeling in terms of a single image—"not a fancy, not a dream, not a vague blur of consciousness, but a clear, unbroken image." "Every element," he continued, "that enters into an imaginative group must be plastic and sensitive, full, as it were, of chemical affinities," which the mind organizes.[1]

From the beginning Fenollosa attacked analytical thinking, the dissection of experience into neat classifications, and proposed that poetry, like painting, should be synthetic. His first published remarks on poetic theory, which appeared in *The Lotos* in 1896, anticipated the later efforts of Ezra Pound and the Imagists to concentrate and condense poetic language in order to charge words with maximum meaning. "Synthetic thinking," wrote Fenollosa,

> demands a pregnant language; rich, juicy, significant, full words, charged with intense meaning at the center, like a nucleus, and then radiating out toward infinity, like a great nebula. This is poetry, the making a word stand for as much thought and feeling as possible, and that through the mutual modifications of the suc-

1. *Imagination in Art* (Boston, 1894), pp. 5, 9. Toward the close of this discussion Fenollosa made his only published reference to Kant, when he compared his description of imagination to Kant's conception of the faculty of judgment.

cessive words. No literary production which does not have this synthesis in its meanings, principle, and illustration, fact and ideal, the organic fibre of the world, all packed away together in its lightest phrases, plays a part in the sphere of literature as a fine art.[2]

In his studies of Buddhist painting, particularly work stimulated by Zen and Tendai precepts, Fenollosa saw nature mirrored in art in an unusual and effective fashion. The artists had aimed to create living forms by ordering the materials of their medium in a way harmonious with the root order of the natural world, an order mirrored not by unartistic realism but by artistic "unrealism." The purpose of the Zen teacher, according to Fenollosa, was to let the student's mind "build up its own view of the subtle affinities between things; to construct an organic web of new categories."[3] In individual confrontation of nature a Zen artist might glimpse the interrelationships of all life. In painting, this sense of interrelatedness was conveyed not only by the heightened suggestion of simple, condensed forms but by using a pictorial shorthand to combine related forms. For example, a pine branch might be arranged in the shape of a stork's leg, or pine needles might be patterned after fish scales (see Illustrations). Actual words, Chinese written characters of an ideographic type, were often used in a painting to add their visual and historical overtones.

The extensive radiations of suggestion which such methods made possible are evident in a traditional Japanese technique for painting the plum, one of the highly regarded "Four Paragons." The plum, first tree of the year to bloom, takes on the shape of a sleeping dragon in old age, but every spring it renews its youth and beauty with vigorous fresh branches crowded with buds and blossoms.

> The tree branches with their interlacings reproduce the spirit of the Chinese character for woman, called JO JI [see Illustrations]. The blossom (2) is painted on the principle of IN YO, the upper portion of the petal line being the positive or YO and the lower being the negative or IN side. This is repeated five times for the five petals of the blossom (3). The stamens (4) and the pistils are reproductions of the Chinese character SHO,

2. "The Nature of Fine Art," *The Lotos*, 9 (April 1896), 756.
3. *Epochs*, 2, 5.

meaning small. For the calyx (5) the Chinese character for clove, CHO (6), is invoked.[4]

Not only did these written characters add the visual overtones of their ideographic roots to a painting's aesthetic "nebula," but they conveyed to Fenollosa a sense of the continuity of the encounters of man's mobile imagination with the flux of the natural world. These characters were evolutionary and sounded overtones which echoed back toward the historic beginnings of language and the liberating transition from scratches to brush-writing.

During Fenollosa's second Japanese sojourn, 1896 to 1900, he turned his attention enthusiastically to Far Eastern poetry and the visual dance of Chinese written characters. On his several Pacific crossings he learned the 214 Chinese radicals which form the base of the written language, and in Japan he studied intensively with his friend Ariga, fascinated by the pictographic and ideographic qualities of Chinese poetry. At the same time he began teaching English to Japanese students, and the problems of grammatical structure posed by translation pressed him to reconsider the basic qualities of language. He turned to Barrett Wendell's *English Composition* for help in presenting the structure of English to his students, but found little he could use. Wendell's analysis of words, sentences, and paragraphs was helpful, but his account of "whole compositions" and stylistic qualities seemed to Fenollosa "weak and misleading." [5] What Wendell ignored was the synthetic quality of composition, an imaginative ordering which could not be broken down into its serial, analytic components. In the Chinese classics, familiar to most Japanese students, even the individual words seemed metaphorical and their arrangement a matter of synthetic composition. Fenollosa, who was teaching Emerson to his advanced classes, was struck by the hieroglyphs of nature evident in the Chinese written language, and he determined to probe their origins.

Ariga took him to Michiaki Nemoto, Japan's leading authority on the *I Ching*, the Chinese *Book of Changes*, an ancient collection of written wisdom. At the heart of the *I Ching* stood bold single images,

4. Henry P. Bowie, *On the Laws of Japanese Painting* (San Francisco, P. Elder, 1911), p. 71. Bowie met Fenollosa in Japan and respected his judgment (see Bowie, pp. 26–27).

5. Mary M. Fenollosa MSS, No. 11, p. 165, Jan. 25, 1898. See Barrett Wendell, *English Composition* (New York, 1892). Wendell was a Harvard professor of Brahmin inclinations and Anglophile tastes.

calligraphic transformations of the 64 hexagrams whose interpretations offered guides for living amidst the flux of the world. These images, or ideograms, provided a medium through which man could link himself to the heavenly and material realms. Here was vivid support for Fenollosa's philosophical idealism and for his recognition of organic flux as well; for change was interpreted by the *I Ching* as the universal principle which generates Being and the world of *Yin* and *Yang*, the opposites of dark and light.[6] The evolution of the images themselves and their commentaries must have seemed to Fenollosa an "Oriental Hegelianism" at its most condensed.

In Chinese characters Fenollosa found the very essence of his earlier definition of poetry, "full words, charged with intense meaning at the center, like a nucleus and then radiating out toward infinity, like a great nebula." In Chinese poetry, which he studied with Kainen Mori, he found words which stood "for as much thought and feeling as possible, and that through the mutual modifications of the successive words." For example, the pictograph of the sun, 日 , might be repeated in many of the words of a single poem in varied ideographic combinations, such as joined with the moon, or hidden by a tree, or lighting speech; and its overtones seemed to Fenollosa to "vibrate against the eye" in fresh poetic patterns.[7]

The contents of the poems also suggested paintings. In his studies of painting he had often encountered poems written on the surface of the paintings, a practice of the great Sung illumination imitated in Ashikaga Japan. He observed in these poems the same qualities of economy, condensation, and suggestion which characterized good painting. Far Eastern poetry tended to confirm "the old dictum that poetry and painting are only varying forms of each other." [8] With the help of Ariga and Mori, Fenollosa began to read Chinese poetry with enjoyment, and in the student *shida's* held frequently at his house he combined readings of classic Chinese poems with discussions of Emerson. The hieroglyphics of Hangchow and Concord had affinities.

Fenollosa's studies of the stylized images of the Noh stage opened

6. This interpretation, one which harmonizes with Fenollosa's philosophical tendencies and ideographic interests, is drawn from *The I Ching or Book of Changes*, the Richard Wilhelm translation rendered into English by Cary F. Baynes (2 vols. New York, Pantheon, 1950).

7. *The Chinese Written Character as a Medium for Poetry* (New York, Arrow Editions, 1936), p. 36.

8. *Epochs*, 2, 37–38.

his eyes further to the possibilities of visual poetry. Noh drama had originated in court performances of the fourteenth century, and under the influence of Zen ideals it developed a simple and concentrated structure focused intensively on psychological insights into the interrelationships of all life. "The Japanese people have loved nature so passionately," wrote Fenollosa, "that they have interwoven her life and their own into one continuous drama of the art of pure living." The Noh gave to this drama a powerful form in which several arts were fused. To Fenollosa, the dances at the core of the performance seemed keyed to a hidden order in the forces of nature. The masked dancer represented

> divine situations and emotions, artistically, with restraint and with the chastening of a conventional beauty, which makes every posture of the whole body—head, trunk, hands, and feet—harmonious in line, and all the transitions from posture to posture balanced and graceful in line. A flashlight glimpse across such a dance is like a flashlight of sculpture; but the motion itself, like a picture which moves in colour, is like the art of music. There is an orchestral accompaniment of flutes, drums, and cymbals, slow, fast, low, passionate, or accented, that makes a natural groundtone.[9]

The patterned movements had a special quality of linear intensity. As the Irish poet W. B. Yeats remarked of the Noh dancers,

> Their ideal of beauty, unlike that of Greece and like that of pictures from Japan and China, makes them pause at moments of muscular tension. The interest is not in the human form but in the rhythm to which it moves, and the triumph of their art is to express the rhythm in its intensity. There are few swaying movements of arms or body such as make the beauty of our dancing. They move from the hip, keeping constantly the upper part of their body still, and seem to associate with every gesture or pose some definite thought. They cross the stage with a sliding movement, and one gets the impression not of undulation but of continuous straight lines.[10]

9. *'Noh'; or Accomplishment, A Study of the Classical Stage of Japan* (London, Macmillan, 1916), pp. 99, 109–10.

10. Introduction by William Butler Yeats to *Certain Noble Plays of Japan*, in Pound and Fenollosa, *The Classic Noh Theatre of Japan* (New York, New Directions, 1959), p. 158. Yeats credited the Fenollosa-Pound translations of Noh plays with helping him invent "a form of drama, distinguished, indirect

For Fenollosa the beauty and power of Noh lay in its concentration, in the unified impression created by harmonizing appeals to eye, ear, and mind; and at the heart of this harmony he again found individuality, the original interpretations of the performers within a framework of tradition. The pattern of musical intervals is structured by *in* on the small drum and *yo* on the big drum, in alternate five and seven note series; and for both singers and musicians the art lies in a delicate balancing of *in* and *yo* by an intense act of inner spirit, very much like the principle of *In Yo* in painting. An actor behind the mask of an old woman does not try to imitate her voice. His voice remains "always the same, his own; yet with that one individual voice of his he must so express himself as to make it clear that it is the mentality of an old woman, or whatever it happens to be, who is speaking. It is a Noh saying that 'The heart is the form.'"[11] As in Sung and Ashikaga painting and in the concentrated, distilled images of Chinese poems, Noh plays used the power of suggestion rather than agglomerate description, bare details so placed as to convey a world.

Fenollosa brought a set of sculptured Noh masks back to the United States, and in his lectures the dramatic tradition of Noh was merged into necessarily brief surveys of Far Eastern literature. He was able to give occasional lectures on poetry alone, but his primary interest was in revitalizing American attitudes toward painting and design. Audience appreciation of Chinese characters and Noh drama required a more specialized training than was needed to sense the relationships developed on the pages of Dow's *Composition*. Accordingly, Fenollosa's extensive notes on Noh and on Chinese poetic language were added to a growing pile of projects in manuscript.

After Fenollosa's sudden death in September 1908, his wife's main concern was to shape his history of Far Eastern art into publishable form. By the spring of 1910, after a year of work, she had a typescript ready for the corroborative detail which could only be supplied in Japan, and she spent the summer in Tokyo assisted by Nagao Ariga and Tomonobu Kano. From Japan she sailed via the Straits Settlements route to London and a final revision at the British Museum.

and symbolic, and having no need of mob or press to pay its way—an aristocratic form."

11. 'Noh'; or *Accomplishment*, p. 52. The five and seven note musical series parallel the alternate five and seven syllable lines in the Japanese "imagist" poems of the *tanka* (31 syllables) and *haiku* (17 syllables) types.

In London she was introduced to William Heinemann and accepted his offer to publish the manuscript. With no limit on illustrations, *Epochs of Chinese and Japanese Art* appeared in October 1912 with nearly two hundred full-page plates in two magnificent volumes.

Poets as well as historians and connoisseurs were excited over *Epochs*. Not only did the pictures have the charm of exotic times and places, but Fenollosa documented the close relation between painting and poetry by quoting such poems as this one, written to fill a free space in the painting it described:

> The night water-clock has already stopped, and the frozen stork has fallen asleep. The dark-headed servant is warming himself by the fire, with his two knees crossed in front of him. Before the napping old man stands a mouth-cracked jar holding a branch of blossoming plum.[12]

The clarity of the image, the suggestive detail, the simplicity of statement appealed to a new generation of poets in revolt against the vague and dreamy mass of rhetoric which fuddled much conventional poetry.

One of the most articulate of these poetic reformers was Ezra Pound, a young American who had come to London in 1908 and by 1912 had published several books of poetry, critical essays, and translations from early French and Italian. Pound met Mrs. Fenollosa in London, probably through Heinemann or Laurence Binyon, the British Museum's Far Eastern art scholar. Pound questioned her at length about her husband's work and their life in Japan and was so enthusiastic about Fenollosa's literary researches that Mrs. Fenollosa promised, on her return to America, to send him whatever translations and notes she had.[13] When Pound received them, he found

12. *Epochs*, 2, 37.
13. This account follows Mrs. Fenollosa's MS, "Ezra Pound," which, despite several lapses in recollection, seems reliable on the point of Fenollosa's papers. Her acquaintance with Pound was supported persuasively by her daughter, Mrs. S. T. Whatley, in conversations with the author in September 1955. The otherwise established version of Pound's acquisition of Fenollosa's work is given in T. S. Eliot, *Ezra Pound: His Metric and Poetry* (New York, Knopf, 1917), pp. 21–22. According to this version it was Mrs. Fenollosa's reading of Pound's poems in *Poetry* that prompted her to send her husband's manuscripts to Pound in London. Pound, himself, has recalled meeting Fenollosa's widow in London at the home of Sarojini Naidu, the Indian nationalist poetess. See "Ezra Pound: An Interview," *The Paris Review*, 28 (1962), 38.

both confirmation of his own direction of development and a strong stimulus to extend his range to take in Far Eastern literature. Fenollosa was passionately convinced that art was the measure of life and civilization; that the individuality of the artist and his art were equally essential—*Epochs* was "a single personal life-impression"; that the "image" in its synthetic unity offered a most significant ordering of infinite possibilities; that Far Eastern art and literature afforded the West new vitality in a historical movement toward a world civilization. At all these points Fenollosa's work quickened Pound's imagination.

For three years Pound worked over Fenollosa's manuscripts, shaping literal translations of Chinese poetry into the forms of *Cathay*,[14] editing Fenollosa's notebooks on Noh drama—texts, history, and details of performance—into final published form in "*Noh*" or *Accomplishment*, and finally, after repeated refusals by magazines, publishing Fenollosa's historic essay, "The Chinese Written Character as a Medium for Poetry." The priority which Pound gave to the poems of *Cathay* reflected the rising tides of Imagism and Vorticism, movements which swirled around the ideal of a language whose "hard light" and "clear edges" could charge words with maximum intensity.

The visual elements in these influential attacks on literary conventions were pronounced. To Harriet Monroe, who was busy in Chicago with plans for *Poetry* magazine, Pound sent an "Imagiste" poem and a note on Whistler, in token of the coming inevitable "American Risorgimento." Whistler, as "our only great artist," deserved a place "at the threshold of what I hope is an endeavor to carry into our American poetry the same sort of life and intensity which he infused into modern painting."[15] Several months later, in *Poetry* for March 1913, Pound outlined his "tenets of Imagiste faith"; the principles could have applied equally well to a Whistler Nocturne or a seventeen-syllable Japanese *haiku*. There were three main points:

I. Direct treatment of the "thing," whether subjective or objective.

14. Compare Fenollosa's literal version with Pound's "Song of the Bowmen of Shu," published in *Cathay* (1915). See Appendix, pp. 251–54.
15. Pound to Harriet Monroe, Aug. 18, 1912, in D. D. Paige, ed., *The Letters of Ezra Pound* (New York, Harcourt Brace, 1950), p. 10. *Poetry* began publication in Oct. 1912 and included both of Pound's submissions.

II. To use absolutely no word that does not contribute to the presentation.

III. As regarding rhythm: to compose in sequence of the musical phrase, not in sequence of the metronome.[16]

Concrete words limited to essentials and combined freely, this was an accurate description of the English translations of Far Eastern poetry which stimulated the imagists. In the Japanese haiku ("The fallen blossom flies back to its branch: a butterfly.") were all the elements of imagism; and in Fenollosa's translations (see Illustrations), Pound probed the written characters themselves to discover images that would render the quality of the poems with visual immediacy. "The image," said Pound, "is the poet's pigment"; it provides a means of focusing an "intellectual and emotional complex in an instant of time." Pound's experience of seeing beautiful girls emerge from a subway was concentrated into a characteristic haiku:

> The apparition of these faces in the crowd;
> Petals on a wet black bough.[17]

Not that imagist poetry was derived exclusively from Far Eastern sources; its roots extended in many directions, into French symbolism, classical Greek, and wherever "clear edges" could be found. Nor was Pound its acknowledged discoverer, the English critic, T. E. Hulme, having proposed similar poetic reforms as early as 1909; and Pound deserted the movement soon after editing its pioneer anthology, *Des Imagistes*, in the spring of 1914. But his influence was central, and "old Fenollosa's treasures in mss," as Pound called them, tended to draw him closer to these "condensed Oriental forms," in which Fenollosa had seen both relief from dead poetic convention and inspiration during "this weak, transitional period of our Western poetic life." [18]

By the summer of 1914 Pound had shifted toward a new focus. With the recurrent watchword, "make it new," Pound's images whirled into vorticism. The "great art vortex" did not survive more than the two issues of its magenta-covered journal, *BLAST*, but its ferment indicated the direction of Pound's development. Again,

16. Pound, *Gaudier-Brzeska* (London, Lane, 1916), p. 96.

17. "In a Station of the Metro" (written early 1913), in *Personae* (New York, New Directions, 1926), p. 109.

18. EFF in *"Noh" or Accomplishment*, p. 100. For the best account of the intricate personal and theoretical patterns of the imagist movement, see Stanley Coffman, *Imagism* (Norman, Okla., U. of Oklahoma Press, 1951).

Illustrations

Ernest Fenollosa ca. 1874

Certificate of authenticity attested by **Kano Yeitan** (Ernest Fenollosa)

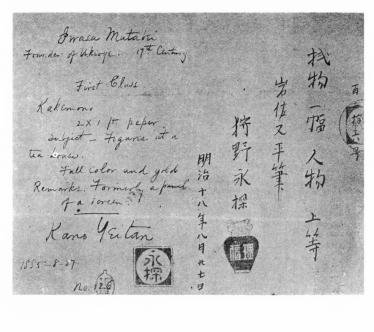

Manuscript translation of a poem by Oshorei (in Fenollosa's hand)

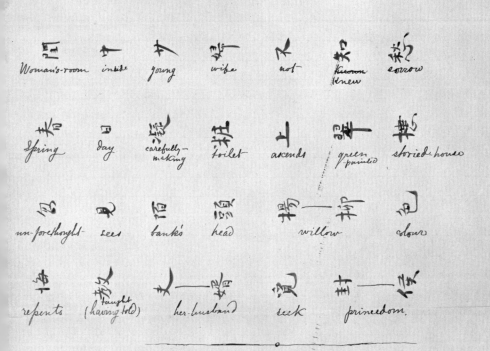

Woman's-room · inside · young · wife · not · knew · sorrow

Spring · day · carefully-making · toilet · ascends · green-painted · storied-house

un-forethought · sees · bank's · head · willow · colour

repents · (having told) · her-husband · seek · princedom.

It is the custom of the Chinese to present a willow-branch to one starting on a long journey (perhaps as whip for the ride-horse). Now a newly married girl had yet no experience of what sorrow was. On a fine spring day she makes her toilet with care and ascends a green-painted balcon. Without fore-thought her eyes fall on a willow tree at the yonder bank, from which she had taken a branch and gave to her husband on parting. The willow is green now as it was then, but the husband is not there. She now experiences what sorrow is and repents having instigated her husband to go on a long journey to try his fortune as soldier.

(by oshorei)

Leonardo da Vinci (Louvre)

Michelangelo, drawing

Kano Tanyu, XVII cent. (part of screen, Museum of Fine
Arts, Boston)

Kano Naonobu, XVII cent. (from screen in ink, Museum
of Fine Arts, Boston)

Two pages from Arthur Dow's *Composition* illustrating line synthesis

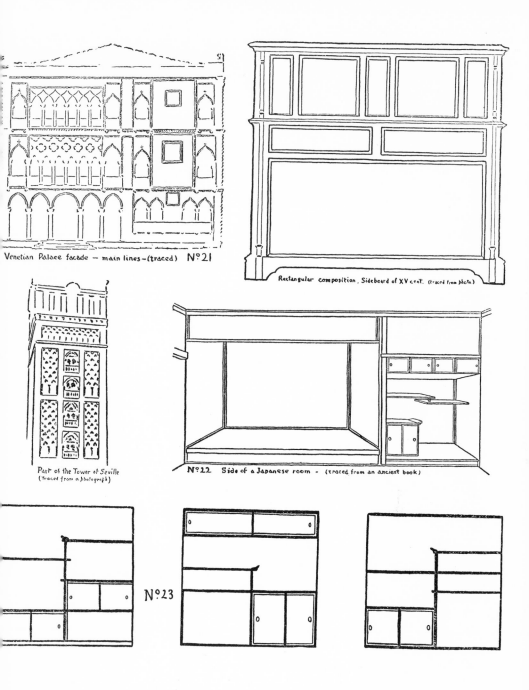

Venetian Palace façade — main lines — (traced)   Nº 21

Rectangular composition, Sideboard of XV cent. (traced from photo.)

Part of the Tower of Seville
(Traced from a photograph)

Nº 22   Side of a Japanese room - (traced from an ancient book)

Nº 23

Abstraction No. 10—Blue Lines (1915) by Georgia O'Keeffe

Natural forms combined in Japanese painting

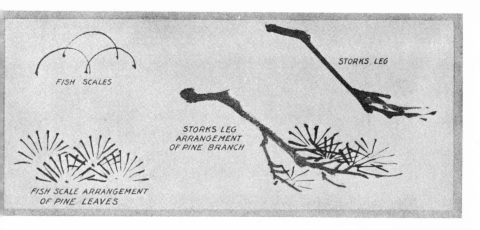

Chinese characters used in painting a plum tree

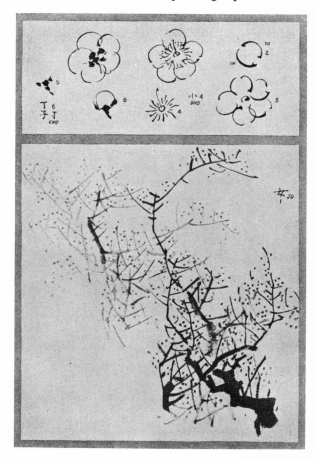

Passage from *The Cantos of Ezra Pound*

Bright dawn 旦 on the sht house
     next day
        with the shadow of the gibbets attendant

The Pisan clouds are undoubtedly various
     and splendid as any I have seen since
at Scudder's Falls on the Schuylkill
     by which stream I seem to recall a feller
settin' in a rudimentary shack doin' nawthin'
     not fishin', just watchin' the water,
a man of about forty-five

     nothing counts save the quality of the affection

     mouth, is the sun that is god's mouth
or in another connection   (periplum)
     the studio on the Regent's canal
     Theodora asleep on the sofa, the young
     Daimio's " tailor's bill "
     or Grishkin's photo refound years after
     with the feeling that Mr Eliot may have
missed something, after all, in composing his vignette
     periplum

(the dance is a medium)
     " To his native mountain "
     Ψυχάριον ἀι βάσταξον νεκρὸν

a little flame for a little
conserved in the Imperial ballet, never danced in a theatre
Kept as Justinian left it
     Padre José had understood something or other
     before the deluxe car carried him over the precipice

sumne fugol othbaer

learned what the Mass meant,
      how one shd/ perform it

the dancing at Corpus   the toys in the
      service at Auxerre

top, whip, and the rest of them.

[I heard it in the s.h.   a suitable place

to hear that the war was over]

the scollop of the sky shut down on its pearl

   καλλιπλόκαμα Ida.
With drawn sword as at Nemi
      day comes after day

and the liars on the quai at Siracusa
         still vie with Odysseus
seven words to a bomb

dum capitolium scandet
    the rest is explodable
Very potent, can they again put one together
as the two halves of a seal, or a tally stick?

        Shun's will and
        King Wan's will

were as the two halves of a seal
      ½s
    in the Middle Kingdom

Their aims as one
directio voluntatis, as lord over the heart
    the two sages united

Ernest Fenollosa ca. 1890

Mary McNeil Scott in 1890

Ernest and Mary Fenollosa ca. 1900

Fenollosa's aesthetics were echoed stridently. Nearly twenty years earlier Fenollosa had called for a poetry of "full words, charged with intense meaning at the center, like a nucleus, and then radiating out toward infinity, like a great nebula," a language concrete and immediate. Now Pound set up the image as the antithesis of static abstractions. "The image is not an idea. It is a radiant node or cluster; it is what I can, and must perforce, call a VORTEX, from which, and through which, and into which ideas are constantly rushing." [19]

Although Pound attempted from time to time to "sort out the arts," to separate them in terms of their most effective forms, he tended to merge them in the poetic structure of *The Cantos*, a cosmic lifework intended to be thoroughly contemporary in its form and virtually limitless in its content. The underlying poetic theories of *The Cantos*, a work begun in 1918 and still in progress, are as complex as the world they seek to create, but three notions are fundamental: "melopaeia," "phanopaeia," and "logopaeia"; and to all three Fenollosa's researches proved relevant.

On the theme of "melopaeia," the ordering of sounds in the ear, Fenollosa indicated that harmonious spacing in terms of intervals is determined by the "heart" of the individual, that although each Noh singer and musician, for example, determines his rhythm independently, all fuse in the unity of the play, the critical element being an original balancing of *in* and *yo* in a delicate interpretation. "Refined harmony," wrote Fenollosa, "lies in the delicate balance of overtones." [20]

Pound's concept of "phanopaeia," the image-evoking quality of poetry, is more closely related to Fenollosa's work. Imagist poetics intensified the evocative role of language, but imagist poems tended to share the limits of their Far Eastern models in that long poems were considered to violate the canons of simplicity and concentration. Could an extended sequence of images preserve an intense impact? Fenollosa's Noh commentaries provided an answer. In the dance sequences of Noh a series of images are created and dissolved, each merging into the next and establishing relationships of heightened intensity.

Fenollosa's speculations proved equally seminal in the development of "logopaeia" in *The Cantos*, a crucial kind of artistic order. Logopaeia involves both sounds and images, but it is essentially a dance of the intelligence among words, a combination of idea-painting and

19. *Gaudier-Brzeska*, p. 106.
20. *Chinese Character*, p. 36.

idea-music. "All that poetic form requires," wrote Fenollosa, "is a regular and flexible sequence, as plastic as thought itself." [21] In Fenollosa's essay on the Chinese written character Pound saw "a study of the fundamentals of all aesthetics"; Fenollosa's ideographic interpretations suggested new possibilities for harmonious spacing in a "dance of ideas."

The music of this dance in *The Cantos* is a personal music composed by Pound from the tones of his own life and orchestrated on a scale which extends over world history and which is keyed to creators of enduring ideas. For example, if it is assumed that every man, especially the creative individual, establishes by the pattern of his life a uniquely pitched tone, then these Confucian "heart's tones" are available for musical ordering, limited only by the hearer's capacity to hold in mind the pitch of a poetically rendered human tone long enough for other tones to "catch up, traverse, intersect it," in a pattern of intellectual harmonics. After defining a series of intellectual tones, Pound attempts to reintroduce them in condensed shorthand form, thereby enabling him to strike multiple tones and overtones in a brief space. To this end, Chinese characters have proved particularly helpful, and Pound's later cantos show a marked increase in Far Eastern elements; for Chinese characters vibrate with an intensity of logopaeia which Fenollosa carefully outlined.

One of Fenollosa's central ideas, supported by his studies of Japanese painting, was that artistic unreality improves on unartistic reality, that in art the basic relationships at the heart of all life are re-created. "Relations," he wrote, "are more real and more important than the things which they relate." [22] By which he meant that metaphor was more penetrating than analytic description, that relations glimpsed as a whole were alive, whereas parts dissected into grammatical categories soon stiffened and died. Indo-European languages seemed to Fenollosa to have buried the eidetic immediacy of metaphor in the dry cubby-holes of subjects, predicates, and weak copulas. How much less intense seemed the phrase "the cup is bright" than the compound picture of "sun-and-moon-cup." The intensity of the Chinese ideograph vibrates against the eye, and in its visual etymology the historical transformation of metaphor is preserved with enriched literary and personal overtones.

"Like nature, the Chinese words are alive and plastic, because thing and action are not formally separated," wrote Fenollosa. Because "na-

21. Ibid., p. 11.
22. Ibid., p. 26.

ture has no grammar" and does not abstract a noun or a "quality" from its rich relationship to life, "grammarless" Chinese is concrete and live; energy is transferred by action without weak copulas. The artificial completeness of a "sentence" is avoided by metaphorical overtones which remind man that "in nature there is no complete-ness," that life is change. Chinese characters, by combining "the vivid-ness of painting" with the "mobility of sounds," create an ideographic dance powerfully suggestive of natural forces.[23]

Sinologists have opposed Fenollosa's sweeping assertions, insisting, properly, that most Chinese characters are phonetic, not pictographic; that educated Chinese readers pay no more attention to etymology than English readers; and that Chinese is not "grammarless." But despite Fenollosa's misleading linguistics, his essay remains a seminal work in aesthetics, an ars poetica which "in its massive conciseness," as a recent critic puts it, ranks with "the great poetic manifestos of the past."[24]

One direct result of Fenollosa's theories is evident in Pound's use of Chinese characters in *The Cantos*. In a novel and intensely per-sonal way he has renewed the metaphorical qualities of individual characters. He has "made them new," cosmopolitanized them (vio-lently by Sinological measure) into visual forms that are as much painting as poetry: designs integrated into the text, their sounds less important than their renewed etymology. Given fresh life in *The Cantos*, Fenollosa's ideographs dance a modern turn to the saying of the ancients, remarked by Kuo Hsi, that "a poem is a painting without visible shape, and a painting is poetry put into form."

The passage from "Canto 77" reproduced (see Illustrations) sug-gests both the complexity and the poetic intensification which an

23. Ibid., pp. 21, 15, 13. For an authoritative appraisal see Roy Earl Teele, *Through a Glass Darkly, a Study of English Translations of Chinese Poetry* (Ann Arbor, Michigan, 1949). Fenollosa's speculations also raise broad questions of the psychology of cultures, questions with which all his work was concerned in one way or another. Fenollosa would have agreed with a later philosopher, Ben-jamin Lee Whorf, who saw every language as "a vast pattern-system, different from others, in which are culturally ordained the forms and categories by which the personality not only communicates, but also analyzes nature, notices or neglects types of relationships and phenomena, channels his reasoning, and builds the house of his consciousness." "Language, Mind, and Reality," in *Language, Thought, and Reality: Selected Writings of Benjamin Lee Whorf*, ed. John B. Carroll (New York, Wiley, 1956), p. 252.

24. Donald Davie, *Articulate Energy* (New York, Harcourt, Brace, 1955), p. 33; Davie's fourth chapter, "Syntax as Action: Ernest Fenollosa," offers a good discussion of Fenollosa's essay.

ideographic dimension provides. The unifying tone of this playful syncopation is established by a highly personalized style of brush-stroke, a reminder that a single selective intelligence is at work and that a man's character leaks through every ink mark.

The characters on the left hand page are 旦 , "dawn," pictograph of the sun risen over a horizon or earth line, and 口 , "mouth." The characters on the right hand page translate from top to bottom: "not one's own spirit and sacrifice is flattery bigosh," with a last inset character, "direction of one's will." At the close of the Canto, Pound suggests a more fluent translation: "To sacrifice to a spirit not one's own is flattery (sycophancy)."

On the purely visual level there are "repeats," which syncopate the flow of attention and suggest that effort to perceive a visual pattern will be rewarded by a heightened awareness of thematic tensions. 旦, "dawn," and 口 , "mouth," are repeated in 祭 , "sacrifice," and in 諂, "flattery." In like fashion the legs, ノ 乀 , in 其 , "one's own," and ハ in 鬼, "spirit," lead to the legs astraddle a horse, 夊 , in 祭. The 厶 in 鬼 is picked up and developed in 也 , "bigosh." The plant deprived of its earth-line, 非 , "not," is contrasted with 而 , a many-rooted plant, the connective "and."

Prior to this passage Pound has established Confucian celestial symbols, particularly the sun, as embodiments of an uncompromising vision of reality. On these terms "sacrifice," 祭 , legs divided over celestial process (i.e. the heavens "above," 二 , compounded with 小, sun, moon, and stars) pulls back dramatically toward the man who saw "bright dawn," 旦 , even though it was "on the sht house" "with the shadow of the gibbets attendant"; and sh'te recalls a Noh hero in the shadows of god-dances.

"Flattery," 諂 , the mouth emitting words, 言 , which cover error, 臽 , moves the eye back across the page to 口 , "mouth," "in another connection," the female principle of love through which man can apprehend the noumenal, through which he can unite with the sexual sun. In this "connection" "flattery" cuts both ways.

By visual progression the legs in 其 , "one's own," and 鬼 , "spirit," separate, as integrity is lost in 祭 , "sacrifice." By another progression of ideas the 厶 in "spirit," what Pound describes as "a source of personally directed energy," [25] is crossed in 也 , "bigosh," to suggest the hand grasping the upper arm in a bending gesture of defiance, a gesture which throws the eye back across to the upper left and the image of Pound watching "Bright dawn on the sht house."

Following this syncopated back-step the page closes with a pictograph of 士 , the "scholar-lord," over 心 , "heart," combined in 志 , "direction of one's will." The focus of attention rests on the Confucian scholar who attempts to act with integrity on a precise definition of his own "heart's tone."

Not only does this Far Eastern ideographic dance support important themes on its own visual level; it establishes "tonal" patterns through an interplay with its Western verbal context. To take one example from many, the ideogram 非 , "not," suggests the wings of a bird "opposing" the air, picking up the bird image of "fugol" (the bird who carried off old friends to death in *The Wanderer*, an Anglo-Saxon classic). The same ideogram relates closely to 韭 , the old seal form for leeks growing out of the ground. Take away the earth and growth is negated. Take away tradition and the Mass (see adjoining line) is negated. Both these visual etymologies support an emotional and intellectual complex, the idea that the priest through Mass transcends the "opposition" of the human and divine natures of Christ and through the Mass renews human contact with the roots of spiritual life.

The contrast between Pound's bold black ideograms and the pallid words they complement emphasizes both the enduring quality of artistic reality and the metamorphoses of artistic forms produced by the shifting sensibilities of individual poets and calligraphers. As each ideograph is stroked, it enters into new relations with its creator, its fellow characters, and the root flux which its metaphoric overtones intimate. The ideographs merge the phenomenal, artistic, and divine elements of life into a Fenollosan "crystallization." In their dance Fenollosa's lotus again emerges as the spirit of individuality, this time in literature, a new complex literature which reflects a world civilization in process.

25. *Confucius: The Great Digest and the Unwobbling Pivot* (New York, New Directions, 1951), p. 23.

You had your searches, your un-
    certainties,
And this is good to know—for
    us, I mean,
Who bear the brunt of our
    America
And try to wrench her impulse
    into art.

You were not always sure, not al-
    ways set
To hiding night or tuning "sym-
    phonies";
Had not one style from birth,
    but tried and pried
And stretched and tampered with
    the media.

Ezra Pound, "To Whistler,
American"

18 · OUT OF ALL THIS BEAUTY
SOMETHING MUST COME

Fenollosa's aesthetic of radical individualism lives on among painters
as well as poets. Again his ideas have stimulated cosmopolitan currents. In this case the historical link was Arthur Dow. The careers of
two talented painters who studied under Dow bear testimony to the
liberating effects of Fenollosa's structural aesthetics on exceptionally
powerful imaginations. Both Max Weber and Georgia O'Keeffe discovered that the language of visual art which Dow formulated gave
coherence to vital centers of their experience. With talents which
neither Dow nor Fenollosa possessed, Weber and O'Keeffe gave substance to the vision of an American art nourished by the art streams
of the world.[1]

1. This chapter was written before Weber's death in 1962. The present tense
is retained out of a sense of the continuing and immediate relevance of Weber's
work.

The art of Max Weber reflects the broad pattern of experiment which has characterized Western art during the last fifty years, a pattern whose appraisal demands the international perspective championed by Fenollosa. Any final consideration of the work of a man like Weber requires a global context; for Weber's imagination has been played on by all the winds of our time. Yet at the base of his eclectic quest lies an emphasis close to Fenollosa's, and his art symbolizes the bold cultural fusions which Fenollosa hoped would enliven American artistic imagination.

Like Fenollosa, Weber is a seeker. "Sensing quality in a work of art is like finding an answer to one's seeking self," says Weber. "Such consciousness of growth is the great revelation in life." Weber is convinced that this grasp of the creative imagination proceeds from within outward, that the growth of plastic intelligence unites interior experience with wider vitalities in ways which renew individual life, and further, that this renewal is an ongoing process, a continual search for new relationships whose "synthesis" enables man to link finite and infinite. Although Weber restricts synthesis to creation and regards appreciation as "analytic," the echoes of Fenollosan thinking are clear. For Weber, as for Fenollosa, the arena for the drama of renewal is the world of objective visual relationships, the world of space "enlivened" and form "illumined." The outer world awakens the potential within the individual by means of the art of seeing. Each encounter generates new experiences made coherent within a temporal framework by the individual's own vital quality.[2]

From the beginning Max Weber was determined to learn how to see. His earliest memories were filled with the colorful rhythms of Russian Judaism, and soon after his family emigrated from Byelostok in western Russia to Williamsburg in Brooklyn, he set out to study art, turning before long to Pratt Institute for practical training. As a teacher of drawing and manual training, for which he prepared, Weber could support himself and work at sharpening his eyes as well.

Weber was seventeen when he entered Pratt in the fall of 1898. He learned to be an expert cabinet-maker and craftsman, but it was Arthur Dow's course in design which fired his imagination. Dow's summons to look at the art of the world with fresh eyes started Weber along the road he has never left. Dow talked of a basic language by which a man might understand the swirl of line and shadow and color which spun his senses around. Dow said that seeing visual relations

2. Max Weber, *Essays on Art* (New York, Rudge, 1916), pp. 9, 14–15, 38, 68.

was like hearing music, and that just as there was more to the beauty of Weber's synagogue choir than the meaning of the words, so there was more to a painting than the representation of something else. To illustrate his points Dow brought in Japanese prints and pattern books. In a beautiful design, said Dow, you can feel the artist's grasp of a unique set of visual relations, a pattern which has a life and a reality of its own.

Weber won a scholarship for continued study, and Dow sent him off to the museums to see for himself what artists had really done. A series of fossil drawings executed at the time by Weber for a paleontologist underscored his strong sense of the evolutionary matrix of life and art. For four years he taught art in American public schools, saving toward the price of an Atlantic passage. He wanted to go to Paris to complete his art training, but the road lead through schools in Virginia and an appointment as head of the Department of Drawing and Manual Training at the Minnesota State Normal School in Duluth. The winters were long and cold in Duluth, but Weber was patient, and in September 1905 he set out on his first and final pilgrimage to Europe. When he returned three years later, it was on the edge of a wave of artistic revolution.

On arriving in Paris, Weber enrolled in the Julian Academy, a training center for academic artists. Under the exacting eye of Jean Paul Laurens he drew figures with photographic precision. But soon he was wandering through the oriental art collections of the Musée Guimet and the African Exhibits at the Trocadero, drawn by what he felt was the emotional force and simple consistency of work condescendingly classified as primitive. His work at the Julian Academy began to reflect the impact of these powerful, simple forms. Where his drafting facility had drawn Laurens' praise earlier, now Laurens criticised Weber's new work by deriding its ox-like solidity.[3] But to Weber solidity seemed closer to art than cleverness; Dow's artistic language freed him from the aesthetic blinders of convention. After a summer in Madrid studying El Greco and Goya, Weber returned to Paris, electing to work from the model at the Academy Colarossi and experimenting freely in his own directions. On a summer trip to Italy Weber found an atmosphere which was both exciting and familiar. Recalling his predawn arrival in Florence and an immediate walk to the Duomo and Giotto's tower, Weber writes,

3. Holger Cahill, *Max Weber* (New York, Downtown Gallery, 1930), p. 8.

It all looked strangely beautiful in the light of early dawn, but it was not strange to me for I had met it in Arthur Dow's class in Brooklyn. "There it is," I said, and I opened my arms to it as to a dear friend who had come back after years of absence. I stood before Giotto's tower following the rhythmic flow and balance of the masses, the sweep of line, my eyes lingering on its colored marble, on the lovely detail, its beautiful proportions and the grand composition of the whole, which I had drawn from pictures, so many times.[4]

The same visual language which enabled Weber to feel the power of the Spanish and Italian masters opened his eyes to the meaning of several experimental trends in Paris. Through Jules Flandrin, an older painter, Weber became acquainted with the work of Cézanne and Matisse. Although Dow's instruction had stressed line and dark-and-light and minimized color, the synthetic method freed Weber's imagination from naturalistic norms. Looking at Cézanne's paintings Weber discovered that color could be used as a primary structural element for planes and bounded shapes. And he was delighted at Matisse's swift and vivid color harmonies, which had drawn the cry of "fauve" from shocked critics in 1905. When Matisse insisted that the whole canvas be charged with life, Weber agreed on the basis of Dow's teaching and his own experience. If forms were distorted in the process, it merely demonstrated the primacy of visual language and its freedom from supposed literary equivalents. In the fall of 1907 Weber helped organize a class to study under Matisse.

Weber's own work began to be recognized by other experimental painters. Weber watched Picasso moving toward cubism and shared the excitement over African sculpture, although to Weber's eye the work of his close friend, Henri Rousseau, the Douanier, had more vitality and insight than most of the "primitives" coming into vogue; and he took Picasso to see Rousseau. Weber exhibited in the Salon d'Automne and at the Indépendants. In 1908 notice of his work reached America. The Paris critics were no longer shocked by experiment; important exhibitions had underscored what the moderns were driving at, and the revolt had gathered its partisans. But one of Weber's canvases was hung upside down, and this made good copy. The *New York Times* picked up the story and added that the young

4. Ibid., p. 10.

man from Brooklyn had also shown "several pictures of an ultra-modern variety, mostly sketches from the nude." [5]

With this scant advance notice Weber sailed back to the United States in December 1908. He found American art circles still largely unaware of events in Paris. Academic work held sway undisturbed. Prospects for an American market for modern work were dark. There were exceptions. Leo and Gertrude Stein had bought several Matisse paintings in Paris, the first in 1905; the next year Michael Stein's wife, Sarah, had brought a Matisse into the United States; and cousin Etta Cone had returned to Baltimore with the beginnings of her notable collection of modern paintings. But these were straws in an expatriate breeze. The first substantial gust of the Parisian revolt blew through the open doors of Alfred Stieglitz's tiny gallery at 291 Fifth Avenue in New York. In April 1908 Stieglitz gave Matisse a first American exhibition and followed with a succession of shows for Cézanne, Picasso, and a growing number of returning Americans, men like John Marin, Alfred Maurer, Marsden Hartley, and Max Weber.

When Weber returned to New York in January 1909, he knew nothing of Stieglitz's new interest, however, and he found the doors of the New York art world tightly closed. There were no open exhibition societies, and group shows without a jury were still in the discussion stage. Dealers' galleries were tied exclusively to conservative art work. Through Abraham Walkowitz, a fellow student fresh from Paris, Weber managed to rent a small gallery in the basement of a picture frame shop on Madison Avenue near Sixtieth Street. Here Weber opened his first American show in April 1909. Arthur Davies, the painter whom Fenollosa had praised in *The Lotos* as "evolutionary," bought two pictures, but the show was a financial and critical flop. Weber applied for a job in the public schools as an art teacher. But neither Dow's recommendations nor Weber's earlier experience and successful examinations could overcome the xenophobia which made Weber's immigrant English a cause for flat refusal.

Alone and penniless in New York, Weber abandoned all thought of returning to Paris but continued to paint. The National Academy bluntly rejected his entries, but welcome encouragement came from Stieglitz, who had heard reports of Weber from Paris. In March 1910 Stieglitz included Weber's work in the first group show of American

5. "Salon Given over to Freak Paintings," *New York Times*, Oct. 11, 1908, p. 3.

modernists,[6] and Weber soon joined the Stieglitz circle, living at "291" and assisting with exhibition hangings. Although his painting was becoming increasingly bold, filled with distorted forms and striking color combinations, Weber continued to study, drawn particularly to the Museum of Natural History, where Mayan and Aztec sculpture and Pacific Northwest totems sounded a note of primitive American strength. Again it was simplicity and basic principles which attracted him. In whatever direction he extended his experimental eye and hand, his base remained synthetic in the sense developed by Fenollosa and Dow. Some unifying emphasis of attention was necessary in any painting or design. "Choose the most interesting or characteristic form or color and relate to that all other things that make the study," wrote Weber in one of the notes he was continually jotting down as he looked at pictures and shaped his own vision.[7]

Despite Weber's staunch adherence to the principles of Fenollosa and Dow, the critics were nearly all hostile. When "291" opened its 1911 season with a one-man show of Weber's recent work, critical notices were harsh and abusive. The *Mail* found their ugliness "appalling"; the *World* saw a "grotesquerie . . . acquired by long and perverse practice." Arthur Hoeber, art critic of the *Globe*, was righteously indignant: "Here are forms that have no justification in nature, but that seem for all the world like the emanations of someone not in his right mind, such as one might expect from the inmate of a lunatic asylum." [8]

To make matters worse, Weber soon lost the support of Stieglitz, on personal rather than artistic grounds. Weber would not grant Stieglitz the fealty sought by the master from his circle. The break was serious, however, for no other support was to be found. Yet Weber

6. The show, entitled "Younger American Painters," grouped the work of Brinley, Carles, Dove, Fellowes, Hartley, Marin, Maurer, Steichen, and Weber. It is of interest that "291" 's first exhibition of painting showed the work of Pamela Colman Smith, an English illustrator whose designs often showed markedly Japanese characteristics. In an article in the *Craftsman* in 1908 she directed art students to follow Dow's *Composition*. P. C. Smith, "Should the Art Student Think," *Craftsman*, 14 (1908), 417–19.

7. Untitled Weber MS, in Stieglitz Collection, Yale Collection of American Literature, Sterling Memorial Library, New Haven, Conn.

8. Cited in Lloyd Goodrich, *Max Weber*, retrospective exhibition catalogue (New York, Whitney Museum, 1949), p. 25. Weber included a realistic life drawing from his Julian Academy work to prove he could "draw."

continued to paint, living at a bare subsistence level. He was still hopeful of sales but unwilling to compromise his principles. When the Murray Hill Gallery presented Weber's work the following year, Hoeber again spoke for the majority: "His pictures this season are rather more pronouncedly revolutionary than the previous collection, and are quite incomprehensible to the present reviewer, who frankly sees in them only distorted notions of art requirements, ugly color, hopelessly stupid drawing, and absurd compositions." [9]

Weber's economic outlook continued bleak. The Armory Show of February 1913 generated a wave of publicity for modern art, and several hundred works were sold off the walls, despite the acid protests of shocked critics. The Revolutionary pine tree, emblem of the exhibition, heralded a new market, but the demand among an excited avant-garde was for the new European "masters"—Cézanne, Matisse, Picasso. Several months later, when Weber was given a one-man show at the Newark Museum (the first museum show for an American modern), there was little interest and no substantial sale prospects.[10]

During the next few years Weber supported himself mainly by work at the Clarence White School of Photography, lecturing in the morning on art appreciation and criticizing photographic design in the afternoon. White, a one-time member of Dow's fine arts faculty at Columbia, was a talented and original photographer; Weber's approach was well suited to the school's aims. Weber's lectures, published in 1916 as *Essays on Art*, indicated the continuing force of the Fenollosa-Dow philosophy of art. "Culture," said Weber,

> will come only when every man will know how to address himself to the inanimate simple things of life. A pot, a cup, a piece of calico, a chair, a mantel, a frame, the binding of a book, the trimming of a dress . . . these we live with. Culture will come when people touch things with love and see them with a penetrating eye. . . . He who appreciates the principles of proportion, harmony, balance, symmetry, in simple objects and in works of art, finds that those qualities are in him, and it is only through things that one discerns himself. These principles tell the spectator that these are principles of life, and man has expressed them

9. Ibid., p. 27.

10. The London critics commented bitingly on Weber's paintings hung in the Grafton Group show of 1913, but Roger Fry wrote Weber encouragingly that he was struck by their "extraordinary power" and their grasp of "the principles of design." Ibid., p. 35.

in form, in things as a part of himself. . . . Thus art and life are not apart. Art foundations life. [11]

Weber went on to describe the onward movement of art and the natural affinity of this movement with "true liberation and the democratization of the races." Art "ferments" human life and makes all men aware of their universal belonging. Whereas war and materialism narrow life's scope, art "opens and universalizes."

Weber's outlook was close to Dow's, but as a poet and artist rather than an aesthetician Weber was skeptical of his own lectures and of all men who accepted theory as real. By his insistence that "it is only through things that one discerns himself," he took issue with all teachers who were not artists first and last. Yet the range of Weber's art and its continuing vitality reflect the fusion of historicism and experiment propounded by Dow. Weber stated explicitly in the '40s that he was still "following Dow's principles." [12]

Weber has responded to nearly all the artistic currents of the twentieth century. His early fauve work was followed by cubist figures and futurist cityscapes, which in turn moved toward semi-abstraction under the renewed influence of primitive art. In the '20s Weber entered a long period of representational work, poetic and religious in mood and filled with figures from a Judaic past, with an interval of social realism in the mid '30s. But he has never been content to stop, and the '40s saw a burst of calligraphic scenes, playful and serious, orthodox and fantastic, followed by a drift back toward abstraction and pure color, always experimenting with forms and materials, with woodcuts, sculpture, even poetry, all at a time when his works were beginning to bring fair prices.[13]

In the midst of all this change Weber has retained his individuality. He has not moved backward and forward so much as outward, in that organic growth which he feels essential to an art that is alive. Although an artist should be richly rooted in the past, he risks death if he stops growing; so Weber asserted in his talks to students at the White School and the Art Students League. Fenollosa would have agreed.

In the years when Weber was lecturing on appreciation and design, tradition had a strong hold on the American art world, and modernist

11. *Essays on Art*, pp. 32, 35–36.
12. Goodrich, *Max Weber*, p. 8.
13. See esp. Max Weber, *Cubist Poems* (London, Mathews, 1914).

art faced a long struggle for acceptance. As might be expected, Arthur Dow was outspoken in support of the new experiments. He interpreted them historically, in relation to well-established precedents in non-Western art, and theoretically, in terms of the universal artistic language which he had been propounding for twenty years. Although reigning art critics and their supporting ranks of dealers and clients were unprepared for modern work, an avant-garde sensibility was well established across the country among Dow's loyal followers in the field of art education. New York's Armory Show of 1913, which is credited with introducing modern art to the general American public, may have caught that public largely unprepared.[14] But by 1913 the Fenollosa-Dow system of art education had been attacking naturalistic aims for twenty years, and its visual grammar offered an excellent means of appreciating all art, however abstract. And Dow's influence increased steadily. Thomas Munro, a leading figure in a new generation of art educators and aestheticians, found that by 1926 Dow had become a symbol for advanced attitudes across the country. "One who looks over the situation in American school art work," wrote Munro, "is constantly impressed with the far-reaching influence of the late Arthur Wesley Dow, of Teachers College, Columbia University. East and west, in state and city school boards, in conventions of art teachers, his name has become a rallying cry for the liberal factions, usually far in the minority, that struggle for advance toward modern methods of instruction." [15] Dow and his missionaries deserve recognition for initiating a shift in American taste which gradually developed a wide market for all phases of modern design from Bauhaus furniture to "Mondrianesque" graphics and calligraphic paintings.

In 1915 Dow was in the thick of the early battles, summoning all art teachers who believed that art structure is fundamental to "welcome the modernists." "There is not only rebellion but revolution in

14. Oliver W. Larkin has stated a prevailing historical view: "In America no pioneers . . . had steadily undermined the naturalistic idea. . . . The American modern faced a public wholly unprepared for what he did." *Art and Life in America* (New York, Rinehart, 1949), p. 354; cf. Dow, *Composition* (see Illustrations).

15. "The Dow Method and Public School Art," reprinted from *Journal of the Barnes Foundation* (Jan. 1926), in John Dewey et al., *Art and Education* (Merion, Pa., Barnes Foundation Press, 1929). In the autumn of 1930, for example, art appreciation replaced drawing as the core of art training in the public schools of New York City; Forrest Grant, director of art in New York's secondary schools, maintained that "all he himself has done is to take advantage of an

the air," said Dow, revolution against the "stereotyped nature-drawing and conventional design" of the art academy. Living color need not be nature's color; modernist painters and designers justifiably demand freedom to create in independent visual rhythms. Dow declared that modernists deserve neither hoots for lack of realism nor applause as the discoverers of rhythm; they are merely continuing in the tradition of Far Eastern painting and handicraft.[16]

Dow made his position even clearer in a talk on "Modernism in Art" to a group of college art teachers. "I confess to sympathy with all who reject traditional academism in art," he declared.

> I often regret the years spent in the Academie Julian, where we were taught by professors whom we revered, to make maps of human figures. I regret still more the persistence of this acade-mism in America and sincerely hope that this association will not permit it to have full sway over proposed new college courses. Japanese art has done much toward breaking the hold of this tyranny, the incoming Chinese art will do more, but it may re-main for modernist art to set us free.

What is needed, Dow urged, are eyes sufficiently trained to distin-guish serious modern art, the work of men of principle, from the fakery of "self-advertisers." An historical perspective shows that revo-lutions in art are nothing new, that they are "the natural result of creative power in man," a sign of life in art. "Efforts of the state or of any ruling body whatsoever to control art or to produce it have always proved failures. The creative artist will not be controlled. He may be excluded from exhibitions, ridiculed and repressed, but he will be free." [17]

The career of Georgia O'Keeffe, one of Dow's most talented stu-dents, illustrates a line of development which recalls, symbolically and historically, Fenollosa's dream of a world civilization. In O'Keeffe's

---

opportunity presented to him to embody Mr. Dow's ideas in an actual public school course." *New York Times*, June 1, 1930, Sec. E, p. 9. In 1941 the cam-paign against "skillful copying" continued under the banner of a creative mod-ern design; "Arthur Dow was the first to start this process long before the of-ficial art schools even guessed there was an issue." Ralph Pearson, *The New Art Education* (New York, Harper, 1941), pp. 40, 239.

16. "The Use of Non-applied Design in Teaching Art," address before Ameri-can Federation of Arts, Washington, D.C., May 13, 1915, in Dow MSS.

17. Untitled MS, pp. 5–9, in Dow MSS.

condensed visual language the female, aesthetic element, which Fenollosa associated with the Far East, flowered in an American idiom, an idiom at once abstract and true to nature. Yet O'Keeffe's art did not take shape in the smooth, unfolding fashion suggested by her mature style. Her early efforts were disappointing and frustrating. Not until she experienced the liberating effects of Dow's language of space-art did her work come to life.

Georgia O'Keeffe was born in Sun Prairie, Wisconsin, daughter of an Irish father and a Hungarian-Dutch mother. She attended school in nearby Madison and later in Chatham, Virginia. At the age of seventeen she entered the Chicago Art Institute; this was in 1904. For three years she studied in the academic tradition, first under John Vanderpoel in Chicago and then in New York at the Art Students League, with Kenyon Cox and William Merritt Chase. Anatomy, perspective, modeled drawing, and historical ornament gave her little satisfaction. Although she won a prize for still life in Chase's class and a scholarship, she saw no reason for further imitative practice. A season of commercial art work in Chicago proved equally unrewarding, and in 1909 she gave up painting completely, returning to her family in Virginia.

The decisive step toward her own natural artistic idiom was taken in the summer of 1912. At the University of Virginia summer school she met Alon Bement, an enthusiastic advocate of Arthur Dow's methods, and she discovered that Dow's artistic language opened up the aesthetic possibilities to which her whole life was keyed. Here was an artistic program based on the unity of artistic activity, a recognition that the individual sensibility which ordered a painting was the same sensibility which furnished a room, chose a dress, or made a walk at sunrise into an act full of beauty. The Fenollosan trinity of line, dark-and-light, and color offered her a grammar for understanding and expression.

That autumn, on Bement's recommendation, she went to Texas as supervisor of art in the public schools of Amarillo. The climate was too dry for the flowers she loved, "but I belonged," she recalled. "That was my country—terrible winds and a wonderful emptiness." [18] After two years in Amarillo, with summers instructing at the University of Virginia summer school, O'Keeffe went to Teachers College,

18. Anita Pollitzer, "That's Georgia," *Saturday Review of Literature*, 33 (Nov. 4, 1950), 42; biographical data from D. C. Rich, *Georgia O'Keeffe* (Chicago, Art Institute of Chicago, 1943).

Columbia, to study under the master, Dow. After two years' work she joined the art missionaries who were carrying Dow's language of space-art across the country. Her new post was head of the art department at West Texas State Normal College.

In Texas she was free to work with all the independence she desired. Moving beyond her monochromatic experiments with charcoal and the Japanese brush, she developed a vocabulary of color thoroughly her own. The simplicity and understatement of her paintings suggested Far Eastern models, but the style was her own. Her best work has a quality of inner concentration matched by controlled technique; the impression is of an intense immediacy and stable duration, at the same time. Many critics have remarked the feminine quality in all her work. To Stieglitz, for example, even her early charcoal abstractions conveyed the essence of woman.[19] Her paintings of flowers seem explicitly symbolic; her later abstractions and landscapes are always sensuous, often with an ascetic clarity.

It is this quality of sensuous immediacy which has led the philosopher F. S. C. Northrop to interpret the art of Georgia O'Keeffe as a herald of the coming fusion of East and West and as an indication of America's crucial role in this fusion. Northrop does not use Fenollosa's term, "fusion," but the drift of his argument in *The Meeting of East and West* (1946) has marked parallels with Fenollosa's earlier vision. The pivotal position of O'Keeffe's painting in Northrop's argument raises a question of the relation of history to philosophy, in this case the relation of Fenollosa's career to Northrop's hypothesis.

According to Northrop's hypothesis, Western culture has directed its energies primarily toward developing the theoretic component of things, a component "logically, systematically, and deductively formulated, and verified only indirectly by precisely and theoretically defined experiments," a component scientifically inferred rather than directly apprehended.[20] In contrast, the civilizations of the East have

19. Stieglitz offered the first exhibit of O'Keeffe's work in May 1916, in a group show at "291," and followed this with an all-O'Keeffe show in April 1917. He arranged her shows at the Anderson Galleries in 1921, 1924, and 1925 and gave regular shows at his "Intimate Gallery" from 1925 to 1929 and thereafter at "An American Place." Stieglitz married Georgia O'Keeffe in 1924. That same year the Boston Museum of Fine Arts acquired a representative collection of Stieglitz photographs, as a result of the enthusiasm of its curator of Asiatic art, Ananda Coomaraswamy, a leading interpreter of East to West.

20. F. S. C. Northrop, *The Meeting of East and West* (New York, Macmillan, 1946), p. 163.

concentrated their efforts on the aesthetic component of things, a self-evident component apprehended immediately and intuitively. The new, world civilization implicit in the meeting of East and West will require "a philosophy grounded in both the aesthetic component and the theoretic component of things as equally primary" in order "to harmonize the genius of Asia with the science of Europe and America," in order to "achieve a society for mankind generally in which the higher standard of living of the most scientifically advanced and theoretically guided Western nations is combined with the compassion, the universal sensitivity to the beautiful, and the abiding equanimity and calm joy of the spirit which characterize the sages and many of the humblest people of the Orient." [21]

What Georgia O'Keeffe's art suggests to Northrop is that the Eastern aesthetically immediate component of things is gaining recognition in the West as a complement to established scientific allegiance and further, that "the culture of the United States is initiating a shift to new philosophical foundations" based on both aesthetic and theoretic components. In such a painting as O'Keeffe's "Abstraction No. 3," for example, Northrop finds "pure fact with all its emotive quale and ineffable luminosity, before the inferences of habit and thought have added their transcendent references to the external three-dimensional objects of common sense or scientific belief, to the theological objects of traditional Western religious faith, or to the future pragmatic consequences of reflective action." [22]

In O'Keeffe's work Northrop sees a new art "indigenously American yet portraying something of universal validity." O'Keeffe becomes the prototype of the new artist, "sensitive to the deeper intimations of her culture" and hinting of the world civilization to come. Her "Abstraction No. 10, Blue Lines" (see Illustrations) is appropriate to a unified civilization both as evidence and prophecy. Its immediacy is aesthetic. Its lines are symbolic: the male and female principles rising from a common base, each distinct and irreducible to the other, yet both united, representing to Northrop the "male scientific component" and the "female aesthetic component" merged in a future already confronted by "the spirit of a free and adventurous United States." [23]

To Northrop, O'Keeffe's art represents a surfacing of the "deeper

21. Ibid., pp. 434, 496.
22. Ibid., p. 162.
23. Ibid., pp. 163–64.

intimations" of American culture, and his quest for a new basic philosophy carries the implication that once such a philosophy is formulated, the resulting relationships of Eastern and Western components will be harmonized. But O'Keeffe's "Blue Lines" have a further historical significance. The presence in O'Keeffe's art of Far Eastern elements transmitted by Fenollosa and Dow and transformed in a series of personal encounters suggests that "the future union of East and West," as Fenollosa called it in 1892, will depend as much on the relationships of individuals at particular times and places as on a philosophic harmony of components.

仁

19 · CODA

The historical situation of the individual Western man as he entered
the twentieth century has been interpreted frequently as a predicament, a predicament created by the loss of unified world views and
an alienation from regenerative experience. This pessimistic historical
mood was stated eloquently in *The Education of Henry Adams* and
in Oswald Spengler's *Der Untergang Des Abendlandes*, both of which
were presented to the general public in 1918. Adams interpreted the
multiplicities of the twentieth century as forces tearing apart the
unified fabric of life once woven around the Virgin of Chartres.
Spengler wrought a powerful imaginative vision of the advanced
decline of Western civilization, a decline evident in modern man's
state of *Wachsein*, or "waking-consciousness," a sterile mode of life
increasingly removed from *Dasein*, or real "being," the source of
harmonious, creative relations with the world. Modern man's attempts to recontact *Dasein* were inevitable failures, and his dream
of progress an illusion. Spengler's morphological structures comple-

mented Adams' "curve of degradation"; and the catastrophes of the twentieth century have offered fresh support.

Current interpretations of American attitudes toward the Far East have extended this pattern of speculation. To Van Wyck Brooks the interest in the East which centered in New England in the '80s and '90s has suggested a "sad and fatalistic" mood of failure, indicative of lost Unitarian hopes and an optimism negated by the bewildering changes which were transforming the American continent.[1] More recently James Baird, stimulated by Jungian theories, has interpreted American voyages to the Orient as searches for live symbols, attempts to rediscover a timeless sacred center unaffected by the disintegrating forces operative in the "profane time" of the modern West.[2] This pattern of individual quest, of which Ishmael is the archetype, Baird describes as an "existential primitivism" at once "atavistic" and "autotypic"—atavistic in the sense that each pilgrim rejects the symbolistic poverty of contemporary culture and turns toward the past, autotypic in the sense that personal experience, emotionally charged, generates the life of the new-found symbol. The Orient, in Baird's view, provides a reservoir of live, "primitive" symbols and an arena for the significant wanderings of Europeans such as Gauguin and a company of Americans led by Melville and including Henry Adams, John LaFarge, Lafcadio Hearn, and Ernest Fenollosa.

Adams, LaFarge, and Hearn do not fit easily in Ishmael's footsteps. And Fenollosa not only bursts out of the category of existential primitivism, he challenges its underlying mood of historical pessimism. That Adams was atavistic is clear, but it is doubtful that during his travels in the East he experienced the sacramental quality of oriental symbols on a deep personal level. Nor does LaFarge's discriminating eclecticism or cosmopolitan frame of reference suit a pattern of rejection, search, and discovery. Hearn's love affair with Japan suggests not so much the symbolistic poverty of Protestant American culture as the discovery of personal happiness in the family life which he had never known; his wife and children and his devoted students gave a new warmth to his life, a new center made more beautiful by the spirit of traditional Japan. Fenollosa, although

1. Van Wyck Brooks, *New England: Indian Summer 1865–1915* (New York, Dutton, 1940), esp. pp. 358–60. The title essay in Brooks' *Fenollosa and His Circle* (New York, Dutton, 1962) avoids this viewpoint but offers no alternative.
2. James Baird, *Ishmael* (Baltimore, Johns Hopkins University Press, 1956). On Near Eastern "polysensua" see Dorothy M. Finkelstein, *Melville's Orienda* (New Haven, Yale University Press, 1961).

"autotypic," belongs not in the pattern of a primitivism which rejects contemporary culture, but in the pattern of a modernism which welcomes multiplicity and change and which remains oriented toward a future alive with hopeful possibilities.

To Fenollosa, when he set out for the Far East at the age of twenty-five, Japan represented an unusual personal and intellectual opportunity, as it did to the first of the "Boston Orientalists," Edward S. Morse. Throughout Fenollosa's life the Far East remained a symbol of the future growth of a world civilization in which East and West would rise to new heights. Both Spengler and Adams made Western culture autonomous, ignoring the potentialities of accelerating contacts with cultures outside the west. Fenollosa's Far Eastern experiences gave him an international perspective which made him aware of prospects for a new growth.

In Fenollosa's view the element most likely to assure the quality of future cultural life was a broadly democratic individuality for which art offered both a metaphor and a medium. The multiple possibilities which would confront the individual aware of various cultural styles would require a developed capacity for free selection and a recognition that life is full of change and contingency. In the name of an emergent free individuality in art and life Fenollosa opposed static absolutes of every variety—academic art, feudalistic society, sectarian religion, rationalistic economics, Aristotelian logic, scientific materialism, and the narrow complacencies of racism. Tradition provided a firm base for evolutionary growth, formalism an unnatural block.

Fenollosa's belief that change itself is welcome and can be made significant by human imagination links him with a pattern of American modernism that includes Walt Whitman and William James as well as Max Weber and Ezra Pound. This pattern of "existential modernism" includes in each instance a series of unique relationships discovered and ordered by a single trained sensibility. Whereas the existential primitive's re-entry into a closed circle of sacred time relieves him of personal responsibility by affording a compulsive "harmony" with the world, the existential modern accepts personal responsibility for achieving some kind of order, if only momentarily and tentatively, in an open world where time's duration is as necessary as change. For change requires time, whether in Whitman's prophetic chants, James' personal empiricism, Weber's "synthetic" paintings, Pound's "dance of ideas," or Fenollosa's artistic histories.

It is within this pattern of modernism that Fenollosa's lotus continues to grow. In the process of its transformation in Fenollosa's imagination and its naturalization in American artistic soil, the lotus becomes a symbol of the historical encounter of free individuality with the limitless possibilities generated by a world in flux. Art points the way toward those styles of life which can take account of change and uncertainties. Just as a painter confronts virtually limitless visual arrangements when he encounters the canvas, so a cosmopolitan individual is aware of many ways of living, and he shapes a pattern appropriate to his individuality. Just as each work of art is unique, a momentary achievement of relations, so individuality is created anew in that series of moments which add up to a single life. What a great work of art and a distinguished cosmopolitan career both do is to communicate intensely a sense of wide-ranging possibilities imagined and the right ones elected. Part of the achievement consists in the reassurance examples provide that an individual human being can encounter uncertainties and order them successfully. The painter's or the scholar's voyage into the unknown, when he returns successful, summons others to dare things new and untried.

Fenollosa saw art presenting a momentary and sufficient ordering of possibilities. Art offered a metaphor of human relations in a world where freedom and individuality were continually threatened. American individualism has long since become a phrase conventional to the point of cant. Fenollosa's radical artistic individualism, symbolized in the lotus, recaptures the revolutionary implications of an American individualism fit in many ways for a cosmopolitan world.

APPENDIX · Three Versions of Bunno's "Song of the Bowmen of Shu"

1. Fenollosa's English Version as Taken from His Notes.

Sai-bi

(At the epoch of the last emperor of the "In" dynasty, there appeared the two powerful barbarian tribes who often invaded the empire, namely: "Kon-i" in the western part, and "Ken-in" in the northern part of China proper. Bunno was the commander in chief of the western princes; he had to dispatch his army to defend against the outsiders under the order of the emperor. In that time he composed this piece, as if he was one of the soldiers, to show his sweet sympathy to them and to soften their grief and pain. As the commander was so kind, the soldiers were glad to serve in his army. This is one of the chief reasons why the "Shu" [Chou] dynasty arose and Bunno was esteemed as a saint.)

We pick off the "Warabi" (an edible fern) which first grow from the earth.

We say to each other, "When will we return to our country?" It will be the last of the year.

Here we are far from our home because we have the "ken-in" as our enemy.

We have no leisure to sit down comfortably (as we did at home) because we have "ken-in" as our enemy.

We pick off the "Warabi" which are soft.

When we say the returning our mind is full of sorrow.

We are very sorrowful. We are hungry and thirsty.

But our defense is not yet settled, so we cannot let our friends return to our country and ask how our family lives.

We pick off the "Warabi" which have become already rough.

We say to each other, "When will we return to our country?" It will be October.

We must be prudent for our affair (which is the order of the emperor); we have no leisure to sit down comfortably.

Our sorrow is very bitter, but we would not return to the country.

What is that blooming flower?

Whose is that chariot? That is our general's.

The horses are hitched already to the chariot; they seem to be vigorous.

How dare we repose? We must conquer the enemy even three times in a month.

Those four horses are tied; they are very strong.

The generals are on their backs and the soldiers are by their sides.

The four horses are well educated; the generals have the ivory arrows and the quivers that are ornamented with the skin of fish.

We must be careful every day, because the enemy is very quick.

Other time when we started the willows are drooping by spring wind.

But now we come back when it snows.

We go very slowly and we are thirsty and hungry.

Our mind is full of sorrow; who will know our grief?

2. Pound's Version in *Cathay* (1915)

Here we are, picking the first fern-shoots
And saying: When shall we get back to our country?
Here we are because we have the Ken-nin for our foemen,
We have no comfort because of these Mongols.
We grub the soft fern-shoots,
When anyone says "Return," the others are full of sorrow.
Sorrowful minds, sorrow is strong, we are hungry and thirsty.
Our defence is not yet made sure, no one can let his friend return.
We grub the old fern-stalks.
We say: Will we be let to go back in October?
There is no ease in royal affairs, we have no comfort.
Our sorrow is bitter, but we would not return to our country.
What flower has come into blossom?
Whose chariot? The General's.
Horses, his horses even, are tired. They were strong.
We have no rest, three battles a month.
By heaven, his horses are tired.
The generals are on them, the soldiers are by them.
The horses are well trained, the generals have ivory arrows and quivers
    ornamented with fish-skin.
The enemy is swift, we must be careful.
When we set out, the willows were drooping with spring,
We come back in the snow,
We go slowly, we are hungry and thirsty,
Our mind is full of sorrow, who will know of our grief?

By Bunno
Reputedly 1100 B.C.

3. Pound's Version in *The Confucian Odes* (1954)

Pick a fern, pick a fern, ferns are high,
"Home," I'll say: home, the year's gone by,
no house, no roof, these huns on the hoof.
Work, work, work, that's how it runs,
We are here because of these huns.

Pick a fern, pick a fern, soft as they come,
I'll say "Home."
Hungry all of us, thirsty here,
no home news for nearly a year.

Pick a fern, pick a fern, if they scratch,
I'll say "Home," what's the catch?
I'll say "Go home," now October's come.
King wants us to give it all,
no rest, spring, summer, winter, fall,
Sorrow to us, sorrow to you.
We won't get out of here till we're through.

When it's cherry-time with you,
we'll see the captain's car go thru,
four big horses to pull that load.
That's what comes along our road,
What do you call three fights a month,
and won 'em all?

Four car-horses strong and tall
and the boss who can drive 'em all
as we slog along beside his car,
ivory bow-tips and shagreen case
to say nothing of what we face
sloggin' along in the Hien-yün war.

Willows were green when we set out,
it's blowin' an' snowin' as we go
down this road, muddy and slow,
hungry and thirsty and blue as doubt
(no one feels half of what we know).

BIBLIOGRAPHY

Part One: Chapters 1–3

Details of Ernest Fenollosa's mode of life derive from the recollections of his stepdaughter, Erwin Scott Whatley, his stepson, Alan Chester, and his daughter, the late Brenda Fenollosa Biddle. Fenollosa's family background in Spain and his Salem boyhood are described in Mary McNeil Fenollosa's preface in Ernest Fenollosa, *Epochs of Chinese and Japanese Art* (London, 1912); genealogical data therein were verified by the late Moncure Biddle. Musical life in nineteenth-century Salem is chronicled in George M. Whipple, "A Sketch of the Musical Societies of Salem," *Essex Institute Historical Collections*, 23 (1886), 72–80, 113–33, and in Thomas Carroll, "Bands and Band Music in Salem," *Essex Institute Historical Collections*, 36 (1900), 265–84. On Manuel Fenollosa's house, 5 Chestnut St., see Richard H. Wiswall, "Notes on the Building of Chestnut Street," *Essex Institute Historical Collections*, 75 (1939), 222. Samuel E. Morison, *Maritime History of Massachusetts* (Boston, 1921) provides the best account of Salem's seafarers. On early American contacts with the Far East, see Tyler Dennett, *Americans in Eastern Asia* (New York, 1922); George H. Danton, *The Culture Contacts of the United States and China* (New York, 1931) describes missionary and mercantile activities 1784–1844; Robert S. Schwantes, *Japanese and Americans: A Century of Cultural Relations* (New York, 1955) is extensive with an excellent bibliographical essay.

Fenollosa's Harvard days are recalled in two of his classmates' memoirs: Arthur Foote, *An Autobiography* (Norwood, Mass., 1946) and Nathan Haskell Dole, "Autobiography," manuscript in possession of Mrs. Margaret Dole McCall, New York, N.Y. Handwritten autobiographies by seniors in "Class Book 1874," manuscript in the Archives, Harvard University, indicate the backgrounds and prospects of Fenollosa's classmates as do *Reports of the Secretary of the Class of 1874 of Harvard College*, Nos. 1–11 (Cambridge, Mass., 1874–1924). These reports include Fenollosa's accounts of his own career at regular intervals as well as a memorial to Fenollosa by Nathan Dole in the 35th anniversary report No. 9 (1909). On Harvard's tonic transition from a college to a university see: W. A. Neilson, *Charles W. Eliot, The Man and His Beliefs* (2 vols. New York, 1926), Henry James, *Charles W. Eliot* (2 vols. Boston, 1930), Rollo W. Brown, *Harvard Yard in the Golden Age* (New York, 1948). See also Samuel E. Morison, *Three Centuries of Harvard* (Cambridge, Mass., 1936). The intellectual flavor of Harvard and Boston are clear in the biographical writings of Mark Antony DeWolfe Howe, in Ralph Barton Perry, *The Thought and Character of William James* (2 vols. Boston, 1935), and in Philip Wiener, *Evolution and the Founders of Pragmatism* (Cambridge, Mass., 1949); George Santayana offers trenchant criticisms of this milieu in *Persons and Places* (3 vols. New York, 1944–51) and *Character and Opinion in the United States* (New York, 1920).

Benjamin Rand, "Philosophical Instruction in Harvard University from 1636 to 1906," Parts 2 and 3, *Harvard Graduates' Magazine*, 37 (1928–29), 188–200, 291–311, summarizes curricular developments. Herbert W. Schneider, *A History of American Philosophy* (New York, 1946) sets Harvard philosophy in a broad context. Herbert Spencer's importance in American evolutionary thought is analyzed in Richard Hofstadter, *Social Darwinism in American Thought* (rev. ed. Boston, 1955); on Spencer's popularizers see Merle Curti, *The Growth of American Thought* (2d ed. New York, 1951); *Evolutionary Thought in America*, ed. Stow Persons (New Haven, 1950) includes an excellent bibliography. On Hegelianism see J. H. Muirhead, "How Hegel Came to America," *Philosophical Review*, 37 (1928), 226–40; Henry A. Pochmann, *New England Transcendentalism and St. Louis Hegelianism* (Philadelphia, 1948) and his comprehensive *German Culture in America: Philosophical and Literary Influences 1600–1900* (Madison, Wis., 1957).

William Knight, *The Philosophy of the Beautiful* (2 vols. New York, 1891–93) summarizes prevailing British and European views and indicates the scantiness of aesthetic speculations by Americans. John B. Montignani, "A Note on the Bibliography of Art: Some XIXth Century American Authors," *Bulletin of the Metropolitan Museum of Art*, 36 (Jan. 1941), 12–16, uncovers early art historians. Kermit Vanderbilt, *Charles Eliot Norton, Apostle of Culture in a Democracy* (Cambridge, Mass., 1959) is a straightforward biography of America's leading art historian of the time; more interpretive is Austin Warren, "C. E. Norton, Apostle to the Gentiles," in his *New England Saints* (Ann Arbor, 1956); Fenollosa probably noted Norton's "Popularizing Art in America," *Nation*, 18 (1874), 170–71, and "The Massachusetts System of Instruction in Drawing," *Nation*, 22 (1876), 252–53. On art educational policies in the post-Civil War decade see: *Reports of the United States Commissioners to the Paris*

Universal Exposition, 1867, ed. William P. Blake, vol. 1 (Washington, D.C., 1870), which includes *Report on the Fine Arts* by Frank Leslie and *The Fine Arts Applied to the Useful Arts,* report by committee of Frank Leslie, Samuel F. B. Morse, Thomas W. Evans; Charles C. Perkins, *Art Education in America* (Cambridge, Mass., 1870); Walter Smith, *Art Education, Scholastic and Industrial* (Boston, 1872); and *Report of the Board of Visitors of the Massachusetts State Normal Art School, January 1875* (Boston, 1875). Neil Harris, "The Gilded Age Revisited: Boston and the Museum Movement," *American Quarterly,* 14 (1962), 545–66, analyzes Boston Museum of Fine Arts trustee backgrounds and suggests the inadequacies of present characterizations of "custodians of culture."

Important cultural connections between the United States and the Old World remain unexplored. Cushing Strout's pioneering work *The American Image of the Old World* (New York, 1963) scants the 1870–1910 reception of European culture. English thought, analyzed splendidly in Walter E. Houghton, *The Victorian Frame of Mind 1830–1870* (New Haven, 1957), and Raymond Williams, *Culture and Society 1780–1950* (London, 1958), has not been connected with an American intellectual milieu strongly attached to British writing during the nineteenth century. Ralph H. Gabriel, *The Course of American Democratic Thought* (New York, 1940, rev. ed. 1956), the best history of nineteenth-century American consensus, skirts debates over the quality of cultural life. Oliver W. Larkin, *Art and Life in America* (New York, 1949, rev. ed. 1960) surveys conditions. John H. Raleigh, *Matthew Arnold and American Culture* (Berkeley, Calif., 1957) focuses on literary theory. David H. Dickason, *The Daring Young Men, The Story of the American Pre-Raphaelites* (Bloomington, Ind., 1953) is fragmentary. On Arts and Crafts see bibliographical comments for Part Four.

Part Two: Chapters 4–8

Western responses to the Far East are described in W. W. Appleton, *A Cycle of Cathay* (New York, 1951), Virgile Pinot, *La Chine et la formation de l'esprit philosophique en France 1640–1740* (Paris, 1932), William L. Schwartz, *The Imaginative Interpretation of the Far East in Modern French Literature* 1800–1925 (Paris, 1927), Earl Miner, *The Japanese Tradition in British and American Literature* (Princeton, 1958). The general account of Japan read most widely in the United States up to 1900 was probably William E. Griffis, *The Mikado's Empire* (2 vols. New York, 1876). Robert S. Schwantes, *Japanese and Americans, A Century of Cultural Relations* (New York, 1955) is comprehensive with an excellent bibliography.

For analysis of Japanese responses to Western ideas I have relied heavily on George B. Sansom, *The Western World and Japan* (New York, 1950). Donald L. Keene, *The Japanese Discovery of Europe* (London, 1952) surveys the pre-Restoration "Western Studies" movement. Chitoshi Yanaga, *Japan Since Perry* (New York, 1949) is filled with information. Extensive material on Japanese conditions is compiled in the series *Japanese Culture in the Meiji Era*, Kaikoku Hyakunen Kinen Bunka Jigyo Kai [Centenary Culture Council], ed., of which the most helpful volumes were: Yoshie Okazaki, ed., *Japanese Literature in the Meiji Era*, Eng. trans. V. H. Viglielmo (Tokyo, 1955); Hideo Kishimoto, ed., *Japanese Religion in the Meiji Era*, Eng. trans. John F. Howes (Tokyo, 1956); Toyotaka Komiyo, ed., *Japanese Music and Drama in the Meiji Era*, Eng. trans. Donald Keene and Edward Seidensticker (Toyko, 1956); Keizo Shibusawa, ed., *Japanese Life and Culture in the Meiji Era*, Eng. trans. Charles S. Terry (Tokyo, 1958); Naoteru Uyeno, ed., *Japanese Arts and Crafts in the Meiji Era*, Eng. trans. Richard Lane (Tokyo, 1958); and Masaaki Kosaka, ed., *Japanese Thought in the Meiji Era*, Eng. trans. David Abosch (Tokyo, 1958). Tendai Buddhism is discussed in Masaharu Anesaki, *History of Japanese Religion* (London, 1930), pp. 111–22. General interpretations of the play of forces in Japan's rapid modernization are made in E. O. Reischauer, *Japan Past and Present* (2d ed. New York, 1958) and Hugh Borton, *Japan's Modern Century* (New York, 1955). George M. Beckmann, *The Making of the Meiji Constitution* (Lawrence, Kan., 1957) shows the role of German ideas. Problems of cultural transition are interpreted in J. W. Hall and Yoshio Sakata, "The Motivation of Political Leadership in the Meiji Restoration," *Journal of Asian Studies*, 16 (1956), 31–50. Delmer M. Brown, *Nationalism in Japan, An Introductory Historical Analysis* (Berkeley, Calif., 1955) treats issues essential for any precise appraisal of the significance of Fenollosa's activities, but his study scants artistic and philosophical currents.

Fenollosa's activities in Japan are recounted in authoritative detail in Mitsugu Hisatomi, *Fenorosa* [*Fenollosa*] (Tokyo, 1957), in Taro

Odakane, "Ernest F. Fenollosa's Activities in the Field of Art," 3 parts, *Bijutsu Kenkyu*, Nos. 110–112 (Feb.–April 1941), 48–62, 82–94, 112–21, and more summarily in Taro Kotakane, "Ernest Francisco Fenollosa, His Activities and Influence on Modern Japanese Art," *Bulletin of Eastern Art*, No. 16 (April 1941), 20–27. Fenollosa's role is minimized in Naohiko Masaki, "The Fine Arts," in Count Shigenobu Okuma, comp., *Fifty Years of New Japan*, Eng. trans. Marcus B. Huish, 2 (London, 1909), 323–57. For Fenollosa's influence on Japanese philosophy see Yujiro Miyake, "The Introduction of Western Philosophy," in *Fifty Years of New Japan*, pp. 226–41, and Gino Piovesana, "Main Trends of Contemporary Japanese Philosophy," *Monumenta Nipponica*, 11 (July 1955), 60–74.

Fenollosa's contacts with Henry Adams, John LaFarge, William Sturgis Bigelow, and Edward S. Morse are sketched in Van Wyck Brooks, *Fenollosa and His Circle, With Other Essays in Biography* (New York, 1962). Morse's impressions of the Far East are recorded in his own writings: *Japan Day By Day, 1877, 1878–79, 1882–83*, with 777 illustrations from sketches in the author's journal (2 vols. Boston, 1917); "Notes on Hokusai, The Founder of the Modern Japanese School of Drawing," *American Art Review*, 1 (1880), 144–48; *Japanese Homes and Their Surroundings* (Boston, 1886); *Glimpses of China and Chinese Homes* (Boston, 1902); Morse's energetic career is recounted in Dorothy Wayman, *Edward Sylvester Morse* (Cambridge, Mass., 1942). *Henry Adams and His Friends: A Collection of Hitherto Unpublished Letters*, ed. Harold Dean Cater (Boston, 1947) and *Letters of Henry Adams, 1858–1891*, ed. Worthington C. Ford (Boston, 1930) include reports from Japan. Ernest Samuels, *Henry Adams, The Middle Years* (Cambridge, Mass., 1958) provides the best account of the circumstances of Adams' visit to Japan; two excellent intellectual portraits are William H. Jordy, *Henry Adams, Scientific Historian* (New Haven, 1952) and J. C. Levenson, *The Mind and Art of Henry Adams* (Boston, 1957). John LaFarge's early appreciation, "An Essay on Japanese Art," appeared in Raphael Pumpelly, *Across America and Asia* (2d rev. ed. New York, 1870), pp. 195–202; see also John LaFarge, *An Artist's Letters from Japan* (London, 1897), *Considerations on Painting* (New York, 1895), and *Hokusai* (New York, 1897); Royal Cortissoz, *John LaFarge, A Memoir and a Study* (Boston, 1911) is appreciative; more theoretical is R. B. Katz, "John LaFarge, Art Critic," *Art Bulletin*, 33 (1951), 105–18. On art education see chapter footnotes and bibliographical comments for Chapter 15.

Part Three: Chapters 9–12

On Japanism in the West Ernst Scheyer, "Far Eastern Art and French Impressionism," *Art Quarterly*, 6 (1943), 116–43, includes a good bibliography. Early collections are reported in Louis V. Ledoux, *Japanese Prints in the Occident* (Tokyo, 1941) and analyzed in René Brimo, *L'Evolution du gout aux Etats- Unis, d'apres l'histoire des collections* (Paris, 1938). Benjamin I. Gilman, *The Museum of Fine Arts, 1870–1920* (Boston, 1920) is an official survey of this Boston museum; early museum objectives are analyzed in Neil Harris, "The Gilded Age Revisited: Boston and the Museum Movement," *American Quarterly*, 14 (1962), 545–66. Newspaper accounts of Fenollosa's work at the museum are included in year by year scrapbooks of museum activities located in the library of the Boston Museum of Fine Arts. Benjamin March, *China and Japan in Our Museums* (New York, 1929) summarizes resources. Edward A. Grant, "A Note on Fenollosa's Attributions," *Boston Museum of Fine Arts Bulletin*, 25 (1927), 83–84, is corrective. On general issues of museum development and education see bibliographical comments for Chapter 14.

Fenollosa's Boston milieu is recalled vividly in Van Wyck Brooks, *New England: Indian Summer 1865–1915* (New York, 1940) and *The Confident Years: 1885–1915* (New York, 1952). Helpful memoirs and biographies include: George Santayana, *The Last Puritan: A Memoir in the Form of a Novel* (New York, 1936), *Persons and Places* (3 vols. New York, 1944–51), *The Letters of George Santayana*, ed. Daniel Cory (New York, 1955); Henry Adams, *The Life of George Cabot Lodge* (Boston, 1911); Edith Wharton, *A Backward Glance* (New York, 1934); Ralph B. Perry, *The Thought and Character of William James* (2 vols. Boston, 1935); Morris Carter, *Isabella Stewart Gardner and Fenway Court* (Boston, 1925), an official account less lifelike than the mordant sketch of Mrs. Gardner in Aline B. Saarinen, *The Proud Possessors: The Lives, Times, and Tastes of Some Adventurous American Art Collectors* (New York, 1958); also Ralph Adams Cram, *My Life in Architecture* (Boston, 1936), Abbott Lawrence Lowell, *Biography of Percival Lowell* (New York, 1935), and Ferris Greenslet, *The Lowells and Their Seven Worlds* (Boston, 1946).

Tensions between aestheticism and Protestantism in the United

States are illustrated in Carleton Mabee, *American Leonardo: A Life of Samuel F. B. Morse* (New York, 1943). Washington Gladden, "Christianity and Aestheticism," *Andover Review*, 1 (1884), 13–24, presents a contemporary argument. Charles Eliot Norton's secular art mission was stated most clearly in journal articles: "The Intellectual Life of America," *New Princeton Review*, 6 (1888), 312–24; "A Definition of the Fine Arts," *Forum*, 7 (March 1889), 30–40; "The Educational Value of the History of the Fine Arts," *Educational Review*, 9 (1895), 343–48; "Some Aspects of Civilization in America," *Forum*, 20 (Feb. 1896), 641–51. Kermit Vanderbilt, *Charles Eliot Norton, Apostle of Culture in a Democracy* (Cambridge, Mass., 1959) offers a balanced estimate; Henry James, "American Art-Scholar: Charles Eliot Norton," *Notes on Novelists* (London, 1914), Paul Elmer More, "Charles Eliot Norton," in *A New England Group and Others* (Boston, 1921), and Austin Warren, "C. E. Norton, Apostle to the Gentiles," in *New England Saints* (Ann Arbor, 1956) are especially perceptive.

Minutes of the full board of trustees quarterly meetings on file at the Boston Museum of Fine Arts document Fenollosa's resignation. Biographical information on Mary McNeil Fenollosa derives from her diaries (see under manuscript sources), scrapbooks of newspaper clippings in possession of Mrs. S. T. Whatley, Montrose, Alabama, and Mrs. Whatley's recollections of her mother's career. Fenollosa's legal wranglings are recorded in papers in the Hall of Records, New York City, in the case of Kobayashi v. Ketcham, February 1897 to April 1897.

Lafcadio Hearn's writings on Japan include: *Glimpses of Unfamiliar Japan* (2 vols. Boston, 1894), *Out of the East: Reveries and Studies in New Japan* (Boston, 1895), *Kokoro: Hints and Echoes of Japanese Inner Life* (Boston, 1896), *Gleanings in Buddha-Fields: Studies of Hand and Soul in the Far East* (Boston, 1897), *Exotics and Retrospectives* (Boston, 1898), *In Ghostly Japan* (Boston, 1899), *Shadowings* (Boston, 1900), *A Japanese Miscellany* (Boston, 1901). *Kotto: Being Japanese Curios, with Sundry Cobwebs* (New York. 1902), *Kwaidan: Stories and Studies of Strange Things* (Boston, 1904), *Japan: An Attempt at Interpretation* (New York, 1904), also *Life and Letters of Lafcadio Hearn*, ed. Elizabeth Bisland (2 vols. Boston, 1906), and *Japanese Letters of Lafcadio Hearn*, ed. Elizabeth Bisland (Boston, 1910). Elizabeth Stevenson, *Lafcadio Hearn* (New York, 1961) is the most complete biography; see also Paul Elmer More,

Bibliography

"Lafcadio Hearn," in *Shelburne Essays, Second Series* (New York, 1905) and Matthew Josephson, "An Enemy of the West: Lafcadio Hearn," *Portrait of the Artist as an American* (New York, 1930).

Contemporary views of Japan's role as benevolent leader of Asia are presented in Kakuzo Okakura, *The Ideals of the East, with Special Reference to the Art of Japan* (London, 1903) and *The Awakening of Japan* (New York, 1904), and in *Japan By the Japanese, Essays on Meiji Japan by Its Leaders*, comp. Alfred Stead (London, 1904). See also Walter C. Young, *Some Oriental Influences on Western Culture, Part I, Japan as Tutor to the West* (American Council Institute of Pacific Relations, 1929). Popular American views of China are analyzed historically in Harold R. Isaacs, *Scratches on Our Minds* (New York, 1958).

Part Four: Chapters 13–16

Fenollosa's campaigns for individuality through art are part of an as yet unwritten history of the relations of culture and democracy in the United States. The complexity of these relations, suggested in Raymond Williams, *Culture and Society 1780–1950* (London, 1958), has been obscured in the influential and pioneer writings of Lewis Mumford by a generalized cultural organicism whose corollaries include self-tutored Americanism and an artistic alienation necessary amid the corrupt materialism of the Gilded Age; see Mumford, *Sticks and Stones, A Study of American Architecture and Civilization* (New York, 1924), *The Golden Day, A Study in American Literature and Culture* (New York, 1926), *The Brown Decades, A Study of the Arts in America 1865–1895* (New York, 1931), *The Culture of Cities* (New York, 1938). Some general problems in the cultural historiography of the period are discussed in my introduction to Dorothy Weir Young, *The Life and Letters of J. Alden Weir* (New Haven, 1960). An important study of vernacular art, John A. Kouwenhoven, *Made in America: The Arts in Modern Civilization* (Newton Center, Mass., 1948), intentionally scants cultural relations with Europe and other parts of the world. Siegfried Giedion, *Mechanization Takes Command, a Contribution to Anonymous History* (New York, 1948), develops broad hypotheses. Henry F. May, *The End of American Innocence, a Study of the First Years of Our Own Times, 1912–1917* (New York, 1959) offers the first general analysis of the related ideas of culture, morality, and progress at the turn of the century, but the idea of culture is confined generally to its genteel Anglophile version. Important approaches through histories of taste are made in René Brimo, *L'Evolution du gout aux Etats-Unis, d'apres l'histoire des collections* (Paris, 1938), Russell Lynes, *The Tastemakers* (New York, 1949), and Aline B. Saarinen, *The Proud Possessors: The Lives, Times, and Tastes of Some Adventurous American Art Collectors* (New York, 1958). Robert H. L. Wheeler's forthcoming history of the relations of leisure, the arts, and higher learning to equality and industrialism in the United States explores conditions ignored in the voluminous analyses of "mass culture" written since the second World War.

The varieties of Chautauqua meetings and programs and their effects have not been analyzed. Harry P. Harrison, *Culture under Canvas, The Story of Tent Chautauqua*, ed. Karl Detzer (New York, 1957), recalls places and personalities. The Arts and Crafts movement receives only generalized treatment in Robert L. Duffus, *The American Renaissance* (New York, 1928); nor does it receive more than cursory consideration in David H. Dickason, *The Daring Young Men* (Bloomington, 1953). The best outline remains Rho F. Zueblin, "The Arts and Crafts Movement," a series in nine parts, *Chautauquan*, 36–37 (Oct. 1902 to June 1903). Materials for a history of the American Arts and Crafts movement are plentiful in magazine files: *Knight Errant* (1892–93) and *Handicraft* (1902–04, 1910–12) from Boston; *Brush and Pencil* (1897–1905) from Chicago; *The Artsman* (1903–07) from Philadelphia; *Craftsman* (1901–16) and *Arts and Decoration* (1910—) from New York; *Philistine* (1895–1915), Elbert Hubbard's journal, and also his Roycroft Press publications; *Modern Art* (1893–97), *House Beautiful* (1896—). For European connections of Arts and Crafts with Art Nouveau see: Nikolaus Pevsner, *Pioneers of Modern Design* (New York, 1949); S. T. Madsen, *Sources of Art Nouveau* (Oslo, 1956); Alf Bøe, *From Gothic Revival to Functional Form* (Oslo, 1957); Henry F. Lenning, *The Art Nouveau* (The Hague, 1951); Clay Lancaster, "Oriental Contributions to Art Nouveau," *Art Bulletin*, 34 (1952), 297–310; and also Ernst Scheyer, "Far Eastern Art and French Impressionism," *Art Quarterly*, 6 (1943), 116–43.

Charles Lang Freer's career as a collector is sketched sharply in Aline B. Saarinen, *The Proud Possessors* (New York, 1958). On issues of museum development and education see Laurence V. Coleman, *The Museum in America* (3 vols. Washington, D.C., 1939), Walter

Bibliography

Pach, *The Art Museum in America, Its History and Achievement*
(New York, 1948), Francis H. Taylor, *Babel's Tower, The Dilemma
of the Modern Museum* (New York, 1945), Alma S. Wittlin, *The
Museum, Its History and Its Tasks in Education* (London, 1949),
Grace F. Ramsey, *Educational Work in the Museums of the United
States* (New York, 1938), and Theodore L. Low, *The Educational
Philosophy and Practice of Art Museums in the United States* (New
York, 1948).

The *Golden Age*, one volume of 319 pages, appeared as an illustrated monthly in five numbers from January to June 1906; it was
published in New York City by the Junior Publishing Co. The magazine foundered after the first two numbers (January and February)
and resumed publication in April with a new editor, Ada Jean McKey,
who worked very closely with Ernest and Mary Fenollosa.

Most helpful for general educational context are R. F. Butts and
L. A. Cremin, *A History of Education in American Culture* (New
York, 1953), John S. Brubacher, *A History of the Problems of Educa-
tion* (New York, 1947), and Merle Curti, *Social Ideas of American
Educators* (New York, 1935). Lawrence A. Cremin, *The Transforma-
tion of the School, Progressivism in American Education 1876–1957*
(New York, 1961) is excellent and with a good bibliography, but art
education is slighted. Frederick M. Logan, *Growth of Art in American
Schools* (New York, 1955) is narrow and distractingly partisan. Vari-
ous representative viewpoints which help define the context for the
Fenollosa-Dow system include: Thomas Davidson, *The Place of Art
in Education*, lecture before the American Social Science Association,
Saratoga, N.Y., 1885 (Boston, 1885); E. D. Starr, "The Aesthetic in
Education," *American Catholic Quarterly*, 16 (1891), 159–70; Walter
S. Perry, "Conditions Underlying Art Education in European and
American Schools," *National Education Association Addresses and
Proceedings*, 1891 (New York, 1891), pp. 765–76; J. M. Hoppin,
Methods of Art Education, paper read at the Congress of Art Educa-
tion of the World's Fair, Chicago, July 27, 1893 (1893); William T.
Harris, "Aesthetic Element in Education," *National Education Asso-
ciation Addresses and Proceedings*, 1897 (Chicago, 1897), pp. 330–38;
Francis W. Parker, "Art in Everything," *National Education Asso-
ciation Addresses and Proceedings*, 1900 (Chicago, 1900), pp. 509–
14; John Dewey, *The School and Society*, based on lectures first given
in 1899 (2d rev. ed. Chicago, 1915), esp. pp. 44–47, 117–18; Frank F.
Frederick, "Study of Fine Art in American Colleges and Universities:
Its Relation to the Study in Public Schools," *National Education*

266

Association Addresses and Proceedings, 1901 (Chicago, 1901), pp. 695–703; Frank Lloyd Wright, "The Art and Craft of the Machine," *The New Industrialism* (Chicago, 1902); L. S. Cushman, "Fenollosa's Theory of Art Development," *Elementary School Teacher*, 5 (April 1905), 473–81; James P. Haney, *Art Education in the Public Schools of the United States* (New York, 1908); Henry T. Bailey, *Instruction in the Fine and Manual Arts in the United States, A Statistical Monograph* (Washington, D.C., 1909); Louis H. Sullivan, "Is Our Art a Betrayal Rather than an Expression of American Life?" *Craftsman*, 15 (January 1909), 402–04; Royal B. Farnum, *Present Status of Drawing and Art in the Elementary and Secondary Schools of the United States*, with 63 plates (Washington, D.C., 1914). A comprehensive survey of conditions before 1900, with key documents reproduced, is Isaac Edwards Clarke, *Art and Industry, Education in the Industrial and Fine Arts in the United States* (4 vols. Washington, D.C., 1885–98). Arthur W. Dow, *Composition* (Boston, 1899) was published in a nineteenth edition in 1938.

Katherine A. Gilbert and Helmut Kuhn, *A History of Esthetics* (rev. ed. Bloomington, Ind., 1953) and Thomas Munro, "Aesthetics as Science: Its Development in America," *Journal of Aesthetics and Art Criticism*, 9 (1951), 161–207, are helpful surveys; see also Bernard Bosanquet, *A History of Aesthetic* (New York, 1892) and G. W. F. Hegel, *Introduction to Hegel's Philosophy of Fine Art*, Eng. trans. Bernard Bosanquet (London, 1886). Lionello Venturi, *History of Art Criticism*, Eng. trans. Charles Marrott (New York, 1936), stands virtually alone, as does the ambitious history by Horace M. Kallen, *Art and Freedom* (2 vols. New York, 1942). There is no history of art history; nor have connections been made with cultural history in histories of aesthetics, criticism, connoisseurship.

Consideration of non-Western aesthetics and criticism, preliminary to less European-centered analyses and histories, has been advanced by the writings of Ananda K. Coomaraswamy, notably *The Transformation of Nature in Art* (Cambridge, Mass., 1934) and *The Dance of Siva* (rev. ed. New York, 1957). Far Eastern writings include: Seiichi Taki, *Three Essays on Oriental Painting* (London, 1910); Henry P. Bowie, *On the Laws of Japanese Painting* (San Francisco, 1911); Kuo Hsi, *An Essay on Landscape Painting*, Eng. trans. Shio Sakanishi (London, 1935); *The Chinese on the Art of Painting*, Eng. trans. Osvald Siren (Peking, 1936); *The Spirit of the Brush, Being the Outlook of Chinese Painters on Nature from Eastern Chin to Five Dynasties* A.D. 317–960, Eng. trans. Shio Sakanishi (London,

1939); Mai-mai Sze, *The Tao of Painting* (2 vols. New York, 1956). George Rowley, *Principles of Chinese Painting* (Princeton, 1947) offers an eloquent introduction.

Representative modern views of Far Eastern art history are Ludwig Bachhofer, *A Short History of Chinese Art* (New York, 1946); William Cohn, *Chinese Painting* (London, 1948), Hoshu Minamoto, *An Illustrated History of Japanese Art*, Eng. trans. H. Henderson (Kyoto, 1935); Robert T. Paine and Alexander Soper, *The Art and Architecture of Japan* (Baltimore, 1955). Good general histories are Edwin O. Reischauer and John K. Fairbank, *East Asia: The Great Tradition* (Boston, 1960), C. P. Fitzgerald, *China* (4th ed. rev. New York, 1954), and G. B. Sansom, *Japan, a Short Cultural History* (2d ed. rev. New York, 1952). Yu-Lan Fung, *A History of Chinese Philosophy*, Eng. trans. Derk Bodde (2 vols. Princeton, 1952–53) is standard. On the development of Western studies of China see Arthur F. Wright, "The Study of Chinese Civilization," *Journal of the History of Ideas*, 21 (1960), 233–55, and Kenneth Scott Latourette, "Chinese Historical Studies during the Past Seven Years," *American Historical Review*, 26 (1921), 703–16. Of particular relevance to Fenollosa's stress on individualism in Chinese art are Joseph R. Levenson, "The Amateur Ideal in Ming and Early Ch'ing Society: Evidence from Painting," in *Chinese Thought and Institutions*, ed. J. K. Fairbank (Chicago, 1957), pp. 320–41, James F. Cahill, "Confucian Elements in the Theory of Painting," in *The Confucian Persuasion*, ed. Arthur F. Wright (Stanford, Calif., 1960), and Tung-chi Lin, "The Chinese Mind: Its Taoist Substratum," *Journal of the History of Ideas*, 8 (1947), 259–72.

Brief posthumous notices of Fenollosa include: Laurence Binyon, "National Character in Art," *Littell's Living Age*, 259 (Dec. 5, 1908), 627–29; G. S. Layard, "The Universality of Art," *Bookman*, 43 (Dec. 1912), 174–76; Ernst Grosse, "Fenollosa," *Ostasiatische Zeitschrift*, 6 (1917), 95–99; S. Miyoshi, "Ernest Fenollosa," *Japan Magazine*, 11 (1920), 281–85; Yone Noguchi, "Japan's Debt to America," *Arts and Decoration*, 15 (June 1921), 84–85. See also Langdon Warner, "Ernest Francisco Fenollosa," *Dictionary of American Biography* (New York, 1930), 3, 325–26.

Part Five: Chapters 17–19

Relations between poetry and painting through the art of writing are indicated in Henry P. Bowie, *On the Laws of Japanese Painting*

(San Francisco, 1911), Chiang Yee, *Chinese Calligraphy, an Introduction to Its Aesthetic and Technique* (2d ed. London, 1954), and Mai-mai Sze, *The Tao of Painting* (2 vols. New York, 1956), which includes discussion of the relations of the *I Ching* with painting.

Roy E. Teele, *Through a Glass Darkly: A Study of English Translations of Chinese Poetry* (Ann Arbor, 1949) is the best introduction to controversy over Fenollosa-Pound versions and theories of Chinese. Achilles Fang, "Fenollosa and Pound," *Harvard Journal of Asiatic Studies*, 20 (1957), 213–38, criticizes Pound's translations in detail. George Kennedy, "Fenollosa, Pound, and the Chinese Character," *Yale Literary Magazine*, 127 (Dec. 1958), 24–36, makes a broadside attack from a linguistic position. More sympathetic is Hugh Gordon Proteus, "Ezra Pound and His Chinese Character," in *An Examination of Ezra Pound*, ed. Peter Russell (Norfolk, Conn., 1950). Pound's use of Chinese is analyzed perceptively in Hugh Kenner, *The Poetry of Ezra Pound* (Norfolk, Conn., 1950). Donald Davie, *Articulate Energy: An Inquiry into the Syntax of English Poetry* (London, 1955) analyzes Fenollosa's poetics in an important context.

The best account of the intricate personal and theoretical patterns of the imagist movement is Stanley Coffman, *Imagism: A Chapter for the History of Modern Poetry* (Norman, Okla., 1951). See also Glenn Hughes, *Imagism and the Imagists* (Stanford, Calif., 1931); John Gould Fletcher, "The Orient and Contemporary Poetry," in *The Asian Legacy and American Life*, ed. Arthur E. Christy (New York, 1942), pp. 145–74; and T. S. Eliot, *Ezra Pound: His Metric and Poetry* (New York, 1917), "The Noh and the Image," *The Egoist*, 4 (1917), 102–03.

John Hamilton Edwards and William W. Vasse, *Annotated Index to The Cantos of Ezra Pound, Cantos I–LXXXIV* (Berkeley, Calif., 1957) is essential. My interpretation of the visual effects and themes in "Canto 77" is based on Pound's writings, Fenollosa's theories, and R. B. Blakney, *A Course in the Analysis of Chinese Characters* (Shanghai, 1928).

Arthur F. Wright, "Professor Northrop's Chapter on the Traditional Culture of the Orient," *Journal of the History of Ideas*, 10 (1949), 143–49, offers a searching critique of an important part of F. S. C. Northrop's influential *The Meeting of East and West* (New York, 1946). Fenollosa's cosmopolitan perspectives are part of a later pattern of speculations which include: Benjamin Rowland, Jr., *Art in East and West* (Cambridge, Mass., 1954), Horace M. Kallen, *Art and Freedom* (2 vols. New York, 1942), Alan W. Watts, *The Way of*

Bibliography

Zen (New York, 1957), *Language, Thought, and Reality: Selected Writings of Benjamin Lee Whorf,* ed. John B. Carroll (New York, 1956), Ivor A. Richards, *Mencius on Mind, Experiments in Multiple Definition* (New York, 1932), "Toward a Theory of Comprehending," *Speculative Instruments* (Chicago, 1955), pp. 17–38, and A. L. Kroeber, *Style and Civilizations* (Ithaca, N.Y., 1957).

B. Manuscript Sources

1. Fenollosa Family Papers

FENOLLOSA, ERNEST

"Poems Written in Boyhood," February 1866–August 1868. 211 pp. Brenda Fenollosa Biddle estate, Haverford, Pennsylvania.

"Pantheism," Harvard University Commencement Parts, 1874–76, signed Ernest F. Fenollosa, April 30, 1874. 12 pp. Archives, Harvard University, Cambridge, Massachusetts.

"Ernest Francisco Fenollosa," Class Book 1874. Pp. 285–90. Archives, Harvard University, Cambridge, Massachusetts.

Letters (6) to Edward Sylvester Morse, 1884–93. Peabody Museum, Salem, Massachusetts.

"East and West," Phi Beta Kappa Society Poem delivered June 1892 in Cambridge, Massachusetts. Freer Gallery of Art, Washington, D.C.

Letters (7) to Robert Underwood Johnson, 1893–98. New York Public Library.

Letter to Isabella Stewart Gardner, n.d. (c. 1894). Fenway Court Museum, Boston, Massachusetts.

Notes on Japanese Career (c. 1894). Harvard College Alumni Office, Cambridge, Massachusetts.

"The Relations of China and Japan," address delivered before the Liberal Club, Buffalo, New York, February 24, 1896. 25 pp. Mrs. S. T. Whatley, Montrose, Alabama.

"An Outline of Japanese Art" (c. 1897). 81 pp. Mrs. S. T. Whatley, Montrose, Alabama.

270

Essay on the philosophy of art, untitled (c. 1898). 21 pp. Ralph Ladd, Cambridge, Massachusetts.

"An Outline of the History of Ukiyoye," first draft begun January 20, 1899, finished February 27, 1899. 146 pp. Mrs. S. T. Whatley, Montrose, Alabama.

Poem by Rihaku (transcribed c. 1899). 1 p. Alan Chester, Cismont, Virginia.

Poem by Oshorei (transcribed c. 1899). 1 p. Alan Chester, Cismont, Virginia.

"Outline Sketch of the History of Doctrines in China" (c. 1900). 763 pp. Alan Chester, Cismont, Virginia.

Letters (40) to Charles Lang Freer, 1901–07. Freer Gallery of Art, Washington, D.C.

Letters (2) to Joel Spingarn, 1901. New York Public Library.

"Landscape Poetry and Painting in Medieval China," Washington, March 17, 1903, lecture 6 in a course of 7 lectures, notebook pp. 101–77. Ezra Pound, Brunnenburg, Tirolo, Italy.

"Report of a Lecture on Japanese Art by Ernest Fenollosa," n.d. 37 pp. Freer Gallery of Art, Washington, D.C.

"Notes Taken Before Mr. Freer's Collection in Detroit," November 4–11, 1907. Freer Gallery of Art, Washington, D.C.

FENOLLOSA, BRENDA (MRS. MONCURE BIDDLE)

"Recollections of My Life in Japan," October 12, 1952. 5 pp. Brenda Fenollosa Biddle estate, Haverford, Pennsylvania.

FENOLLOSA, MANUEL

Music Composed for Piano, 1842–63. Music Collection of Essex Institute Historical Society, Salem, Massachusetts.

FENOLLOSA, MARY MC NEIL

Daily Journals: July 28, 1890, to July 23, 1891 (1 vol., 200 pp.); April 17, 1896, to December 31, 1899 (19 vols., 3654 pp.); February 11, 1902, to June 25, 1903 (1 vol., 165 pp.). Mrs. S. T. Whatley, Montrose, Alabama.

Notes on death of Ernest Fenollosa, the preparation of *Epochs of Chinese and Japanese Art*, and on Ezra Pound (c. 1948). 6 pp. Mrs. S. T. Whatley, Montrose, Alabama.

Walpole Galleries Sales Catalogue no. 139, Jan. 27 and Jan. 28, 1920, New York City, lists "Library and MSS of the late Prof. Ernest F. Fenollosa" on pp. 7–19, 50–60, approximately 200 items.

2. Other Personal Papers

Dole, Nathan Haskell. Autobiography. Mrs. Margaret Dole McCall, New York, New York.

Dow, Arthur Wesley. Papers. Ralph Ladd, Cambridge, Massachusetts.

Freer, Charles Lang. Correspondence. Freer Gallery of Art, Washington, D.C.

Gardner, Isabella Stewart. Journals and Guest Books. Fenway Court Museum, Boston, Massachusetts.

Johnson, Arthur W. Papers of relating to Arthur Wesley Dow. Ralph Ladd, Cambridge, Massachusetts.

Mendenhall, Thomas Corwin. "Autobiographical Notes." Thomas C. Mendenhall, II, Northampton, Massachusetts.

Morse, Edward Sylvester. Papers. Mrs. Russell Robb, Concord, Massachusetts, and Peabody Museum, Salem, Massachusetts.

Weber, Max. Papers. Stieglitz Collection, Yale Collection of American Literature, Sterling Memorial Library, New Haven, Connecticut.

C. A Chronological List of the Published Writings of Ernest Francisco Fenollosa

"Poem," delivered at Harvard College Class Day Exercises 1874, *Baccalaureate Sermon and Oration and Poem Class of 1874,* Cambridge, Massachusetts, John Wilson, 1874.

"Bijutsu Shinsetsu" (Truth of Fine Arts), *Meiji Bunka Zenshu* (Collection of Works on Meiji Culture), Tokyo, Nihon Hyoronsha, 1928–30, *12,* 157–74.

"Nihon Bijutsu Saiko Ron" (On the Revival of Japanese Art), *Dai Nippon Bijutsu Shinpo,* No. 6 (1884).

Review of the Chapter on Painting in Gonse's L'Art Japonais, reprinted from *Japan Weekly Mail,* July 12, 1884, Boston, James R. Osgood, 1885.

"Nippon Gadai no Shorai" (The Future of Themes in Japanese Painting), *Dai Nippon Bijutsu Shinpo*, Nos. 19, 21 (1885).

"Gadai ni Bukkyo o Mochiuru no Tokushitsu" (Merits and Defects of Using Buddhist Themes in Art), *Dai Nippon Bijutsu Shinpo*, No. 20 (1885).

"Dai Ikkai Kangwakai Taikai Jusho Sakuhin Hihyoo" (Comments on the Prize-Winning Works Submitted to the First General Meeting of the Kangwakai), *Dai Nippon Bijutsu Shinpo*, Nos. 19, 23 (1885).

"Nippon Bijutsu Kogei wa Hatashite Gaikoku no Jukyu o Kanki suru no Chikara Auru ya Ina ya" (Do Japanese Arts and Crafts Have the Capacity to Interest Foreign Markets?), *Dai Nippon Bijutsu Shinpo*, Nos. 25, 29 (1886). This article is an excerpt from a speech made by Fenollosa at the ninth regular meeting of the Kangwakai in November 1885; the complete text of this speech is printed in *Dai Nippon Bijutsu Shinpo*, Nos. 43, 44, and 45.

"The Pictorial Art of Japan," *Blackwood's Edinburgh Magazine*, 141 (1887), 281–90. This was an unsigned review of William Anderson, *The Pictorial Arts of Japan*, London, 1886.

"Reisei no Sangenso" (The Three Elements of the Sublime), *Tetsugakkai Zasshi*, No. 16 (1888).

"Nihon Bijutsu Kogei on Shorai Ikan" (The Future of Japanese Arts and Crafts) (1889), in Okabe Munahisa, ed., *Naigai Meishi Nihon Bijutsu Ron* (Essays on Japanese Art by Foreign and Japanese Authorities).

"Nara no Kobijutsu" (The Ancient Art of Nara) (1889), in *Naigai Meishi*.

"Ukiyoye-shi Ko" (Considerations on the History of Ukiyoye), *Kokka*, Nos. 1, 2, 4, 6, 8 (1889–90).

"Bijutsu Tetsugaku Gairon" (Outline of the Philosophy of Art), *Kokka*, No. 3 (1889).

"Bijutsu ni Ararzaru Mono" (What Is Not Art), *Kokka*, No. 5 (1890).

Letter from Fenollosa to James R. Chadwick relating to purchase of the Morse Collection, in *The Morse Collection of Japanese Pottery*, Boston, 1891, pp. 4–6 [pamphlet].

"The Significance of Oriental Art," *The Knight Errant*, 1 (1892), 65–70.

"Chinese and Japanese Traits," *Atlantic Monthly*, 69 (1892), 769–74.

Hokusai and His School, Catalogue of Special Exhibition Number One, Boston Museum of Fine Arts, 1893.

East and West, The Discovery of America and Other Poems, New York, Crowell, 1893.

"Contemporary Japanese Art," *Century,* 46 (1893), 577–81.

"Studying Art—Discussion," *Proceedings of the International Congress of Education, Chicago, 1893,* New York, National Educational Association, 1894, p. 472.

Catalogue of a Special Exhibition of Ancient Chinese Buddhist Paintings Lent by the Temple Daitokuji of Kioto, Japan, Boston, Museum of Fine Arts, 1894.

Imagination in Art, Boston, Boston Art Students Association, 1894.

Catalogue of an Exhibition of Japanese Paintings and Metal Work Lent by Mr. F. Shirasu of Tokio, Boston, Museum of Fine Arts, 1894.

"Ancient Chinese Paintings," *New Cycle,* 8 (1895), 555–60.

Introduction to *Special Exhibition of Color Prints Designed, Engraved, and Printed by Arthur W. Dow, April 18–June 1, 1895, in the Japanese Corridor,* Boston, Museum of Fine Arts, 1895.

Mural Painting in the Boston Public Library, Boston, Curtis, 1896.

The Masters of Ukiyoye, a complete historical description of Japanese paintings and color prints of the genre school as shown in exhibition at the Fine Arts Building, New York, January 1896, by W. H. Ketcham, New York, Knickerbocker Press, 1896.

"The Symbolism of the Lotos," *The Lotos,* 9 (1896), 577–83.

"The Nature of Fine Art," *The Lotos,* 9 (1896), 663–73, 753–62.

"Color Studies," *The Lotos,* 9 (1896), 771.

"Art Museums and Their Relation to the People," *The Lotos,* 9 (1896), 841–47, 929–35.

"The French Salon of 1896," *The Lotos,* 9 (1896), 950–61.

"An Exhibition of Japanese Color Prints" (unsigned), *The Lotos,* 9 (1896), 634–36.

"Arthur W. Dow" (unsigned), *The Lotos,* 9 (1896), 709–10.

"Lectures at the Metropolitan Museum" (unsigned), *The Lotos,* 9 (1896), 731–33.

"The Fine Arts" (unsigned column appearing also as "Lotos Leaves" and "Art Notes"), *The Lotos,* 9 (1896), 637–41, 727–30, 811–16, 986–90.

"Japanese Art from the World's Point of View," *Far East* (an English edition of *Kokumin no Tomo,* Tokyo), 2 (May 20, 1897), 196–201.

"The Abuse of the Nude in Art," *Far East*, 3 (Jan. 20, 1898), 39–45.

Catalogue of the Exhibition of Ukioye Paintings and Prints Held at Ikao Onsen, Uyeno Shinzaka, from April 15 to May 15, 1898, Tokyo, Bunshichi Kobayashi, 1898.

"Outline of Japanese Art," *Century*, 56 (1898), 62–75, 276–89.

"The Coming Fusion of East and West," *Harper's*, 98 (Dec. 1898), 115–22.

"Japan's Place in History," *The Orient* (*Hansei Zasshi* transformed), 14 (1899), 9–15.

"Epithalamial Ode," *Japan Weekly Mail*, Yokohama, 33 (May 12, 1900), 462; a poem of 243 lines "On the Marriage of H. I. H. The Crown Prince of Japan."

"Wood Printing in Color" (unsigned), *Japanese Paintings and Modern Wood Prints Made in Japan for J. B. Millet*, New York, American Art Association, n.d. (c. 1900), pp. 7–9.

Catalogue of the Exhibition of Paintings of Hokusai, held at the Japan Fine Art Association, Uyeno Park, Tokyo, from January 13 to 30, 1900, Tokyo, Bunshichi Kobayashi, 1900.

"Notes on the Japanese Lyric Drama," *Journal of the American Oriental Society*, 22 (1901), 129–37.

An Outline of the History of Ukiyoye, Tokyo, Bunshichi Kobayashi, 1901.

"Possibilities of Art Education in Relation to Manual Training," *National Education Association Addresses and Proceedings*, 1902, Chicago, U. of Chicago Press, 1902, pp. 564–70.

"The Place in History of Mr. Whistler's Art," *Lotus*, 1 (1903), 14–17.

"The Fine Arts," *Elementary School Teacher*, 5 (Sept. 1904), 15–28.

"Japanese Pictorial Art, Rare Screens, Prints, and Paintings," *Catalogue of the Art Treasures Collected by Thomas E. Waggaman*, New York, American Art Association, 1905, pp. 560–85.

"The Roots of Art," *The Golden Age*, 1 (April 1906), 160–63.

"The Logic of Art," *The Golden Age*, 1 (May 1906), 230–35.

"The Individuality of the Artist," *The Golden Age*, 1 (June 1906), 280–85.

"The Collection of Mr. Charles L. Freer," *Pacific Era*, 1 (Nov. 1907), 57–66; portions reprinted as "The Charles L. Freer Collection," *Academy Notes*, Buffalo Fine Arts Academy, 4 (Nov. 1908), 93–95.

Catalogue of the Exhibition of Ukiyoye Paintings and Prints at the

*Yamanaka Galleries, 254 Fifth Avenue, New York, February 27–
March 14, 1908*, New York, Alexander Press, 1908.

"Modern Spanish Art to the Fore in the Salon of Nineteen Hundred
and Eight: Decadence of French Influence," *Craftsman*, 14
(Sept. 1908), 571–87.

Epochs of Chinese and Japanese Art, An Outline History of East
Asiatic Design, edited by Mary Fenollosa, 2 vols., London, Heinemann, 1912; new and revised edition with copious notes by Professor Petrucci, New York, Stokes, and London, Heinemann,
1921.

L'Art en Chine et au Japon, adaptation et préface par Gaston Migeon,
Paris, Hachette, 1913.

"The Classical Drama of Japan," *Quarterly Review*, No. 441 (Oct.
1914), 450–78.

"Ernest Fenollosa's Work on the Japanese 'Noh'," ed. Ezra Pound,
Drama, No. 18 (May 1915), 199–247.

Cathay, translations by Ezra Pound for the most part from the notes
of the late Ernest Fenollosa and the decipherings of Professors
Mori and Ariga, London, E. Mathews, 1915.

Certain Noble Plays of Japan, from the manuscripts of Ernest Fenollosa, chosen and finished by Ezra Pound, with an introduction
by William Butler Yeats, Churchtown, Dundrum, Cuala Press,
1916.

'Noh'; or Accomplishment, a Study of the Classical Stage of Japan, by
Ernest Fenollosa and Ezra Pound, London, Macmillan, 1916.

The Chinese Written Character as a Medium for Poetry, an Ars
Poetica, with a foreword and notes by Ezra Pound, New York,
Arrow editions, 1936; another edition, New York, Kasper & Hor-
ton, n.d. (c. 1950). This was first published in Ezra Pound, *In-
stigations of Ezra Pound*, together with an essay on the Chinese
written character by Ernest Fenollosa, New York, Boni & Live-
right, 1920.

Ursprung und Entwicklung der Chinesischen und Japanischen Kunst,
Ger. trans. F. Milcke und Shinkichi Hara, 2 vols. Leipzig, Hierse-
mann, 1923.

Japanese Noh Drama Given for the First Time Outside of Japan,
staged by Michio Itow for the Thursday Evening Club, including
"The Story of Hagoromo" translated by Ernest Fenollosa and
Ezra Pound, n.p., 1923.

Introduzione Ai No (by Ernest Fenollosa and Ezra Pound), con un dramma in un atto di Motokiyo—Kagekiyo, tr. dall'inglese di Mary de Rachewiltz, Milano, All'Insegna del Pesce D'Oro, 30 October, 1954, 2d ed. 1956, 3d ed. 1958.

Nishikigi, a cura di Ernest Fenollosa, ed. Ezra Pound; introduzione ai No di W. B. Yeats, tr. dall'inglese di Mary de Rachewiltz, Milano, All'Insegna del Pesce D'Oro, 1957.

Catai Di Ezra Pound, a cura di Mary de Rachewiltz 5 pp. manoscritto di Ernest Fenollosa, Strenna Del Pesce D'Oro, 1960, All'Insegna Del Pesce D'Oro, Milano, 1959.

L'Ideogramma Cinese Come Mezzo Di Poesia, Una Ars Poetica, introduzione e note di Ezra Pound, versione dall'inglese di Mary de Rachewiltz, Milano, All'Insegna Del Pesce D'Oro, 1960.

Alcuni Nobili Drammi Del Giappone, dai manoscritti di Ernest Fenollosa scelti e finiti da Ezra Pound, introduzione di W. B. Yeats, versione dall'inglese di Mary de Rachewiltz, Milano, All'Insegna Del Pesce D'Oro, 1961.

INDEX

Clarke, Isaac E., 78 n.
Clarke, Purdom, 172 n.
Clarke, Samuel Behler, 24 n.
Colarossi Academy, Paris, 232
Collections. *See* Art
Colombo, Ceylon, 131
Color: a Chinese view of, 174 n.; in
Composition, 188; EF on, 81, 202–
03; transforms American school-
rooms, 189–90; Weber on, 233, 237.
See also Brush
Columbia University, 178 f., 192 f.,
195; EF at, 198
Columbus, Christopher, 137
Columbus, Ohio, 157
Commercialism, 39, 47, 74, 99, 126,
179, 181, 183 n. *See also* Art
Composition, 156, 161, 187 ff., 193 f.,
221, 235 n.; French trans., 194. *See
also* Art education, Dow
Concord, Mass., 126, 219
Cone, Etta, 234
Conformity, 4, 16, 126, 159, 166, 199
f. *See also* Individuality
Confucian Analects, 131, 177
Confucianism, 83, 95, 128, 135, 148,
203, 207 f.; Pound's, 226, 228 f.
Congo, 141
Coomaraswamy, Ananda, 241 n.
Cooper Union, N.Y.C., 154
Copley Society, Boston, 172
Corcoran Gallery, Washington, D.C.,
29
Corot, Jean B. C., 182
Cortez, Hernando, 10, 23
Cosmopolitanism, 3, 6 f., 23, 32, 50,
58, 67, 85, 92, 96 f., 115 f., 149, 208
f., 212, 245 ff.; H. Adams's, 68;
American, 57, 115; in American
painting, 230–43; Dow's, 186 ff.,
197, 238 f.; EF's, 6 f., 10, 23, 32, 50,
58, 68 f., 71 f., 75, 92, 104, 149,
208 f., 245–47; Hearn's, 141–47;
H. James's, 3; Japanese, 85, 96 f.;
Jarves's, 62; LaFarge's, 61, 68, 74;
Norton's, 115; in poetry, 215–29;
Pound's, 222–29; Weber's, 231–37;
Whitman's, 20, 32, 35 f., 57. *See*

also Eclecticism, World art, World
civilization
Cox, Kenyon, 240
Crafts, 48 n., 130, 147 f., 192, 210,
231, 239. *See also* Arts and Crafts
Craftsman, 210 f., 235 n.
Craftsmen, National Society of, 210
Cram, Ralph Adams, 133 n.
Crane, Walter, 91
Crawford, F. Marion, 104 n.
Creole, 141
Crowninshield family, 12 n.
Cubism, 233, 237
Cultural characteristics: China, 95 f.,
98 f.; the East (Far East), 7, 96–
100, 125, 128;
Japan: artistry, 72–74, 163; ear-
nestness, 40; industrial efficiency,
163; loyalty, 42, 45; militarism, 8,
83, 129, 132, 149, 163; nature
domesticated, 143; nature sensitiv-
ity, 73; primitivism, 36, 75; self
multiple, 145; xenophobia, 132, 134,
136, 149; *see also* Japan;
Latin, 140 n.; Protestant, 14, 110,
113 f., 140 n., 245; the West, 7, 57,
96–100, 125, 128, 145, 244 ff.
compared: China and Japan, 95 f.;
East and West, 96–100, 125, 128;
U.S. and Europe, 43 f.; U.S. and
Spain, 15
Cultural pluralism. *See* pluralism
Culture. *See* civilization
Culture epoch theory, 191, 205–09

Dance, 139, 166, 198, 218, 220 f.,
225 ff., 247. *See also* Arts compared,
Noh
Dante, 68
Darwinian. *See* Evolution
Davids, Rhys, 103
Davies, Arthur, 124, 234
Davis, Hayne, 166
Dayton, Ohio, 157
Death, theme of, 17 ff., 31 f., 79 f.,
111 ff., 121, 144, 211 f.
Debs, Eugene Victor, 159
Decentralization, 178

Index

Japanese art *(continued)*
232; prints exhibited in Japan for first time, 148; prints a Western vogue, 48, 60 f., 91, 122, 147, 190 n., *see also* Hiroshige, Hokusai, Utamaro; situation ca. 1878, 46–48; in U.S. schools, 189 f., 239; Western knowledge of, 60–62. *See also* Brush, Buddhism, Kano, Sesshu, Tosa

Japanese architecture, 210

Japanism: in Boston, 89; in West, 60, 89

Japon Artistique, 131 n.

Jarves, James Jackson, 27, 61 f., 182

Jefferson, Thomas, 27

Jewett, Sarah Orne, 105 n.

Jizo, 110

Jones, Owen, **61** n.

Journal of Speculative Philosophy, 25, 26

Journalism, 199

Judaism, 231, 237

Julian Academy, Paris, 180, 232, 235 n., 239

Jung, Carl G., 245

Kaga province, Japan, 37, 38

Kaibun, 93

Kajin No Kigu (Strange Encounters of Elegant Females), 84

Kanai, Noboru, 39 n.

Kanawoka, 210

Kaneko, Kentaro, 48, 135 f.

Kangwakai, 54 f.

Kano, Asaoka, 49

Kano, Eitoku, 49, 55

Kano family, 46, 47, 49, 51, 53, 55, 64, 81, 83, 135, 188, 205 n., 208

Kano, Hogai, 55 f., 66, 81 f., 98, 188 n.

Kano, Jigoro, 39 n., 136

Kano, Katsukawa, 49

Kano, Tomonubu, 49, 55, 57, 193, 221

Kano, Yeishin, 55

Kano, Yeitan (EF), 5, 55

Kano, Yeitoku. *See* Kano, Eitoku

Kano, Yushin, 81, 85

Kant, Immanuel, 216

Kanze, 138 n.

Karma, 133, 141

Kearney. *See* Miss Kearney's School

Keats, John, 216

Keion, 92

Keitoku, Abbot Sakurai, 63, 98

Kentucky, 158

Ketcham, William H., 132

Kindergartens, 178, 187, 190

Kingston, N.Y., 169

Kipling, Rudyard, 6

Kirby, T. E., 171 n.

Kiritsu Kosho Kaisha, 37, 63 n.

Kiyonaga, 155

Knight Errant, 116, 182

Know-Nothing party. *See* Nationalism, American

Kobayashi, Bunshichi, 132, 134

Kobe, Japan, 120

"Kobinata," Mobile, Ala., 3, 4, 6, 197 f., 210

Koga Biko, 49

Koizumi, Yakumo (Lafcadio Hearn), 144. *See also* Hearn

Kokka, Bijutsu Zasshi (Journal of National Art-Flowering), 82

Kokoro, 143

Kokugaku-in (Academy of National Letters), 84

Kola the Parsee, 180 n.

Komachi, Sekidera, 138

Komaji, Aiba, 86 n.

Komparu, 138 n.

Koopman, Augustus, 171 n.

Korea, 84, 129, 158 n.

Korin, 49, 181, 193

Kotakane, Taro, 81 n.

Koyetsu, 170, 174 n.

Krapp, George, 166, 198

Kuki, 56, 136

Kumamoto, 143

Kunisawa, 47

Kuo Hsi, 9, 157, 176, 227

Kuroda collection, 49

Kwannon, 110

Kyoto, Japan, 49, 93, 106, 131, 167

Laboratory School, University of Chicago, 168, 191 f.

Lacquer, 14, 70, 156

West Texas State Normal College, 241

Wharton, Edith, 105 n., 107, 113

Wheeler, Benjamin Ides, 139 n.

Wheeler, Candace, 162 n.

Whistler, J. A. M., 4, 90 n., 181, 188; EF on, 173–74; Freer collects, 170–72; Pound on, 223, 230

White, Clarence, 236

Whiting, Lilian, 103 n.

Whitman, Walt, 20, 26 n., 32, 35 f., 57, 153, 162, 180, 244, 246

Whitney, 171

Whorf, Benjamin Lee, 227 n.

Wilcox Co., Ala., 231

Williamsburg, Brooklyn, 231

Wilshire, Gaylord, 166

Winckelmann, Johann J., 76

Winona Lake, Ind., 3, 153 ff., 196, 209

Women: and the arts, 90; feminine principle, 240 ff.

Women's clubs, 90, 101, 122 f., 126, 159, 163

Women's rights, 198. See also *New Cycle*

Wordsworth, William, 133

World art, 56, 77, 92 f., 116, 171, 173 ff., 230 ff.

World civilization, 3, 8, 54, 56, 92, 94, 96–100, 124 f., 127 ff., 176, 205, 209, 229, 239, 241–43, 246–47; art as medium for, 54, 92, 124, 205, 215; China as possible synthesis, 136; Japan as possible key, 96; scholarship reveals, 209; symbolism of, 125; U. S. belief in, 6, 20; U. S. moving toward, 3, 242, 247. *See also* Cosmopolitanism, East and West fusion, Eclecticism, World art, World history

World federalism, 166

World history, 6, 25, 50, 54, 58, 67, 139, 155, 204 ff., 209, 211, 226, 229

World literature, 215–29

World's Parliament of Religions, Chicago (1893), 102, 180 n.

Wright, Frank Lloyd, 162

Yale College, 20

Yamana, Kanga, 55

Yamanaka, 211 n.

Yamashiro, Japan, 53

Yamato, Japan, 49, 53

Yeats, William Butler, 220, 221 n.

Yerkes, Charles Tyson, 171

Yin-Yang. *See* In-Yo

Yokohama, Japan, 37, 44 n., 64, 85, 143

Yumedono, Buddha of the, discovered, 52

Zen (Ch'an) Buddhism, 207, 208, 217, 220